# SKIBBEREEN

## RESCUED FOLKLORE

Mike Baldwin

First published in Great Britain in 2022

Cover image from C. F. Weiland, Allgemeiner Hand Atlas (Weimar: Geographisches Institut, 1835).

The texts which form this book are transcribed from the School's Collection with the kind permission of the National Folklore Commission, University College Dublin. https://www.duchas.ie/en

This volume is dedicated to the children of Skibbereen's schools who so diligently rescued and preserved these stories.

## EDITOR'S NOTE

This book is a direct transcription of volumes in the collection of the National Folklore Commission, University College Dublin. Every effort has been made to preserve the text as originally written. Spellings, both in English and Irish, have been maintained where possible, as has grammatical form other than where the lack of (or excess) punctuation makes reading difficult or alters meaning. Some Irish phrases have been translated and the editor accepts responsibility for errors incurred in doing so.

## ACKNOWLEDGEMENTS

Thanks are due to those who have been instrumental in the writing of this book, most notably the National Folklore Collection, University College Dublin, for permitting the use of the School Collection documents, and the National Library of Ireland for allowing the use of many of the images contained here. Special thanks are owed to Sheila and Jean who, by selling so many copies of my first book, *Mizen: Rescued Folklore*, made this one possible. Above all, I owe a huge debt of gratitude to my parents, Kathleen and George, and my grandmother, Johanna Cleary (nee Downey) (from Goleen), who introduced me to West Cork, and to my grandfather, James Cleary (from Durrus), of whom I have heard a lot but was never fortunate enough to have met.

# Contents

# Illustrations

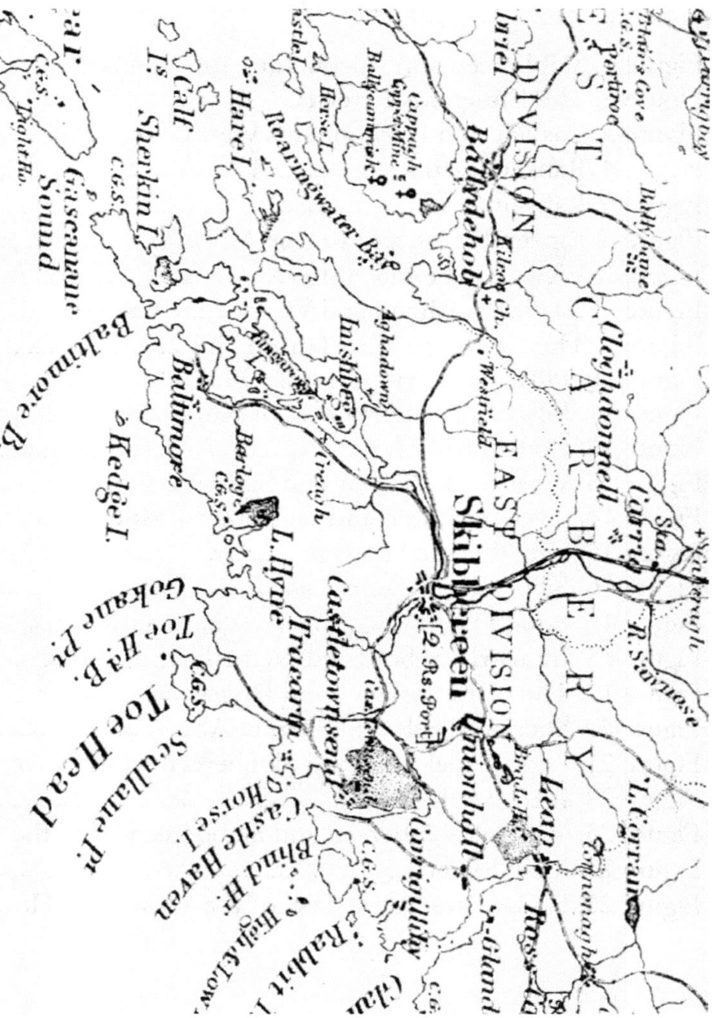

Figure 1. Skibbereen and surrounding townlands (Stanford, 1887).

# INTRODUCTION

Not so long ago, the hearth was the heart of the home, vital and essential, the giver of warmth, light and nutrition. At night, we gathered around it talking, telling stories, playing music and singing. Perhaps we watched the flames dance, imagining foreign lands and mythical peoples in the flickering light. Fire was of even greater importance to our nomadic ancestors, the first farmers. No doubt they also warmed themselves there, eating, talking and singing, but fire offered them safety too. And it was around these fires and hearths that many of the stories in this book were sparked into life, skilfully kindled and shared to entertain. They spoke of local news and characters, recalled and revised old histories, warned of risk, and explained natural and supernatural phenomena. With these fire-lit gatherings, the people waked their dead, and mourned those who'd left for foreign lands often never to return, leaving behind them a poignant aphorism.

Níl aon tinteán mar do thinteán féin
*There's no hearth like your own hearth*

In one sense, it's a comforting phrase: that feeling of arriving home after a hard day's work to loved ones and homely comfort. But for those who'd emigrated in search of a better life, it speaks of longing and loss. It is found in many languages – There's no place like home; home is where the heart is – home is where the hearth is... It refers to the buildings in which we live, but also the communities from which we hail; places that, for most, brings sanctuary. Attachment to home grows stronger when we leave, and for those who leave unwillingly, the pull - the call home - is surely stronger. Such is the case for the people of West Cork who throughout history have been touched by occupation, famine, civil war, and emigration. Here, during An Gorta Mór, on the edge of Europe but close to the bright lights of great European cities, many left for a new world. Others, perhaps taking the proverb to heart, but more likely thwarted by poverty, remained, and many thousands died.

West Cork, in some ways, is a remnant. It sits on the edge of the European continent, bordered to the west and south by the Atlantic Ocean and Celtic Sea. It is periglacial, windswept, wave-ravaged, and rain-soaked, and at its heart is Skibbereen. Those who are unfamiliar with this small country town may know of the aforementioned history. Perhaps they've heard the song, *Dear old Skibbereen*, for there cannot be many continents on which it hasn't been sung. However, those who *know* twenty-first century Skibbereen will recognise it as a vibrant and fiercely proud town surrounded by beautiful countryside and breath-taking sea views. Should our ancestors return today, Skibbereen would be familiar. They would recognise its streets and townlands, its rivers, loughs, fields and rolling hills, and its rugged coastline. Place- and family-names would be familiar too, and the welcome from the people would be unchanged - open, friendly and warm. Amongst the farms and small businesses, they may be surprised to find tourism, a mainstay of the local economy, but also innovation; Skibbereen's relative remoteness engenders a forward-looking, self-sufficient attitude backed by the ties of family and community.

Skibbereen is rich in folklore, and folklore, in the seen-it-all twenty-first century, is an odd thing. On one hand we might consider it an old-fashioned remnant of our past. On the other, it offers a vivid and vibrant connection with our ancestors. Where many countries, particularly in the west, have lost touch with their oral heritage, in Ireland it is very much alive. What is more, it continues to live in songs, stories and landscapes, and hence each generation discovers it anew. The tales published here are a rare survival, for whilst many countries blithely allowed their folklore to petter out, the Irish Folklore Commission's decision, in 1937, to instruct the nation's schools to collect stories from their localities, was inspired. It recognised that the newly formed nation's folklore had been compromised by centuries of occupation, and that irrevocable loss was likely. They saw that the salvation of the nation's folklore might become a valuable part of future identity as it was in the past, and they were right. These stories and histories are transcribed from the archives of the National Folklore Collection, encompassing the writings of students from 17 national schools at Abbeystrowry, Aghadown, Castlehaven, the Convent of Mercy, Corravoley, Creagh, Dooneen, Drishanemore, Heir Island, Kilcoe, Lisheen, Lissalohorig, Lough Hyne, Ringagrogy and Sherkin Islands, and Skibbereen town. It is to these students and their teachers that we owe a debt of gratitude for preserving a wonderful part of our heritage.

# ABBEYSTROWRY

Co. Chorcaighe
Bar: Cairbre Thiar
Par: Abbeystrowry (An Sciobairín)
Scoil: An Mhainistir
Oide: Dd. MacCarthaigh

ABBEYSTROWRY, a parish in the barony of Carbery East, in the county of Cork, and province of Munster, Ireland; containing part of the market-town of Skibbereen. It is intersected by the river Ilen, near which are the remains of an abbey, from which the parish takes its name; but of whose age and founder nothing is known. Less than two-thirds of the land in the parish is under cultivation, the remainder being waste or bog. The bog is not very extensive, and the rest consists of rocky hills, with small tracts of pasture scattered here and there. Farming has not made much progress. It is said the old wooden plough is used still. At Derrygoole there are some slate quarries, but they have not been worked very extensively or profitably. Here are several fine residences of the gentry, as Hollybrook, Lakelands, Abbeyville, &c.

*The National Gazetteer: A Topographical Dictionary of the British Isles*, vol, 1
(London: Virtue, 1868), p.4.

# ABBEYSTROWRY
# Local Folklore and Stories

# A Thief's Treasure

There was a thief long ago and he used to go around stealing by night. Once he was found out and was to be hanged because it was said that he had gold hidden somewhere. He was told he would be let off if he told where the gold was hidden. He said some of it was in Bán Cham, which is the name of a fort in Lassanaroe, and more of it in Coolnaclehi. Some years ago, a man named Eoin Sweeny working for Mr O'Donovan found a gold ring while digging potatoes. It is said there is gold hidden there still.[1]

# ABBEYSTROWRY
# People, Places and Property

# Local Heroes

Long ago, men and women were very powerful. They used to walk long distances going to fairs and other places. When there was not any train or motor car, the people used to walk to Cork from this district. One morning, a woman from Whitehall went walking to Cork. She left home about seven o'clock and she carried a basket of butter on her head. She reached Cork about midday. There she sold the butter and brought a basket of groceries. Putting the basket on her head, she started off for home. She reached home early in the evening, and she was not a bit tired. The woman's name was Mrs Desmond.[2]

In olden times, men were great runners, walkers, jumpers, swimmers, singers, dancers, boxers, bowlers, and weight throwers, and some of them brought great honour to their country, even in foreign lands. There was a man named Micheal Daly of Coolbawn who was a great bowler. It is said that a better match was never seen in Ireland than one which he had with a man named Kane from the same district. From Dreeny Bridge to Morgan's Gate, the contest was very keen, and a tremendous crowd followed it to the end.[3]

# The Corran

The Corran is situated in the land of Mr Patrick O'Driscoll in the townland of Skeagh, which is in the parish of Aughadown. The Corran is a large circular mound of stones of an area of about a hundred square yards, and the centre of it is about twelve feet high. It is said that a chieftain was buried there about three-hundred years ago, and that everyone that attended the funeral put a stone on top of the grave. This was how they raised the big mound of stones there. Years after he was buried, it is said that he was often seen riding a white horse round the Corran.[4]

# The Blessed Well

There is a blessed well in our land which is the townland of Barnagoulane in the parish of Aughadown. The name of the field is 'Páirc an Tobair Beannaithe', which means the field of the blessed well. The well was blessed by a saint some years ago. It is in the corner of the field about five or six feet from the ditch, and there are steppingstones going into it. Any person around that had any defect and that knew of the well went to it. Every person that came to the well left some token after him. There is a bush growing beside the well, and the bush was covered with bits of cloth that the people left after them. Some years ago, there was a man ploughing in the field and he cut a rod that was growing beside the well to drive the horses. When he went in for his dinner, he put the rod on the ridge near the plough. When he came back to his work again, he found it growing in the place where he'd cut it.[5]

# Story of an Old Church

Long ago, there was an old Catholic church in the townland of Abbey, a short distance from the Abbey school. A small part of the ruins where it was built is still to be seen. There was an aisle and three galleries in it, and a thatched roof. Mass was said every Sunday morning there by a priest who lived near the place. It was very convenient to the country people, but very few of them are living now that attended it. It was closed when Skibbereen church was built. I heard that my grandfather attended mass there when he was young.[6]

## ABBEYSTROWRY
# Local Customs

## Marriage Customs

Near the north end of the island of Cleire, a pillar-stone (gallaun) may be seen standing upright and about four feet high. In the centre there is a circular opening. There is an ancient tradition connected with it. In former times, this was a marriage stone where lovers met and became engaged. As no jeweller flourished on the island and engagement rings were not to be obtained, the lovers adopted the custom of plighting their troth by shaking hands through the circular opening. The mutual vows made on such occasions were strictly observed. The gallaun is looked upon as a venerable relic connected in some way or another with the worship of the druids.[7]

Collected by Máire Ní Cheadagáin from her mother

## ABBEYSTROWRY
# The Natural World and Weather Lore

## The Year of the Big Snow

There was a very heavy fall of snow on the sixth of February in the year 1855. It covered mostly all the small houses, and it was over the doors of the big houses. The snow was falling for three days and for three nights. It was on the ground for five or six weeks before it all melted away. When the people got up in the morning, they had to shovel away the snow from their doors. There was a man who had three cows and they were under the snow for three weeks. They lived on the top of a ditch and they had nothing to eat except the green furze bushes. There were a great many cattle and sheep found dead on the ground when the snow melted.[8]

# CORK CONSTITUTION

### 20 February 1855

## The Weather

The snow with which the country was visited during Wednesday night and Thursday and Friday, ceased about half-past nine p.m. on Friday evening. On Saturday there was a frost, and on Sunday a partial thaw, to which a frost succeeded, rendering the roads exceedingly difficult and dangerous to travel. The west of the county has, it is stated, experienced a heavier fall of snow than other localities, and the mails to and from thence cannot be expected for some time. The traffic between Bantry, Skibbereen, Clonakily, Macroom, Youghal, Fermoy, Midleton &c. and Cork, has been totally stopped. At the Corn Market on Saturday, but five loads of wheat and oats were brought in: yesterday eight loads arrived, two of which were from near Mallow; the carried stated that the latter had been three days on the journey. The carriers state that the roads are blocked up to a great depth, in many places fully ten feet. The Great Southern and Western, and Cork and Passage Railway trains are again running, but the Bandon line is still impassable. Upwards of one hundred men however are employed in clearing the snow from the rails, and it is expected the trains can be resumed today. One consequence of the present state of the roads is the extreme scarcity of milk and vegetable, which it is almost impossible to procure.

# The Thunderstorm of 1907

There was a great thunderstorm in the month of February in the year 1907. The people said that it was the worst storm they ever remembered. It blew slates off houses and hardly left a tree standing. It blew iron off outhouses and off sheds, and it carried it a great distance away. There was a man who had a couple of tons of hay in a shed. When he arose in the morning and went to the haggard to give hay to his cattle, there was not hay nor shed in the haggard before him. He looked for the iron and he found some of it about a mile from the house.[9]

## Signs of Rain

It is a sign of rain if the sky is dark or cloudy, if the moon looks pale, the stars are dim, or if there is a circle round the moon. If the cat sits by the fire or the dog eats grass, rain will follow. If the birds fly low, or if the seagulls come inland, it is another sign of rain. If there is a blue blaze in the fire or when the wind blows southwest, when the soot falls from the chimney and when blue light is seen in the fire, it is a sign of rain.[10]

# ABBEYSTROWRY
# History and Archaeology

## The Barnagoulane Mass Rock

There is a mass rock in our land which is in the townland of Barnagoulane, parish of Aughadown. It is built in a lonely part of a field surrounded by hills. It is built up with small stones covered by a large flat stone. It is about four feet high. It is now covered with moss, heather and some wildflowers. Whenever the field in which it is built is tilled, the rock is not touched. It was erected in the penal days when the priests were hunted. It is said that while the priest was celebrating mass, a man would be up on the hill close by watching for fear that the army would come and kill the priest. I heard that my great-grandfather attended mass there when he was young. There are old roads leading to it from north, south, east, and west where the people used to come from to attend mass.[11]

Collected by Síobhan ní Carthaigh, Barnagoulane
From Florence McCarthy, Barnagoulane

## The Mohona Mass Rock

There is a mass rock in the land of Mr O'Driscoll in the townland of Mohona, parish of Aughadown, where mass was celebrated in the penal days. The rock is still to be seen. There are shelves in it that served as an altar. There is also a blessed well carved in a rock nearby and it was supposed to be blessed long ago. It never went dry. A short distance away there is a large stone where someone was always watching for fear the soldiers would come and kill the priest.[12]

Collected by Áine Ní Ghogáin, Mohanagh
From Michael Goggin, Mohanagh

# An Gorta Mór

It is doubtful if in the history of the world there ever occurred such a pitiful calamity as the great Irish Famine which began in the autumn of 1845, and lasted through '46 and '47. Many stories are told of the most heroic charity shown towards one another by the poor sufferers. A poor man was known to have shared his scanty meal with another at the public works only to die of starvation himself on his way home. Another man was known to have fallen dead at his cabin door with a parcel of meal in his possession which he had brought five miles but would not taste it until he shared it with his starving family. Skibbereen is said to have been one of the worst plague spots in Ireland during the famine. It is said that hundreds of bodies were thrown into two great pits to the right of the gate of the Abbey cemetery, which is about a mile from the town, shroudless and coffinless.

The mysterious disease which destroyed half the crop of 1845 and almost all the crop of 1846 is commonly known as the blight. At first a brown spot appeared on the leaf of the potato, soon the spots became bigger, and the stem became brittle and fell off. It was first noticed in the middle of September 1845 on the coast of Wexford, but soon spread inland over the country. It is said that twenty hours after it appeared, a field of potatoes was found to be utterly destroyed. It was also found that potatoes, healthy apparently when pitted, were a mass of rottenness when the pit was opened. Various remedies were tried to keep them sound but failed. We are told that in Spring 1846, the people made all the efforts they could to procure the means of cropping the land again. They begged and borrowed the money for seeds. They planted potatoes more extensively than ever before, nearly 2,000,000 acres being under the crop. The potato crop looked very promising at the end of July. All over the country might be seen fields of green waving potatoes in full flower. In the beginning of August, a strange white fog appeared which brought the blight, and almost in a single night it destroyed the potato crop of 1846 all over Ireland.[13]

# Carew

Carew and his army camped in a field called 'Carraig an Saghdúir' in the land of Mr Tim Collins, in the townland of Reencorran, on their way to Dunboy Castle. On that night, they seized cattle and went to the farmers houses in the district and took all the eggs and butter they had in the house with them, and they destroyed all the cream and mixed it with the milk. In the morning, before they went away, they milked the cows and destroyed some of the crops. The men hid themselves for they were afraid the soldiers would take them away and make them fight.

There is a high rock about 17 feet high in the same field and it is said that a soldier was found dead there the next morning, and he was buried near the rock and that is why it is called 'Carraig an Saghdúir'[i].[14]

---

[i] Carraig an Saghdúir' - Rock of the Soldier.

# Aghadown

Co. Chorcaighe
Bar: Cairbre Thiar
Par: Achadh Dúin
Scoil: Achadh Dúin
Oide: Máiréad Sweetnam
13.11.38 – 12.38

AGHADOWN, or Aughadown, a parish in the eastern division of the barony of Carbery West, in the county of Cork, province of Munster, Ireland, 4 miles to the southwest of Skibbereen. It is situated on the river Ilen, which is navigable, and communicates with Baltimore harbour near Cape Clear. It includes the islands of East and West Calf, East and West Innishbeg, Hare, and Scheams. About one-third of the land is rock and bog, the rest is cultivated, and the soil by the river is very fertile. There are ruins of a castle erected in 1495, and of an abbey called the Abbey of Our Lady. Aghadown House stands on high ground and is surrounded by fine woods. Fairs are held on the 6th May and the 7th October for the sale of cattle, sheep, &c.

*The National Gazetter: A Topographical Dictionary of the British Isles*,
vol, 1 (London: Virtue, 1868), p.32.

# Aghadown
# Local Folklore and Stories

# Hidden Treasure

In the parish of Kilcoe, there is a place called Skeaghanore where there is a whitethorn bush, and gold is supposed to be buried near it. Skeagh or Sceaċ means whitethorn, and ór, gold. The old people say that it is still there and as not yet been found.[15]

Collected by Peggy Swanton, Church Cross, Skibbereen
From Patrick O'Driscoll, aged 85, Aghadown, Skibbereen

## How Skibbereen got its name

Long ago, where Skibbereen now stands, there was a hamlet where very dishonest people lived, and while the industrious men of honest people were away from home working, the good women of the house would make a bastible cake. The name of such cake is even now called the 'billeen'. The youths of the hamlet would snatch the opportunity to slip into the house and steal the billeen out of the bastible. 'To scub' means to whip or snap or steal. A raid was organised, the hamlet was burned, and the bad people hunted, and the place got the name 'Skub-bileen' meaning 'the place where bread was stolen.' Time has altered the spelling.[ii][16]

Collected by Peggy Swanton, Church Cross, Skibbereen

---

[ii] This apocryphal story is of the type that was circulated to explain why something was so. Other explanations of why Skibbereen is so named relate it to the word, 'skiff', meaning a small boat used to cross a river, or 'skibb', apparently meaning little boat harbour.

# Historical Tradition

On Coosheen hill on the side of Mount Gabriel there is a ruin of an old white castle, once the seat of the O'Mahoneys. Turning north towards Hungry Hill can be seen the beautiful country as it runs down to Dunbeacon Castle, once the home of Chieftain O'Sullivan whose ruins now stand at the edge of Dunmanus Bay beneath the shadow of Mount Gabriel. Chieftain O'Sullivan had one child, a daughter, Rosaleen. She was beautiful and fair, and the poets described her as the 'Rose of the Valley.' She had a lover, Owen O'Mahoney of White Castle. When her father heard of her friendship with O'Mahoney, he was very angry as Owen could never hope for more than a younger son's share. One evening as Rosaleen came home after a walk with her lover, she was brought into her father's presence to meet Chieftain O'Driscoll of the Three Castle Head. He was known to Rosaleen who thoroughly disliked him as an elderly bachelor who drank a lot of rich wines, boasted of his castles, and all that he had killed. When Rosaleen heard he had come that day to ask for her in marriage, and that her father gave consent, she was horrified. She told her father she loved O'Mahoney and would not marry any other man; her love for Owen was dearer to her than her life. Her father listened not to her pleading, but set the day for her wedding to O'Driscoll, giving Rosaleen one week to forget O'Mahoney. During that week her father kept her a prisoner in his castle. But love finds a way. She got a letter from Owen telling her he would meet her on horseback outside the castle. Rosaleen was anxiously waiting for Owen's arrival. They were preparing the feast for her wedding to O'Driscoll when Owen came along. He took her by the hand and helped her to get on the horse, and they rode off over the hills. They fixed the day for their wedding and got married. A few days later Rosaleen's father came and apologised for being so hard on her.[17]

Collected by Peggy Swanton, Church Cross
From Mr Lannin, aged 98 years, Church Cross

# Aghadown

# People, Places and Property

# A Local Hero

I listen to many stories round the fireside, but the other day I heard about a neighbour of ours, Fineen McCarthy, who lived in a thatched cottage in the townland of Rahine. He was great grandfather of John and Jerry McCarthy who still live there. His daughter went to America about 1830, and at that time the mail car which ran from Bantry to Cork three days a week, was the only means of conveyance. There was no railway beyond Cork. She forgot her ticket, and Fineen saw it on the dresser when he returned with his donkey after putting her on the mail car. That was midday. He set off to Cork as fast as he could walk, and just got to her when the coach was leaving for the American liner at Queenstown, and gave her the ticket. She was delighted and had not missed it. He returned, no boots on him, and came over the hills of Corran, some little distance from Leap. There they were dancing at the crossroads, so he joined in the sport. He proceeded and arrived at the Abbey graveyard two miles from his home at twelve o'clock. He was so tired after his great walk and feat of endurance that he slept there for the night and arrived home at dawn.[18]

Collected by Anna Trinder, Church Cross, from Owen MacCarthy

McCarthy's sporting escapades were reported in the *Skibbereen & West Carbery Eagle*.

It is recorded that two adventurous characters, one named McCarthy from Baltimore, and another Donovan, a shoemaker, from Skibbereen, in order to astonish the natives and hand down their names to prosperity, jumped across the top of the tower [of the church on Sherkin] – a distance of 8 to 10 feet, so that they had death staring them in the face should they have jumped too far and gone over the parapet, and death at their heels, had they been unable to complete the jump. However, we are happy to announce, though neither appeared to have studied the motto "discretion is the better part of valour," that they both accomplished the jump in safety, and one of them is alive at the present day.

Sketches in Carbery, *Skibbereen & West Carbery Eagle*, 24 October 1868, p.2.

Figure 2. The Emigrants Farewell, Mary Frances Cusak, *An Illustrated History of Ireland* (Kenmare: Kenmare Convent, 1868), p.33 recto.

# Travelling Folk

Very many travelling folk visited this district long ago. The most of them are very poor. The only one I know now is John Boyd. He sells small articles very reasonably, such as hairpins, safety pins, hair clips, laces, pens, pencils, looking glasses, and scissors. He generally stays one night in houses where he is most welcomed. The local people gather around him and many comical stories he tells, and new ones from distant places. He is a splendid fiddler and a good night dancing is enjoyed when he arrives. There were others in the days of yore. I often heard my grandfather tell of Collins from Ross. He was a great fiddler too and was welcomed in this district. He was very poor and stayed for a night in a few houses in the townland. He was found dead in a brake of furze near Ross. Then there was John Relihan from Millstreet. He told funny stories of the travels. He was not a musician. He wore no shoes and his toenails were four inches long. He died at eighty years.

By far the most interesting character of a traveller around here was "Dan the Piper". He rode on a donkey as he was paralysed from the hips down. He was comical and jolly and played the bagpipes which he got as a present from a Mr Townsend of Castletownsend. He had no money and depended on the people for his needs. He was most welcome. He generally remained a few days in a house in the townland. He often stayed at Driscolls or Proness.[iii] There is a famous character for dancing and comics named Jack Roche who is one of his descendants. Mrs Grace was also another traveller, but she was very dirty, and people tried to get rid of her as quickly as they could. She dressed in a bonnet and cape and carried her clothes in a red handkerchief. She stayed for a week or longer in houses she frequented. She often told stories of her travels. Miss Nancy was a more interesting traveller. She had knowledge of many cures. There was a delicate boy round here who had a bad stomach. She cured him with the emission of sheep. She carried various homemade ointments and cures and herbs with her. She was always welcomed in the houses where people were ill.[19]

Collected by Peggy Swanton, Church Cross
From Patrick O'Driscoll, aged 85 years, Aghadown

---

iii Proness – a variant of Prohoness or Prochanas, a townland near Aghadown.

# Aghadown: My Home District

I live in Ardralia in the parish of Aghadown and the Barony of West Carbery. There are twenty families in the townland, sixty-seven people in all. The most common family name is Evans. There are five families of them there. The houses were mostly thatched in the old days but when the farmers were compensated for their improvements under the Land Act, nearly all the houses were raised and slated. They got the slate from the local quarry of 'Beann Dub' between Ross and Leap. Now there is only one house thatched. They do not know Irish except a few words here and there. There are three people over eighty there. Robert Evans is the oldest. He is ninety-four years.

Houses were more numerous before the famine time. There were a hundred houses there, the remains of some of them can be seen today. The famine effected the district very sorely. Hundreds died with hunger and dropsy. Some of the young people were deported and sent to America. The place is mentioned in the ballad, 'The Sack of Baltimore'. These hookers crossed from stormy Schull in this skiff from Affadown. This parish is Aghadown or Achadh Duín but the local people say Affadown, and that is how it is in the old church records. The land is hilly, but ready to produce crops. There is usually a great crop of oats and potatoes better than in any other district for miles around. The Islen [sic] river flows past Ardralia. The wood of Creagh can been seen across the estuary, and some of Carbery's hundred isles.[20]

Collected by Peggy Swanton, Church Cross

# Letterscanlan: My Home District

I live in Letterscanlan in the parish of Aghadown and the Barony of West Carbery. Long ago it was much more thickly populated that it is at present. There are three families in the townland of Letterscanlan, Brookes, Lynch, and Cummins. There are eleven people in it. Letterscanlan got its name because long ago there lived a family of Scanlans and they gathered all the letters from the people of the district.[iv] They paid a man to deliver the letters from the stagecoach and then he collected letters also. Some people brought letters to the Scanlan's house. They took them to the mail car which travelled twice a week from Cork to Bantry. They met it at Foherlagh Cross. There is still a family of Scanlans living in the parish of Aghadown near the site of the old town of Aghadown. Den Scanlan is a mason. He is the last of the name around.[21]

Collected by Evelyn Brookes, Church Cross

# Holy Wells

Saint Ciaran spent much of his life in the island of Cape Clear in the parish of Aghadown. Just as we enter the island at the main pier, we see a large stone. It is called Cloċ Ciarán. On the top is the print of his hand which must have been a large hand. A few yards from it is a holy well called Tobar Ciarán which is supposed to cure diseases of all kinds. Large numbers of pilgrims visit it in the evening of the forth and the morning of the fifth of march, which is a strict holiday on the island. Some pilgrims take away some of the water. They go 'round the well on hands and knees reciting prayers. Then they wash in the water rubbing the effected part and the disease is cured. Some relics of clothes, beads, or money are left at the well, usually on a whitethorn bush near it. The water must not be used for household purposes.[22]

Collected by Peggy Swanton, Church Cross, obtained from the natives during a visit to Cape Clear

---

[iv] Perhaps another apocryphal tale. Letterscanlan is anglicised from the Irish, Leitir Scanláin - leitir meaning hillside. The mostly likely translation of Letterscanlan is Scanlan's Hillside.

# Fairy Forts

There are a number of forts in the vicinity of the school. They are known as forts or raths or lisses, and are all within view of one another in Knocknaraha, in Letterscanlan, Rahine, and Cnoc na Mála. They are all circular in shape and are never interfered with. Children will not even pluck a flower off them for the fairies would follow them. The Irish are supposed to have built them for protection from the Danes.

There was a man named William Bryan of Maryville, Enniskeane, Co. Cork who got two of his working men to dig out a fort. It covered about an acre, four feet above the level of a fine, large field. The following year one of the men broke his leg and died of poisoning in it, the other man died of fever, and William Bryan himself got an incurable disease of the intestines. Ever since, nobody even thinks of interfering with a fort.

There are many stories told about the forts. There are little men resembling leprechauns seen on the Rahine fort. One time they were seen stealing potatoes from the owner of the fort. He fired at them from the bedroom window but the more he fired and talked, the more they laughed and went off with their potatoes. Lights are often seen on it, and music and dancing heard.[23]

Collected by Nan Swanton, Church Cross
From Patrick O'Driscoll, aged 85 years, Aghadown

# Local Place Names

Aghadown (Aċadh Dúin), Dún meaning a fort, and Aċadh (Achadh) means a tract of land without a boundary. It was within this century that the land was divided and ditches built. Before that time people staked the animals. Cnoc na Rátha (Knocknaraha): The hill of the fort or rath. The rath was where Mr Trinder's house now stands. Guirtín Ruadh (Gorteenroe) means the little red road - the red earth gives it a reddish hue. Fasagh: This signifies a wilderness. Lahirtanavally means the site or ruin of the old 'baile' or collection of houses. Foherlagh means forest land. Skeagh means whitethorn Raithín means the site of a rath. It is on Mr Beamish's land, and many lights and fairies are seen near it.[24]

# The Local Roads

There is a road running from Neill's Cross to Foherlagh Cross and it is called Carbery's road. It is one of the most beautiful roads, especially at this time of the year because its sides are one long stretch of whitethorn for nearly four miles. This road was made by the Carberys after the time of the famine days to help the poor people. They worked from sunrise to sunset for a penny a day. It was men from Ross that made Carbery's road because the people in this district would have nothing to do with the new road making. They believed misfortune would overtake them if they had anything to do with it. These men had their food at Rahine where William Sweetnam lives now. His grandmother was a Ross girl by the name of Kingston. She was the only woman these men knew in the district. She gave them plenty of 'ropey milk' and yellow meal, boiled. They had their own bread. When she visited her home in Ross on horseback behind her husband, they always gave her a great welcome for her kindness to them.

# The Building of Roads

There is a field at the righthand side of Carbery's road just at Foherlagh Cross and it belonged to Dan Donovan. Mass was said there in penal days. There is a rock in the field that acted as an altar. It is called Páirc an Aifrinn. There is another road running off Carbery's road at Reenamurragha Cross and extending down the townland of Gorteenroe. This too was planted on either side with blackthorn and whitethorn by the Carbery landlords of the district. It is called O'Driscoll's road for a man by the name of O'Driscoll who was the contractor. It once ran through a thickly populated district but now it only acts as a passage to three houses, and some of it is grown over with briars. This road passes a right-angled rock in William Sweetnam's field at Knock where mass was said in the penal days. It is called Páirc an Caspuig still.

The new road along the Islen [sic] river was made during the famine times, from the new bridge out to Church Cross. The old road from Skibbereen runs over the hill from the new bridge through Mohone and Gurteenroe where it reaches Carbery's road. Long ago, this road ran through Mr Fynns field at Church Cross over the Srucan Caol which runs at the back of the school. Many old tales of feats of strength are told by the old people of this district.

It is over this old road, which is rough and hilly, that the old stagecoach and mail car ran from Skibbereen to Schull in the old days. None of the people of this district worked on the new road from the new bridge to Church Cross.

Before the bridges were made, the rivers were crossed by means of fords. There was a ford at the new bridge and a ford near Aghadown graveyard. People waited for low water before they brought coffins across. Horses swam across the Islen river.[25]

Collected by Peggy Swanton, Church Cross
From Patrick O'Driscoll, aged 85 years, Aghadown

# Old Schools

There was an old school in Con Harrington's house in Kilnagospah. The teachers taught the subjects in Irish, and Irish was the home language of his pupils. Reading, writing and arithmetic were taught from slates. The old Irish folk songs and ballads were sung round the fireside.[26] The Abbey school is known as the Poor School locally.

Collected by Nan Swanton, Church Cross
From Patrick O'Driscoll, Aghadown

# Local Happenings

The ruins of an old house are still to be seen in the townland of Ardralla, Church Cross, Skibbereen, Co. Cork. It is situated about ten feet from the River Ilen in a field belonging to a man named Dick Draper. It belonged to the Beechers, an old family of this district before the Irish Free State soldiers took it over. At that time, rebellion was drawing to a close as the Republicans split. The side which formed the Free State were stationed in this house when the Republicans burned it. The four walls stand a witness to these terrible days. Mrs Beecher and her family went to America, and Dick Draper bought her land.[27]

Collected by Peggy Swanton, Church Cross, Skibbereen

# Old Houses

One night last year I heard Dan Lynch of Letterscanlan telling a story about the kind of houses that the people had long ago. They were made of stone, and the walls were at least eighteen inches thick so that any rain or dampness could not get through them. The roofs were thatched, some of the wealthier folk had them slated. The floors were made of clay. Some people had only one room, the kitchen. A small hole in the wall was their window. In bad weather, they kept this stuffed with rags and paper, and in fine weather they took out the paper and rags so as to give them light. The people made candles of their own as it was the only kind of light they could afford. They made them with fat, and poured the tallow into a shape and ran a string through. It hardened after a while, and they were able to use it as a candle.

When they went 'sgoireacting',[v] they took a sod of turf which was left behind the fire and turned a couple of times till the fire got into it. This they held with an instrument like a tongs to light them over the hillside paths. These often fell asunder and left them wandering over the hillside. They are not as safe as the lanterns of today. Sometimes they blamed Jack o'the lantern for leading them astray. The only way they would get the better of him was by turning their coats inside out.[28]

Collected by Evelyn Brookes, Church Cross
From Dan Lynch, aged about 70, Church Cross

---

[v] Sgoireacting is an Irish term for storytelling.

# AGHADOWN
# Farming, Trade and Crafts

# Basket Making

In this district the only craft that remains of the past is basket making by Mr Tom Kearney, Ardralia, Church Cross, Skibbereen. This craft was practised by his ancestors for centuries. He collects twigs each autumn and has them growing around his cottage. When they are cut in autumn, they spring up again in the spring, and in that way, he can have a good supply each year. He takes large numbers of panniers to Skibbereen each market day. He sticks some strong twigs in the ground and interlaces them with more pliable ones. He has a sharp knife for cutting them, and sometimes he uses his billhook. It is his only means of living in his cottage. Baskets are also made by Mr John Shanahan who only makes them for local farmers. They supply the twigs, and give him days working for his bother making the panniers. He is a farmer.[29]

Collected by Peggy Swanton, Church Cross

# Clothes made locally

Long ago most people made their own clothes. There was generally a spinning wheel in every house, and the woman of the house made clothes for her husband and children with it. First, she spun the wool and then carded it, then knitted stockings with the wool. She made frieze and flannel trousers out of the wool, and also flannel coats and jackets for the men.

There was a tailor that lived in a small, thatched cottage in Cnocgorm. His name was John Hern. He made the richer people's clothes. As he was working, he kept singing the following rhyme. "That the stitch may tear, and the clothes may wear to keep John Hern's pockets full of money.[30]

Collected by Anna Trinder, Church Cross
From Patrick O'Driscoll, aged 85, Aghadown

# The Local Fairs

Long ago, the local fairs in this district were held at a place called Pig's Bridge at the right-hand side of Aghadown School. All the people came there from the district around. The buyers generally came from Cork on the stagecoach to the turnpike where it stopped, and there they got out and walked to Pigs Bridge where the fair was held. The women sold butter, eggs, jam, apples, oranges, sweets, pears, bananas, and such like. They sold them very cheaply so that they made good sales, and profit on them too. When the people sold horses, colts or mares, they believed it to be very unlucky if they did not give the halter with them. When a bargain was made between two people, they clapped their hands together and said, 'take him or leave him'. When a buyer bought pigs, he marked them with a sharp knife so that if anything happened to them it was easy to know it. Special fairs were held at Pigs Bridge for bonhams, horses and sheep. The horse fair was held on the twentieth of August in this district. The bonhams fair was held on the first Monday in every month. All the people gathered together with their cribs of bonhams and sold and bought. When everybody was sure they had made a good profit for themselves, they went to the public house where now there is a graveyard and had what they called 'a good drink'.[31]

Collected by Evelyn Brookes, Church Cross
From Patrick O'Driscoll, aged 85, Aghadown

# AGHADOWN
# Local Customs

# Local Marriage Customs

Marriages take place in West Cork during Shrove, especially on Shrove Tuesday. It is considered a lucky time, whereas the month of May is considered an unlucky month. As the old saying goes, 'Marry in May you will rue the day'. The young man and young woman are brought together by making a match. If money and stock are agreeable to both parties, the match is made. Sometimes people to be married only meet once or twice before. Sometimes the match is broken for a trifling thing.[32]

# Homemade Toys

A great many people long ago made their own toys because they were too poor to buy them, such as dolls, pat guns, catapults, model-turnips, whistles, snares, toy cars, bird-baskets, rattle-boxes, daisy-chains, and necklaces. Dolls were made of rags stuffed with corn. Pat guns were made with elder sticks. Catapults were made with rubber. Whistles were made with horse chestnuts. Snares were made of wire. Bird-baskets were made with sticks braced in a proper position. Rattle-boxes were made with rushes. Toy cars were made of little laths nailed together. Necklaces were made of Indian corn painted different colours. A turnip could be shaped into the head of a man putting a red paper inside the face, and a candle lit to make him look like a ghost.[33]

Collected by Peggy Swanton, Church Cross

# Local Customs

The spilling of salt is considered a sign of a quarrel, as also is the crossing of two knives. Three candles lit together are regarded as a sign of a wedding or a wake. To sing at one's meal is a sign of disappointment, as also is meeting a person on the stairs. Seeing a red-haired woman in the morning is an omen of ill-luck. A dog crying in the night is a prophesy of death. Sparks jumping towards a person from the fire indicate, it is said, a promise of money. A cat with his back to the fire or seagulls inland are portents of broken weather. To carry round inadvertently a lighted lamp in one's hand, or to put on an article of clothing inside out, are considered signs of good luck. To come across a pin in the morning or a four-holed object like a button, is a great promise of good fortune - "Meet a pin and pick it up, all-the-day you will have good luck." It is not right to dip a milky vessel into a well, milky water must not be thrown into a stream but on dry ground. The person who pours out the first cup of tea of a meal must also pour out the others. The afterbirth when a cow calves must be placed on a nearby hedge. It is lucky to be licked by a cow. It is not customary to comment on the condition of cattle and horses without adding, "God bless them!" No important work is started, nor no journeys undertaken on Monday. Before a new dwelling is inhabited, sheep must be housed there first. It is unlucky to find a strange pig in one's garden or to leave empty spaces in ridges. When a farmer kills an animal for table use, it is never one of his own rearing. After the cream has been churned, nobody leaves the dairy without giving the handle a few turns lest the butter would not come. Large candles are lit in every window of the home on Christmas night. The Christmas candles are kept burning all night, and no door is locked or barred. Slips of seasonal flowers, whitethorn, and furze, cherry and apple blossoms, are plucked before sunrise on May morning and brought into the house to usher in summer. Bonfires are lit in the fields on St John's Eve and the farm stock are supposed to receive a blessing if the fire is brought amongst them. The kitchen chairs are cleared off lest the holy souls should want to sit at table during the night.[34]

Collected by Evelyn Brookes, Church Cross
From Patrick O'Driscoll, Aghadown
Originally obtained from Evelyn's grandmother

# The Lore of Certain Days

There are certain days of the week that are lucky and unlucky for removing from an old house to a new house. The lucky days are Tuesday, Thursday, and Saturday. All the others are considered unlucky. There are also lucky and unlucky days for marriage.

> Monday for health
> Tuesday for wealth
> Wednesday the best day of all
> Thursday for losses
> Friday for crosses
> Saturday no good at all.

It is also believed by people that it is unlucky to go to see a sick person on a Monday and Friday. It is also unlucky to turn the mattress of a sick person's bed on Friday. There are lucky and unlucky days for birth.

> Monday's child is fair of face
> Tuesday's child is full of grace
> Wednesday's child is full of woe
> Thursday's child has far to go
> Friday's child is loving and giving
> Saturday's child has to work for his living
> The child that is born on the sabbath day
> is bonnie, handsome, bright and gay.[35]

# Games I Play

I play a great many different games in school and at home such as rounders, hide and seek, Jenny Joe, black man, goat in the garden, nuts, may I please, frog jump, rats and rabbits, the farmer wants a wife, oats and beans and barley grow, drop the handkerchief, stack, and the jolly miller.

In autumn we have great sport picking blackberries and taking them home to make jam. In summer we go fishing in the river and we catch a few small fish with our fishing rods. In winter we make bird-baskets and snares for rabbits and birds. We make the bird-baskets with sticks traced one after another, and set them. Then the birds go in and the basket falls down.

Quats is a very old game in this district. It is played very much still. You get one big stone and go away a little distance and take another in your hand and try to get it on the big stone. If it gets on the big stone, you get ten; if it gets near the stone you get five. You could get any number you like up to forty to make the game.

Jenny Joe is another old game also. One must be Jenny Joe, and another a maid, and they go into a room, and the rest come to see her, and something is supposed to be wrong with her each time that you cannot see her, until the maid says she is dead, and we must bury her now. Everybody helps to take her to the grave in which she is buried. She jumps up out of the grave and hunts them all, and the one she catches is supposed to be Jenny Jones next.

Hide the thimble is a very old game. Two people go into a room and hide the thimble, and the rest stay out until they are told that it is hidden. Then they all come in and look for it, and the one that finds it, he and his companion hide it next time.[36]

Collected by Evelyn Brookes, Church Cross

# AGHADOWN
# Local Cures

## Local cures

Donkeys milk is a cure for whooping cough.

The food the ferrets leave behind is a cure for sore eyes.

The sheep's milk is a cure for measles.

The wild sage is a cure for rheumatism.

Goose grease is a cure for thrush in a baby's mouth.

The golden dandelion is a cure for the pip.

The penny leaf and dandelion mixture is a cure for sore corns.

The yarrow makes an ointment used for wounds.

Coarse salt warmed is a cure for a sore throat.

The leaf of the tobacco is good for boils.

Celery is also a cure for rheumatism.[37]

Collected by Evelyn Brookes, Church Cross

# AGHADOWN

# The Natural World and Weather Lore

# Weather Lore

Moon:     When there is a star near the moon it is a sign of rain.
A ring around the moon is a sign of rain.
The moon turned like a boat is a sign of rain.

Sky:     A mackerel sky is a sign of rain.
No cloud in the sky is a sign of fine weather.
When the sunrise is coppery it is a sign of rain.
When there is a red sunset it is the sign of a good day.

Rainbow:     A rainbow in the morning is a shepherd's warning.
A rainbow in the night is a shepherd's delight.

Sun:     When the sun goes down very red it is a sign of fine weather.
When the sun goes down pale it is a sign of bad weather.

Birds:     A great number of rooks in a field is a sign of rain.
When the swallows fly low it is a sign of rain.
When the sea gulls are crying it is a sign of rain.
When the swallows fly high it is a sign of fine weather.
When there is a rook on the gallán stones it is a sign of rain.

Clouds:     When there is a cap on Mount Gabriel it is a sign of rain.

Damp:     When there is a sheen on the rocks it is a sign of fine weather.

Insects:     When the crickets are singing it is a sign of rain.
When the mosquitoes are flying in groups near the earth it is a sign of rain.

Animals:     When the dog eats grass it is a sign of rain.
When the donkey neighs it is a sign of rain.
When the goats come home early it is a sign of bad weather.
When a horse shivers in his stable it is a sign of thunder.
When the cat scratches the timber it is a sign of a gale.

| | |
|---|---|
| Smoke: | When the smoke falls down it is a sign of rain. |
| | When the smoke goes up straight it is a sign of calm weather. |
| Fire: | When there's a blue light in the fire it is a sign of rain. |
| Cuckoo: | When the cuckoo comes late it is the sign of a good year. |
| Fowl: | When the fowl run from the fowl-house and eat the grass, it predicts rain.[38] |

## Severe Weather

I heard Mrs Shannon tell a story about a storm that happened in the year 1902 in the summertime. There was terrible thunder and lightening, and hailstones. The flashes were so great that they could see all the countryside around. They saw the hay being taken down the river by the flood; the corn was broken down to the ground. The cattle were killed and drowned. The hailstones were so big that it broke the leaves off the turnips and mangolds. The trees were torn from the ground. She said it was the worst night she ever remembered. The country was in a desperate condition after that summer storm.[39]

Collected by Evelyn Brookes, Church Cross
From Mrs Shannon, aged 70 years, Church Cross

# Bird Lore

A great many birds live here in this district such as robins, blackbirds, thrushes, seagulls, linnets, yellow hammers, hawks, pheasants, woodcocks, magpies, rooks, wrens, ravens, pigeons, and swans. The swallows, corncrakes, and cuckoos come from Africa in April. The robin is supposed to get his red breast as he mocked our saviour on the cross. It was really in the spring time that Jesus was crucified, and this is why the robin's breast is redder at that time. The thrush is supposed to get his speckled breast from some seeds that were thrown at him by a woman as he passed the door of her house. The blackbirds build their nests in a bush and lay about four eggs. The seagulls build their nests in a low rock near the sea. The hawk builds on the top of a very high tree. The little lark builds in a low marshy place. The cuckoo is a very lazy bird for she does not build any nest. The magpie is too clever for her. She throws her egg out whenever she sees it in her nest. There is a rhyme made up about the magpie.

One for sorrow,
two for luck,
three for marriage,
four for death,
five for silver,
six for gold,
seven for a story that will never be told.[40]

# Aghadown
# Local Songs

# An Aghadown Caoine

It was on a rainy Monday. A fair gale blew, and my sons left us half an hour before sunrise to fish in the sea. My children were driven far away to be drowned. This year has been the year of my rain forever.

Cormac, my eldest child, with his gun could kill every kind of bird that fled in the air. The wild goose and wild duck; the partridge, the grouse, and the black plover of the lonely mountains.

Cormac, my dear! Flower of young men: who was mild and well educated – was just, and clean, and good. Oh, glorious King of Heaven! If you had spared him to me. It was the loss of him that broke my heart completely. I might – I could have parted with the rest.

Donal, my dear Donal, the youngest of my sons! It was this day fortnight he was washed on shore, without strength or life in his body. I saw him as he lay lifeless on the shore; and my heart was cold, and dead, and motionless at the sight.

Children! Dear children! Do you pity me? Do you see me? Look on me, your poor father crying and lamenting for the life of his life – the soul of his soul! What is he now? A broken-hearted man, weeping along in the coldest corner of the stranger's home.

Great is my grief and sorrow! Sadness and tears weigh heavy on my Christmas. To have my four young and stout men thrown on the will of the wild waves! If the great ocean, or the dark caves of the ocean would restore three bodies that now lie in it, how should they be caoined and lamented in Affadown.

Great is my grief and sorrow, that you did not all go from your father on board ship; or if my sons left me for a season, like the wild geese, to go to another land, then might I have expected from my master to the help of my four mild and clever young men at some future time.

Martin Selina, *Sketches of Irish History, Antiquities, Religion, Customs, and* Manners (Dublin: Robertson, 1844), p.336.

This caoine, or death song, transcribed and translated from Irish at the time, was composed by a man named Donoghue of Aghadown, whose three sons and son-in-law were lost at sea in around 1780.

> The caoine is kept up while the funeral procession is on the way to the place of interment. Three or four relatives, each carrying two bottles of whiskey, walk with the criers to refresh them occasionally with that cordial for every care. When the procession enters the burial ground, the caoine ceases while they walk three times around it, all the while repeating the creed. During the interment, the caoine is resumed and when the grave is closed, all the people kneel round it to offer up prayer for the departed soul.
>
> Martin Selina, *Sketches of Irish History, Antiquities, Religion, Customs, and Manners* (Dublin: Robertson, 1844), p.149.

# AGHADOWN
# History and Archaeology

# In the Penal Days

In penal days, there were houses built in secluded places in this district where the mass was said. Carraig an Aifreann is the name of one of Mr Donovan's fields at the right-hand side of Foherla Cross, Skibbereen. The rock is still to be seen where mass was said.

There is a field on Mr Sweentnam's farm in the townland of Knockanmoholagh, about a mile distant from Carraig an Aifreann, in a secluded glen. The field is called Páirc an Caspuig. The rock is there the size and shape of an altar.

There was a priest pursued by the Red Coats in the penal days. He escaped as far as Drom Caol, a hill near Ballydehob. The Red Coats were only yards from him when a horse appeared and landed the priest on the other side of the hill. The print of the horse's hooves and the priest's hands and knees are still to be seen on the rock. He then ran on as the horse disappeared. He came to a field where two young men and one crippled old man were sowing oats. He told the story to these men and asked them to untackle the horse and to drive him one mile. The old man, who as a protestant, was reluctant at first as he said the crows would eat all the grain. However, when he understood the good priest's story, he consented, and instead of driving him one mile, the young man drove him six miles from Muinntir Mháire where the field was situated. He returned when he had left the priest a safe distance from the Red Coats, the field was sown, and ever since, nobody has seen a crow, or more correctly a rook, pitch on that field. The farm now belongs to Mr Swanton.[41]

Collected by Nan Swanton, Church Cross
From Patrick O'Driscoll, Aghadown

# Famine Times

The Great Famine affected this district very much. It was much more thickly populated before that time. In the townland of Rahine, there were at least nineteen houses where three now stand. In the townland of Cnoc Gorm there were thirty-two houses where six now stand. There were over a hundred houses in Ardralla where twenty-one now stand. There were nine houses in one field at Rahine where only a couple of foundations are to be seen. The remains of these thatched houses and mud cabins are still to be seen.

The blight came and the potatoes blackened in the ground in this district. It was called the Black Failure. In 1847 the people cut the eyes from the decayed potatoes and stuck a feather of about two inches in each eye. These they sowed, broadcast like grain, and there was a wonderful crop of potatoes.

The people ate yellow turnips, raw flesh of stolen beets, grass, and Indian meal if they had any little money. They got a little help sometimes from the better-off people. They died in hundreds on the roadside and in their homes. There was a man nicknamed Rackateen who was employed to draw the bodies in his donkey cart to the Abbey graveyard. The plot where he heeled the bodies from his cart can still be seen with an iron cross bearing the following inscription: 'Erected to the memory of those departed ones who fell victim to the awful famine of 1846 and 1847. "Eternal rest grant unto them O Lord, and let perpetual light shine on them."'

There is a saying prevalent in this district, "Your legs are as crooked as Tom Gearns." Tom Gearns looked as if he was a victim of the famine, so Rackateen put him as he thought dead in his donkey cart with nine others. They were all heeled into the hole and Tom Gearns did not fall into place exactly. He got a stroke of the shovel on the knees. He screamed, so Rackateen took him up, but his knees were broken. He went back to Skibbereen in the donkey cart and lived to be an old man, but his knees were stuck together and very crooked.

There was a family of MacCartys in Gortín na gCloċ in the townland of Cnoc Gorm. They stole yellow turnips from Hemmings of Newcourt House, now occupied by Mrs Truder. They were reported to the authorities, were all deported to America, and were never heard of again.

There was another man lived in the bottom of Reencairn in the townland of Skeagh. He lived in a mud cabin and died of cholera, the fever which followed the famine. He was dead a week when he was found. There was a rock in front of his door, so he was heeled over the rock into a hole. The grave is still to be seen marked by five flags, one at the top, and one at the bottom and three opposite the rock. They are all about two feet high.[42]

Collected by Nan Swanton, Church Cross
From Patrick O'Driscoll, Aghadown

## Local Monuments

There is a very interesting circle of stones at Reencairn in the townland of Skeagh, Skibbereen. An old chieftain is supposed to be buried there. There was a door with hinges which opened down to the vault below in olden days. Now the stones are falling down, and through interference by animals the entrance is no longer visible. There is a magnificent view over Carbery's Hundred Isles and miles of countryside from this cairn. About fifty years ago large numbers of gentry came to enjoy the scenery and bracing air of the cairn, as it is locally called. As a visitor mounts the height of this hill to a place called the Cnap, the view is still more entrancing. The spires of twenty-one churches can be seen from it on a clear day, and a wide expanse of sea.

When Carew was going to destroy Dunboy Castle, he encamped with his army at the cairn for some time. They stole cattle and all the food they needed but otherwise they did little harm in this district.

The galáns are large stones on the top of the Galán mountain in Foherlagh, another monument of the past.[43]

Collected by Nan Swanton, Church Cross
From Patrick O'Driscoll, Aghadown

# CASTLEHAVEN

Co. Chorcaighe
Bar: Cairbre Thiar
Par: Castlehaven (Gleann Bearcháin)
Scoil: Baile an Chaisleáin
Oide: Seán Ó Donnabháin

CASTLEHAVEN, a parish in the eastern division of the barony of West Carbery, in the county of Cork, province of Munster, Ireland, 4 miles to the southeast of Skibbereen. It is situated in a picturesque district on Castlehaven Bay, or harbour, and was the site of a castle belonging to O'Driscoll, which was given up by him to the Spaniards, on their effecting a landing there in 1601. Some traces of the walls are yet to be seen. Off the coast are several small islands, and the rocks called the 'Stags'. The ancient name of this parish was Glanbarrahane. The church, built about 1827, is a handsome structure of freestone, with a good tower. There is a large chapel for Roman Catholics, and parochial and other schools. Castle Townshend, Point House, Drishane, &c., are the chief residences. The title of Earl of Castlehaven was held by the Touchet family.

*The National Gazetter: A Topographical Dictionary of the British Isles,*
vol, 1 (London: Virtue, 1868), p.511.

# CASTLEHAVEN
# Local Folklore and Stories

## The Goose of Death

Long ago there was a man dying. His wife was very sorry for him. She said she would rather die herself than the man. Some boys who knew she was sorry said they would frighten her. They plucked a goose and put it down through the roof of the house. When she saw the goose, she thought it was death. She pointed to the door of the room where the dying man was. She said, "Mar shíos atá sé" [He's down there]. When the time came, she did not want to die.[44]

Collected by Cáit Ní Mhuirthuille, Baile an Chaisleáin
From Michael Hurley, Farrandaw

## The Dead Brother

Long ago there was a man living in Castletownsend whose brother died in Tipperary. The man set out with a jennet and cart to bring home the corpse.[vi] When he was coming home, the jennet could not go up a hill, so the dead man jumped out and said he would walk up the hill. When they got to the top, he got into the coffin again. They were passing a public house and the dead man said, "Are you thirsty?". The other man said, "I am choked with thirst." The dead man said that the jennet would stand and the living man could have a drink. He went in and stayed inside for about an hour. The dead man jumped out of the coffin and went into the public house. He beat his brother and got into the coffin again. He was buried in Castlehaven graveyard.[45]

---

[vi] Jennet – a female donkey

## The Bull of Shepperton Lakes

Long ago, people went fishing in the Shepperton Lakes by night. One night, a man went fishing alone, and a bull came up out of the lake to him and followed him home. The man locked the door, but the bull broke in and the man got a stick and got hold of his tail and did not stop beating him until the bull went into the lake again. This went on for about four nights until the man was cutting furze and a hare with three legs jumped out of the bush which he was cutting and went over a fence. The man went after the hare but when he got over the fence, he saw an old woman near it and she said, "I have you at last."[vii] The man went to bed that evening and died there.[46]

## The Devil Dog

There was a man working with Dr Levis long ago. One night, he was coming home from Skibbereen and he saw a nice small dog in front of the car. He took the dog home and kept it for a few days. One day, he beat the dog because it would not go out for him. The next day he saw an old woman sitting near the milestone which is two miles from Skibbereen. The woman spoke to him and said, "I was the dog that you beat, and you must leave the country or I will kill you." The man went for the priest and told him. The two went to the place and the priest told her to leave the world. The woman went up in the air with flames of fire coming out her eyes and mouth. She was a devil who came to kill the man.[47]

---

vii In the past, hares were believed to be the animal incarnation of witches.

## The Cats

One night a man was passing Smorán Wood on horseback. About ten thousand cats came out and attacked him, but he killed one. One of the cats spoke to another and said, "He has killed Móithirín an lúchair the head of us." At that time cats used to come into the houses and stay there for a time. When the man got home, he told his wife about the cats. There was a cat on the hearth and it heard him. Its name was Gill Droy, and it crept up behind him and choked him. Then it walked out the door. Another night a man was passing the same place and he saw two or three cats coming out to him and one of them said, "Tell Gill Droy that Moll Paevin is dead." The man went home and told his wife. There was a cat on the hearth and it said, "I am Gill Droy and I am thankful for telling me."[48]

## The Bansidhes

One night, a man was coming home from work, and when he came into the yard, he saw bansidhes at the door.[viii] They would not let him in, and the cock began to crow. People had the hens in their kitchens in a coop at that time and the cock on a pole of wood over the door. When the cock began to crow, the bansidhes let the man in. His supper was ready except to take the potatoes out of the pot. When the man put his spoon into the pot to take out the potatoes, a bansidhe's hand threw it out. This kept on for a few minutes and the man got a fright because he heard the bansidhes crying outside and he ran away to bed. Shortly, the cock began to crow again, and the crying stopped. When the man got up in the morning, he found the cock dead with a sighle-buidhe pin driven through its comb. It is said that a cock has power over a bansidhe.[49]

---

[viii] Bansidhe (banshee) – meaning woman of the fairies – a female spirit and harbinger of death.

## Jack Barry and his Master's Goods

Long ago, there lived a faithful servant named Jack Barry who served his master for many years. In course of time his master died, and Jack expected some of his clothes, and he also had a wish for the gold watch and chain which his master usually wore. Time passed and Jack got nothing though he was still working in the house. At last, his patience gave way and he dressed himself as a ghost. One night, when the family was gathered in a room, they heard the voice of their father, as they thought, saying, "Give all my old clothes to Jack Barry. Give my gold watch and chain to Jack Barry". Next day Jack Barry got all he wished.[50]

## The Lost Bowling Ball

There was a man living in Castletownshend long ago. One day, as he was bowling along the road, the bowl went in over the ditch. The man went looking for it but the first thing he saw inside the ditch was a number of ducks belonging to his uncle. He looked and looked for the bowl, but he could not find it. Next day, as he was going to his uncle's house, he went looking for the bowl but he could not find it. He went to his uncle's house and he got his breakfast there, and when he was eating a duck egg, he found the bowl inside it.[51]

## The Leaping Man of Castletownshend

There was a man living near Castletownshend who used to tell of the leaps he gave. One day, there were people playing football in the Barn field. There was a wall surrounding this field about twelve feet high. This old man was going to the field to see the men playing. He did not go in through the gates but the high wall. That evening, there was a dance in Myross and this man was going there. The day was very wild, and no boat could go across. So, this man jumped and landed on Cat Island. He then took a step and landed in the sea, and he had no time to sink for he took the jump straight away and landed on Myross side.[52]

## The Voice from the Ditch

Once upon a time there was a man who used to go to his neighbour's house every night. One night, as he was passing a graveyard on his way home, he heard a voice inside the ditch saying, "One to me and one to you." He thought that it was God and the Devil in the graveyard sharing the souls of the people who were buried there. He ran back and told the man of the house what he heard. They came back to the place and they heard the voice again. They went in and they found two boys sharing buttons which they were pitching during the day.[53]

# A Hidden Treasure

On the top of Cnoc Droma, where an old fort is situated, a hawthorn bush grows on the bounds ditch. In the distance it has the appearance of a lion's head. The old people say that underneath it is a crock of fairy gold, and on moonlit nights, the fairies are seen dancing around it.[54]

# The Girl in the Lios

Long ago, it was said that the fairies lived in lioses, and when they would take a person down there, if the person touched anything, they would be kept. One day, they took a girl down in the lios, and they put a sick fairy in her place. They had a lovely dinner laid out for her and they tried to coax her to eat something, but she had heard of their trick, and she would not touch anything. The fairies were very cross, and they had to leave her out of the lios and bring back the sick fairy.[55]

# The Fairy Dance

One day, a man was going to a fair in Schull. He had no clock and he started away after his supper. As he was travelling along, he heard music playing. He went into the house and remained all night dancing with the company. He gave sixpence to the fiddler and when the day dawned, he went to the fair. When he was returning home from the fair, he went into the house again and he said to the woman of the house that he danced his 'nough last night. The woman said she did not see or hear anyone, only when she was brushing the floor in the morning, she found a sixpence. He said that he gave the fiddler that sixpence last night.[56]

## The Words of St Paul

There was a minister there long ago and before he went to the church, he sent his servant to the butcher, named Paul, for meat. When the boy returned, the minister was preaching and he said in the sermon, "What did St Paul say?" The boy stood up and said, "He said you will get no more meat until you pay for what you have eaten."[57]

## Mistaken Words

There was an old man travelling along the road and he had no English. He met a funeral and he said, "God bless your work". The people replied, "That is not what you should have said but, the lord have mercy on the dead." Going on further, he saw men pulling two cows out of a bog and he said, "The lord have mercy on the dead", and the men replied, "That is not what you should have said. You should have said, you have one out and I hope it will not be long until you have the other out." Going on further he met an old man that had one eye out. He replied, "You have on eye out and I hope it will not be long until you have the other."[58]

## The Priest and the Lights

One night a priest was going to a sick call. As he was travelling along, he met three lights, two bright and one dim. The first light said, "I am a child baptised by a priest and I am in heaven." The second light said, "I am a child who was baptised by a nurse and I am in heaven." The dim light said, "I am a child who was not baptised, and I am not in heaven." There was a pool nearby and the priest baptised the dim light and they disappeared.[59]

# Myles in the Ashes

There was a woman long ago and she had a son, eighteen years, who never went out, so they called him Myles in the Ashes. His mother was getting alarmed so she went for advice to a very wise old man who told her to stay away for two of three days until her son would get hungry. On the fourth day, she came to the house, and she saw her son outside it, and he was eating a big bowl of ashes. He welcomed her and said that it was time for her to come back. She was delighted to see him outside the door, for she thought he might turn his hand to something. So, he said to her, "This is a fine country and it is time for me to make my own living." So off he went and bid his mother goodbye. He was travelling along looking for a job and when the night was coming on, he saw a light glimmering in the valley. He went towards it and he asked if the man of the house was in, and the answer was yes. This man was the owner of a corn mill and anybody he would leave in charge of it by night would be dead in the morning. He hired Myles in the Ashes as a night watchman and promised him any wages he would demand if he came back in the morning. He was sitting at a little post in the mill when he heard a strange noise coming towards him. He saw a ghost coming towards him who had killed all the other watchmen. They began to fight and kept at it until Myles in the Ashes drove him out through the window, and he was never seen since then. He went home in the morning to his master who was delighted to see him alive, and brought him in, and gave him a lump sum of money, a new suit of clothes, and kept him on a week's holiday. The news of this man called Myles in the Ashes spread all over the country and a gentleman nearby, having heard of him came and hired him, as his home was haunted for many years. He had about twelve men in care of his place, and they had a row with Myles in the Ashes because they did not want him there. He beat the twelve of them and when the master saw he was such a powerful man, he was getting in dread himself. He thought of a plan to get rid of him and told him that he forgot his daybook in hell last week and wanted him to go back for it. Away he went and whatever road he took, he got there. They asked him where was he going, and he said that he was going for his master's day-book that he forgot last week. When they asked him his master's name, they told him that there was no such man and that he had forgotten nothing. Myles in the Ashes said, "That will not do me.

I must do my master's bidding," and he said, "Come now small devil and big devil of ye, let ye walk out before me to prove to him that I was here, and that there was no message." So, he drove them all in front of him right up to the man's hall-door. The man said that he would give him all his money and his daughter to marry if he took them away again. So, he drove away the devils and banished the ghosts that were in the man's house. He married the man's daughter and lived happily ever afterwards.[60]

## The Old Woman and the Roasted Cat

There was an old woman long ago and she had one son. His name was Mickie. There were only the two living in the house together. One day, the old woman got angry with Mickie as he would not do what she told him. She said she would not bake bread for him and so she did not. One day, she put a cake in the bastible to bake, and she went out in the garden planting flowers. Mickie came in and he put a cat in the bastible and ran away with the cake. The old woman came in and she found the horrible smell. She took the cover off the bastible and found the roasted cat. This old woman and Mickie, her son, lived in the townland of Bluid.[61]

## The Man, the Fairies and the Dead Horse

There was a man living in Leitir tSin Lis whose horse died. One night, the man was coming home from Skibbereen. The horse had been dead nine years. The man saw the horse with the fairies and he made a grab for him, but the horse was too lively, and he drove out of the man's sight. The man told Father Hennessy, and the priest told him to go to the spot with a bottle of holy water and sprinkle it on the fairies and the horse. The man did it, and the fairies disappeared, and the horse stood in front of him. The man took him home and he lived nine years after.[62]

# The Knight of the Glenn

Long ago, there was a gentleman living in Gleann Baracán. His title was Knight of the Glen. He owned a famous horse called Steed of the Bells, because it had many bells hanging from its neck. Many people tried to steal it, but when it heard them, it rang the bells. The gentleman had soldiers hired to guard it. When they heard the bells ringing, they came out and carried the robber in and threw him into a room filled with boiling lime. There was a king in Ireland at that time who had three sons. The queen died, but as she was dying, she asked the king to send their sons to a college to learn. Soon after, the king married again. The new queen was very mean and was not liked by the poor. One day, she was speaking to a woman. When she was going away, the woman said, "Goodbye now Your Majesty, and may the devil break your neck." The queen asked the woman why she said that. The woman told her that the three princes wanted the throne from the queen's son, their stepbrother. The queen said that she'd like to know how to get the best of them. The woman took out a magic pack of cards and told the queen to play against the princes. The queen invited the princes to the palace, and they came. While the feast was going on, the queen took out the pack of cards and told the princes to play in turn. She said that the loser should do whatever the winner told him. They agreed. The first two princes lost but the other won. Then the queen said that the two princes who lost should bring the Steed of the Bells to her, and the third prince said that the queen should live in prison till his brothers would return. The three princes set out and they came across an old man on the way who was lame. He told them that he'd go with them. When they came to the stable door, the horse rang the bells.

The four men were carried before the Knight of the Glen who gave them a chance if they told good stories. The old man told a story of how he had been at a giant's castle, who had only one eye. He heard a woman speaking to a baby. He asked her whose was the baby and she told him that it was the giant who had brought it and told her to kill it. The old man said to kill a pig instead and put the baby's finger on top. He got food from her and then he saw the giant coming up the path. The woman told him to hide in a room. He did and he saw a few dead men on the floor. He lay down with them, but the giant came in a looked around to see the freshest man to eat. He cut a piece out of the living man's side, so that was the reason why he was lame. The giant ate it and fell asleep. The man got up and bandaged his wound. He reddened the poker in the fire and drove it into the giant's eye. Then he ran away, but when the giant woke up, he threw a magic ring and it landed on the man's toe. The man had to cut off his toe and throw it into a river. The giant called to the ring and asked it where was it, and it told him. The giant jumped in after it and was drowned. Then the Knight of the Glen said that he was the baby, and that he'd give them the Steed of the Bells. When the princes returned, the queen jumped out of a window and was killed. The three princes got the kingdom then.[63]

# CASTLEHAVEN
# People, Places and Property

# The Parish of Glenbarrahane

The gleann from which the parish derives its name is situated at the western side of Castlehaven (Figure 3). Just above the strand is the cemetery which contains the ruins of an old church, the date of which I have not ascertained, and on the left-hand side of the stream above the cemetery is the holy well, Tobar Bhearchán, to which a few people pay visits still on December 3$^{rd}$. The modern name of the parish is Castlehaven and I have been informed that the popular affectation in the past was Paróisde a'Ghleanna. Across the harbour is Myross (Midhe Ros) parish which is under the administration of the same parish priest. Although the Irish language has survived among some of the older people in Myross, it must have ceased to exist in this area for a considerable time. On my first visit to Castletownshend (the village on the sea-front of Castle Haven) I found that even the oldest inhabitants did not know Irish, an event which may be attributed to the fact that the principal residents were either English or of English descent.

On this side, the whole sea-front is private property of the Townshend, Chavasse, Coghill, and Somerville families who have from time to time settled here. The native lords of this area were the McCarthys of whom the O'Driscolls were vassals. The Cromwellian Settlement bestowed their lands on the Townshends, Colonel Richard Townshend being the first Cromwellian lord of this portion of Carbery. Below the village of Castletownshend (Baile Chaisleáin) are the ruins of what appear to be an old fortress or castle (Figure 3). I was told by Colonel Somerville, who claims descent from him, that this was the original castle of Col. Richard Townshend, but local tradition has it that the castle was that inhabited by McCarthy. A story concerning the confiscation says that when Townshend came to take up the estate, he refused to disturb McCarthy, and that the two families lived together in the old castle till the Chieftain's death.

On the wall of the protestant church in Castletownshend are carved side by side the arms of the McCarthys and Townshends, said to commemorate the friendship between the two families. Two versions of this story exist locally - one that McCarthy's son and Townshend's daughter fell in love with each other, and when the son died, McCarthy, in grief, gave the property to his adopted daughter.

CASTLEHAVEN HARBOUR

COUNTY OF CORK

Figure 3. Castlehaven Harbour (top) ref. ET A94. View of the harbour and castle, Castlehaven (bottom) ref. PD 1974 TX 4 (6). Photos used with the kind permission of The National Library of Ireland.

Another telling is that McCarthy loved the English maid, whose name was Hildegarde, and when she died he grieved, and left to her father the land which he intended for her. I have heard that a poem describing this love affair was published about sixty years ago in *The Lamp*, but I have not succeeded in finding anybody who knows even a part of it.

Near the old castle ruin is Swift's Tower where Dean Swift is reputed to have done some of his writing when he visited the area.[ix] He also stayed for a time at Bawnlahan in the parish of Myross, overlooking Glandore Harbour, and it is probable that his *Carberiae Rupes* was written in one of these places.[x] The modern residence of the Townshends, called the Castle, formerly The Castle House, is situated closer to the village.

Beside the cemetery at Castlehaven stood, about ten years ago, the ruins of Castlehaven Castle, described by Don Pilib O'Sullivan in connection with the war of O'Neill and O'Donnell. Porto Castello, as it is called by O'Sullivan, played a very important part in connection with the Battle of Kinsale. Both O'Sullivan and Carew give accounts of a battle fought in the harbour, and while the former claims that Admiral Levison and his ships were driven off with loss of some vessels at the harbour's mouth, Carew claims victory for the British fleet. Local tradition says that inside Reen Point, on the eastern side of the harbour, lies a Spanish Vessel laden with gold, but that misfortune is sure to follow anyone who seeks the treasure.

Castlehaven Castle was fortified by a combined garrison of Spanish and Irish and withstood the assault of Admiral Levison of the British fleet. The ruins of this castle were in a fair state of preservation about fifteen years ago, but the lower portion of the wall showed signs of weakness, and the great pity was that nothing was done to prevent the collapse of the entire ruin a few years later. It is said that stones had been removed for road metaling many years ago and this vandalism could certainly bring about the unfortunate collapse which only left only a confused pile of stones.

---

[ix] Dean Smith refers to the author Jonathan Swift who was Dean of St Patrick's Cathedral, Dublin. Swift spent four months travelling on the southern and western coasts of Ireland in 1723. It is believed that Cabery Rocks (*Carberiae Rupes*) was written then.

[x] A full translation of *Carberiae Rupes*, Carbery's Rocks, is reproduced on pages 100 and 101.

Raheen Castle (Figures 4 & 5), almost opposite Castletownshend on the Myross side of the harbour, was a stronghold of the O'Donovans, who had another and older castle at Castle Ire behind the National School at Union Hall. Very little of the latter remains but a great part of Raheen Castle still stands in the townland of Raheen.

Further traces of the Spanish Occupation exist in the townland of Reen directly opposite Castlehaven castle. These are the Spanish Graves, the Spanish Trenches and the ovens. The late Admiral Boyle T. Somerville, who was tragically shot in his home a few years ago, took a great interest in local history and made several archaeological surveys in West Cork. He made excavations in Reen to prove the identity of the Spanish field ovens, which are stone lined trenches a short distance inside Reen Point. Before making his researches, he consulted me about the probable meaning of the ovens. He surmised that the probable meaning was Uaimh and had heard from a local resident - a non-Irish speaker - that the old people called it the Bácúis, which he did not understand. On hearing the meaning of Bácúis, he set to work and uncovered the stone lined trench. The Spanish trenches close to the sea-front inside Reen Point can still be clearly discerned though now nearly filled as a result of cattle travelling over the ground for over three centuries. The Spanish Graves on the side of the highest hill over the harbour are clearly discernible. Three of them are clear enough to distinguish as separate graves, and there are probably three more in the rough ground. The headstones though now nearly covered are still discernible. These are the graves of the men who were killed in the sea-battle against Admiral Levison in 1640. It is said that the guns of the British Ships were of such short range that the failed to hit the trenches inside Reen Point.

The River is the name given to the upper reaches of Castlehaven, though only a few small streams find their way into this inlet. It is navigable up to Leabaidh, but at low tide even small boats cannot navigate the muddy channels up to Rineen, where are still working the corn mills, though the large mill (Figure 6), which was water-driven, now rests idle, its place being taken by modern oil engines. Most of the residents of the little village of Rineen have one or more members of their families employed in the local mills.

Figure 4. Raheen Castle by J. S. Flemming (1853) ref. PD 1974 TX 10 (12),
used with the kind permission of The National Library of Ireland

Figure 5. Raheen Castle, photo by Fergus O'Connor, ref. OCO 101. used with
the kind permission of The National Library of Ireland.

Along the sides of the river on the eastern side are Raheen Castle already mentioned, and the once beautifully wooded Leacha Riabhach. In this wood, a portion of which has been left standing, is a little bower called leabaidh an fhile where Seán Máighistir Ó Coileáin is reputed to have composed his songs. It seems a fitting setting for An Buachaill Bán.

Maidin lae ghil fá dhuille chrainn ghlais
Doire im aonar cosi imeall trágha
i bhfís trím néaltaibh do dhearcas spéir bean
Ag teacht ó thaoibh dheis na mara im dháil

Above Leaca Riabhach in the Townland of Cappagh is an old ruin of Stuacín Church, the walls of which are in a fair state of preservation. In the time of Seán Ó Coileáin, this church was in use, and the story is told of a blind man called Scúirdín who came to mass there one Sunday. The dog started to bark just before Mass began and the priest ordered the people to drive out the dog, but the congregation taking no action, the priest came down to the door, kicked the dog out and killed it. Seán, commenting on the event, is reputed to have said "Ní bás gan sagart fuair madra Scúirdín".[xi]

Further up towards Rineen, where a stream from Fórnocht joins the sea at high water, is Beal a'Chinn Mara (pronounced locally Bélicín Mara). Near the bridge (Figure 6) stood another church built by one of the O'Donovans of Bawnlahan. This man, a Catholic, is reputed to have been of a tyrannical disposition, and made a regulation that the priest should not use the church except when he himself was present. The priest celebrated mass in his absence and on his return home he had the church thrown down, and thenceforth ceased to practice his religion. He married a protestant who refused to bring him a priest when he felt his end coming, but his importunities must have been too much for her to bear, so she bribed one of her workmen to dress as a priest and to make pretence of administering the Last Sacrament. The sick man died but the workman who impersonated the priest hanged himself.

---

[xi] Scurry's dog did not die without a priest

Figure 6. Rineen Bridge (top) ref. L_CAB_05219. Rineen Mill (bottom), ref
L_CAB_05218. Photos by Robert French (1841-1917), used with the kind
permission of The National Library of Ireland.

This story is reputed locally to be true, and only a few years ago the last surviving member of the family whose ancestor perpetrated the sacrilege died in the parish of Myross.

St Patrick's Cross is a crudely carved Celtic Cross which stands in the Castletownshend wood opposite Leaca Riabhác, on the western side of The River. Nobody seems to know its origin, but Admiral Somerville believed it had no historical significance, that it was probably placed there for ornament by some one of the Townshends before the wood grew. At present, it is hidden from view by a wilderness of scrub briars, and saplings or suckers from cut down trees.

The Castletownshend Wood, opposite Leacha Riabhác, extends from the village for over half a mile along the water's edge, and the two wooded hills sloping down to the sheltered creek present a very beautiful prospect with the rugged hills of Fórnothz (anglicised Forenaught) in the background. On a height over the wood is erected a crude arch known as Pércín Nelson. The hill itself, the highest in the Castletownshend demesne, was a famous landmark for fishermen approaching the harbour. The Pércín was evidently the original name of the hill. The rustic arch was erected by a body of British Sailors who entered the harbour after the Battle of Trafalgar, but it was thrown down one night during the Anglo-Irish war. When I came to this parish in 1923, the Pércín was strewn with stone from the Nelson monument, some of them were thrown down the side of an adjoining precipice. In 1924, Colonel Somerville asked a number of local men to give their services freely for the re-erection of the monument and the arch again stands reproduced from a photograph of the original. Most people think it is not as high. There are two lakes in the wood. The larger, called Lake Bean Uasal in the ordinance Survey map, is scarcely deserving of the name lake as it is gradually filling with rushes; the smaller one is little more than a pond surrounded by a morass. The hills around these lakes are beautiful in summer with magnificent display of rhododendrons. Between the lakes and the Pércín are traces of tillage and the foundations of houses. It appears that many evictions took place from time to time to extend the demesne. The wood does not reach the present road from Castletownshend to Rineen, and it is said that an English visitor said to the Madam Townshend of the time, that the beauty of the demesne would be enhanced by an unplanted belt. To secure this within the demesne, the tenants were evicted and caretakers appointed in their stead.

Smaller holdings farther north were provided for the evicted tenants. About 80 years ago, or probably much farther back the land was again sold to tenants at a high price and at a heavy annual rent, with the result that in proportion to their acreage, the present holders are paying higher land annuities than their neighbours. These are Daniel Collins, Gurranes, Jerome O'Regan, Kilangil, Con Cahalane, ditto, Jas Dinneen, ditto, and Martin Moloney, Carriglishane (Carraig Tighe Sheáin). Kilangil is also called Kealangile, and Keelahangil. The latter is the commonest pronunciation. There is above The Pound (in Gurranes) an elevation called Langley's Height, and the late Jas. M. Burke B.L., T.D. in his writings suggests that it got its name from the family Angley (Aingle) now extinct.

Baile an Aifrinn is the name for a large field nowadays known as Drishane Side, sloping down to the harbour between the village and Castlehaven Cemetery. Traces of the old road through this field are clearly discernible. Here, in the Penal Days, was either a chapel or shelter for saying mass, the exact site being unknown. Overlooking the sea, there was a chance of escape for the priest and people should the enemy approach.

At the southwestern end of the field are the remains of an old mill, and a narrow bridge still stands much raised above the surface on both sides. It would appear that carts were not used in crossing it, or else the road foundation has been removed to a great depth. The mill has closed long before living memory, but it is known that the owner was an O'Driscoll. The mill was closed down after the death of a worker named O'Regan who was accidentally crushed in the machinery. The roof was removed something over 50 years ago and the wood, which was very sound, was used by local carpenters in the construction of houses in the parish.

The Dutchman's Cove is a small inlet below the Milleen, as it is popularly called. It lies directly opposite the harbour's mouth, and it is known that at least three ships were wrecked here, one a Dutch vessel. The last lost here was called the Aconomy.

Trágha ligeach lies about 3½ miles west of Castletownshend. I have given this strand it's popular pronunciation, but in the locality some of the old people think it should be Trágha na gCloch which would be quite appropriate as it maybe even Trágh Shligeach. In this area the emphasis is on -ach.

In 1823 a battle was fought between the police, assisted by the Coastguards, and the local people who resisted payment of the tithe Rents. Women joined in the fight to assist their menfolk and one woman struck down a policeman with a stone. He was struck by the others and was killed. One of the tenants named O'Regan was also killed. He is buried in Castlehaven. The following are the only pieces I could find of the poem describing the battle.

> Ocht gcead ar míle, trí agus a fiche le'nais
> Mar a leagadh an pílear agus in a chroidhe níor fághadh prab.
> Tá an pílear sínte gan brigh 'na chab
> Agus Pilib Ó Laocha an tríomadh ceach

The policeman was named John Crowe and he is reputed to have cried out when at the mercy of his attackers. "Mercy, mercy, for poor John Crowe".

Currabeg Fair: Currabeg is situated in the northern side of the parish and here a fair used to be held up to about 65 years ago. The fairs usually ended in faction fights and in the last of these a man named Thomas Brown was killed. Three families of the Brownes live in the parish, two at Killangil and one at Móm a'bhualachám.

## Carbery's Rocks
By Jonathan Swift (c1723), translated from the Latin by Dr Dunkin

> LO! from the top of yonder cliff, that shrouds
> Its airy head amid the azure clouds,
> Hangs a huge fragment; destitute of props,
> Prone on the wave the rocky ruin drops;
> With hoarse rebuff the swelling seas rebound,
> From shore to shore the rocks return the sound:
> The dreadful murmurs Heaven's high convex cleaves,
> And Neptune shrinks beneath his subject waves:
> For, long the whirling winds and beating tides
> Had scoop'd a vault into its nether sides.
> Now yields the base, the summits nod, now urge
> Their headlong course, and lash the sounding surge.
> Not louder noise could shake the guilty world,
> When Jove heap'd mountains upon mountains hurl'd;

Retorting Pelion from his dread abode,
To crush Earth's rebel sons beneath the load.
Oft too with hideous yawn the cavern wide
Presents an orifice on either side,
A dismal orifice, from sea to sea
Extended, pervious to the God of Day:
Uncouthly join'd, the rocks stupendous form
An arch, the ruin of a future storm:
High on the cliff their nests the woodquests make,
And seacalves stable in the oozy lake.
But when bleak Winter with his sullen train
Awakes the winds to vex the watery plain;
When o'er the craggy steep without control,
Big with the blast, the raging billows roll;
Not towns beleaguer'd, not the flaming brand,
Darted from Heaven by Jove's avenging hand,
Oft as on impious men his wrath he pours,
Humbles their pride, and blasts their gilded towers,
Equal the tumult of this wild uproar:
Waves rush o'er waves, rebellows shore to shore.
The neighbouring race, though wont to brave the shocks
Of angry seas, and run along the rocks,
Now pale with terrour, while the ocean foams,
Fly far and wide, nor trust their native homes.
The goats, while pendent from the mountain top
The wither'd herb improvident they crop,
Wash'd down the precipice with sudden sweep,
Leave their sweet lives beneath th' unfathom'd deep.
The frighted fisher, with desponding eyes,
Though safe, yet trembling in the harbour lies,
Nor hoping to behold the skies serene,
Wearies with vows the monarch of the main.

## Biddy and Jerh.

These were husband and wife who lived in a little house near the entrance gate to Rinneen House. When the owner of the house went in or out with his horses and carriage, either Biddy or Jerh went to open the gate, and they often got a few pence when visitors came. Biddy was a good-humoured woman who used to say a lot to amuse the visitors, and as a result she always got more money that Jerh when she went to open or close the gate. She never wore shoes except when going to mass or to town. One day a very swanky crowd arrived in a carriage at the gate. Being barefoot, she was afraid the strangers would not like her, so she said to Jerh, "Run out and open the gate, Jerh, as you have the shoes. Jerh's reply was, "Let you run out, Biddy, as you have the tongue."

## Horse Island

Horse Island is the modern name for Oileán Mholugha. The late Admiral Somerville was the first to give me the Gaelic name and he said it was believed that Molugha, sister of St Bearcán is buried there. About sixteen years ago some men employed in repairing the fence over a cliff uncovered a skeleton in a stone coffin. This grave was one of many in a disused cemetery on the island. At the South-eastern end is a circular tower, the origin of which is not known. The island has been uninhabited for about fifty years and only dry stock are kept grazing there. In Myross I was told how it got the name Horse Island. A farmer left a young mare on the island for over a year without any other animal of her kind. To his surprise she produced a foal the second year and this was reputed to be the progeny of a sea-horse! The Island is situated outside the harbour's mouth on the western side. Very fine sandstone has been removed from it for building. The Protestant Church in Castletownshend is built from stone obtained in Horse Island. Much of it shows the effect of weathering.[64]

## Sherkin Abbey

There is a wishing chair in Sherkin Island. It is situated on the top of an abbey and there is a graveyard round it (Figure 7). It is very high.

## Tobairín Handsome

There is a well inside the fence on the right below the river's cross called by the above name. Being in a shaded place, the water is always cool, and in years gone by when the farmers in the district were making butter at home, the neighbouring women used to bring their butter there to wash it in the warm weather. How it got its name is not known.[65]

## The Parish Churches

In the townland of Bawn was situated the first chapel built after the penal times, but two parties to a faction fought in the grounds of the church one Sunday after mass, so the building, which appears to have been a small one, closed down. The next church was in Fahoura on the old road passing through Raheen from the river's cross, but only a small piece of ivy-clad wall remains to mark its site. Being on the borders of Raheen, it was also called Raheen Church. The modern church, which was built a little over 100 years ago, also stands in Fahoura but there are no parochial records to give it the date of its creation nor of the parish priest of the time.

The story is told of the headless horseman who was seen riding past Raheen church, and here is another tale of the same road. A man going home from a wake alone on a moonlit night met a rider on horseback coming towards him. He saw the rider was a stranger but had no fear, so he addressed him. "Where are you going so late, Sir?" The stranger replied, "I am going to midnight mass on Cnoc Droma." There is no record of a church on this hill, but there is a stone marked with a cross.[66]

INISHERKEN

Figure 7. Views of Sherkin Abbey from *The Illustrated London News*, 27 August 1887, p.247, (top), and S.C. Hall, *A Week at Killarney* (London: Virtue & Co., 1850), p.58, (bottom).

## The School Yard

On the ground where the school was built, there was once a haggard where a lot of corn used to be threshed. When the first threshing machine came to the district it was tried here, and the local farmers brought their corn here to be threshed. As now, the neighbours came to assist each other at the meitheal, and the work lasted for a week. The men had to work very hard, and one who was getting tired thought of a plan to stop the machine. He quietly slipped a mouse into the ear of one of the four horses working the machine. The animal got restive and had to be untackled, so the men had a rest while another was being provided to take its place. The owner of the place at the time was named Swanton.[67]

## The Factory Hill

There are traces of houses on the side of the road where it is believed the workers in the linen factory lived, but there is no trace of the factory itself. It is thought to have been on the land now occupied by Mr James Dinneen, Kilapil. The latter is only about ten years in residence there.

# CASTLEHAVEN
# Local Customs

## The Wagtail

It is said to be very unlucky to kill a wagtail and children grew up with a great love for this little bird. Very likely the old people made up the pishogue as they knew it was a very useful bird for destroying the wireworm. That is why they said it was unlucky to kill it.[68]

## The Spider

It is a very common belief that anyone who kills a spider will meet with some misfortune. In the old times, people shore the sheep and spun the thread at home. They wound it into big balls which they hung from the rafters of the loft, which was the name given to the second floor of the house. The spiders made their webs over the balls and so kept the moths from eating the thread. That is very likely the reason why the old people said one should never kill a spider.[69]

## The Christmas Candle

This candle is about two feet long. It is hard to get a candlestick to suit it, so a turnip is scooped out to hold it. The turnip is then covered with coloured paper and holly sprays, but sometimes the turnip is carved into patterns on the outside with a few holly sprays stuck in it. It is lighted [sic] on Christmas Eve at nightfall and must not be quenched before midnight. Some people keep the candle lighting [sic] all night and put it out when they are going to first mass on Christmas Day. In the country, all the windows in the house have candles and no blinds are drawn, so it is a lovely sight to look around on Christmas night all over the country. Only when a death takes place in the house during the year are the windows left without light. This custom is kept up on the eve and day of Christmas, New Year, and Little Christmas. On Christmas night, the first Christmas candle is lighted by the father of the family and the mother quenches it. It used to be the custom to have the first candle lighted on Christmas night also lighted for some time on each of the twelve days of Christmas.[70]

# The Cockcrow

First cock-crow was after midnight, and no one should leave the house before that time as the fairies were out until cockcrow. Second cockcrow was about 4am and that was the time for the farmers to get up and get ready for the fair. When the cows rise up in the stall is about 5am.[71]

# Piseóga

A bride on the day of her wedding should wear something old, something new, something borrowed, and something blue. The bridegroom should not see the bride's wedding dress until she arrives in it at the church. When the bride gives her dress to be made, she should not see it again until it is finished, unless she makes it herself. She will not live long is she sees another person sewing it. The bride must be the last person to leave the house when going to the church to be married. She must never reach the church before the bridegroom.[72]

# Time by the Sun

Not long ago, a great many people could tell the time by the sun. Watches and clocks were not very plentiful years ago and people knew the time by the position of the shadows. In the morning, the sun's rays fell on a certain mark on the floor or wall, and the shadow of the chimney on some place outside showed midday. In the evening, the shadow of the chimney on some part of the roof told the old people the time. An old woman in Kilhanghil was called Pug na Corcán because she had a broken pot with three legs on top of a stick in the haggard. She could tell the time very correctly from the way the sun made shadows with the broken edges of the pot. The shadows thrown by the legs of the pot also helped her to get the time.[73]

## Superstitious Sayings

It is not right to bring an article made of steel into a house on your shoulder for you would grow no more.

Foreign cows wear long horns.

It is not right to look behind when riding a horse after midnight.

It is not right to be out at one o'clock or two o'clock in the night.

It is unlucky to cry after the dead.

It is not right to go home alone after midnight.

It is unlucky to carry the dead the short road to the grave.

It is lucky to get married on Saturday or during shrove.

It is unlucky to get married during lent.

It is not lucky to have a wedding meet a funeral.[74]

# CASTLEHAVEN
# The Natural World and Weather Lore

# Signs of Rain

The roar of the waterfall in Smithfield can be heard far off. The roar of the sea outside Horse Island is another sign. The dog eats grass and the cat sits with its back to the fire. Frogs are heard croaking in the bog above the school. Old people get pains in their bones. Seagulls are seen coming in from the sea and the curlews are heard crying. The latter reminds me of an incident which occurred when I was a boy. An old man was saving late upland hay about the end of August in my home locality. As he worked, the curlews flying overhead commenced their cry, and the old man looking up said, "The Divil take ye for cuírliúns, ye were the bad séuds coming into the country", so apparently, he blamed the effect for the cause.[75]

# CASTLEHAVEN
## Local Songs

## Sweet Castletownsend Demesne

The following poem attributed to Seán Ó Coileáin was supplied by Pádraig Ó Mathúna. In verse V he refers to Leaca Riabhach which unfortunately is much denuded of its trees now. In a part of the wood which has not been destroyed is a little bower called Leabhaidh an Fhile. Here, Seán Máighistir, as he is known locally, composed many of his poems and he had a lovely setting for his poem, An Buachaill Bán.

### Sweet Castletownshend Demesne

Your gentle sweet muses assist me,
And join in my sweet vocal lays,
In praising this sweet habitation,
Where nature its beauty displays.
I've roamed through all parts of this nation,
And travelled both Paris and Spain,
But found none so truly delightful,
As sweet Castletownshend Demesne.

The fruit trees of this habitation,
Are growing spontaneously rare,
The peach, quince, the plum and the cherry,
The apple and nectarine pear.
Oh! Were I the great Julius Caesar,
Or Nelson who once ruled the main,
I'd resign all those favours and titles,
For sweet Castletownshend Demesne.

Meandering streams from pure fountains,
In cataracts gently do glide.
The pheasant, the woodcock and partridge,
Are abounding by each waterside,
Where the shellfish, the trout and the salmon,
The pike-fish, the roach and the bream,
Add beauty to nature's productions,
In sweet Castletownshend Demesne.

The loveliest landscape of Nature,
Mount Eagle most pleasing to rove,
The valleys romantic and charming,
Surrounded by sweet shady groves,
Where the cry of the hounds and the horn,
Reached each neighbouring plain,
Arousing the deer from their arbour,
In sweet Castletownshend Demesne.

To walk on a fine summer's morning,
'Tis pleasant in May or in June,
To sail up that beautiful harbour,
To view Leaca Riabhach in full bloom,
Where the ships from the remotest regions,
With gold from the Peruvian main,
Are riding in safety at anchor,
Beneath Castletownshend Demesne.

Here's a health to our youthful Commander,
Who fought like a hero in Spain,
With laurels of honour and glory,
With battles victoriously gained.
Many fortune attend his proceedings,
And bring him safe home to remain,
He's the pride of his country and people,
He's Colonel John Townshend of fame.[76]

Figure 8. Castletownshend (top), F. O'Connor Collection,
c1900-1939, NLI. Ref: OCO 273. View of the Castle,
Castletownshend (bottom), photo by
R. French. Ref: L_ROY_04912,
Used with the kind permission of the NLI.

# CASTLEHAVEN
# History and Archaeology

# The Famine

Many people in this locality died during the famine period, and scores were taken from the Skibbereen Workhouse to the famine plot in the Abbey burial ground, Skibbereen. An old man named Barry of Rinneen died, and as the people were afraid to go to his house. His mother took the body on her back up to Forenaught where she buried it without coffin or sheet. The field where he lies is known as Páirc na marbh.[77]

The following was told me by Patrick O'Brien, Lettertinlish. The bottom of Forenaught was spotted with houses at that time, and they were all starving, so they went up to Townshend's fields and hunted a couple of bullocks down the wood. They drove them into the slab below Rineen, and while alive they commenced to cut up the animals and eat the raw meat. As my informant put it, you could hear 'em screeching in the slab and the people ating 'em. When they had satisfied their hunger, they gathered up what was left of the animals and buried the remains in Forenaught. The field is now called Páircín na Feola, and the inlet at Rineen where the beasts were caught in the Slab is called Cuaisín a Tarbh (probably should be Cuaisín na dTarbh).[78]

# Syrian Remains in County Cork

About four miles from Skibbereen, as we go to the picturesque village of Castletownshend, the road seems barred by an abrupt hill, on the summit of which we may observe, what appears a wall of dark grey stone. A rugged road leads up to this, and when we gain the highest point, there breaks upon us as beautiful a view as can be found in any part of Ireland. A vast horizon of open sea extends as far as the eye can reach […]. So splendid is the panorama, so lovely the details of the view that spreads before us when we reach the summit of Knockdrum, that at first we little regard the old grey wall which attracted our upward steps (Figure 9). But, when we look more closely, we find that this wall, though now only five or six feet high, encloses a circular space of about 300 feet in circumference, and is ten or eleven feet in breadth. This great circle has but one entrance; at one side of which stands a pillar stone, with a rudely sculpted cross carved at its top (Figure 10), and on the other there is a recess carefully made in the thickness of the wall which may have been the post of a sentinel, or possibly the cell of an immured anchorite.

In the centre of the enclosed space there are the foundations of a small building, which we believe to have been a little church, eighteen feet in length and breadth, with a semi-circular apse; and in close proximity to this are a series of underground rooms of different sizes with flat flag roofs and narrow connecting passages, so narrow that when one tries to crawl through them there is a strong probability that one can neither advance nor recede; the rooms or cells are from six to twelve feet in length and a good deal less in breadth, while they are only about three feet high at present; but as there is a great deal of rubbish on the floor, they may originally have been higher. In Professor Stokes' Lectures on the Celtic Church, an account is given of the cashel or sacred enclosure in the island of Innismurry, which is said to correspond closely to some early Syrian Christian buildings in Brittany and elsewhere. It is worth noting that if instead of ascending the hills of Knockdrum we turn to the left of the road which leads to Castletownshend, we shall find three tall monolithic pillars, still upright, a fourth prostrate beside them (Figure 11).

Rev. Canon John R. Brougham, 'Syrian remains in County Cork', *Journal of the Cork Historical and Archaeological Society*, ser. 1, vol. 2, no. 20 (1893), pp.154-156

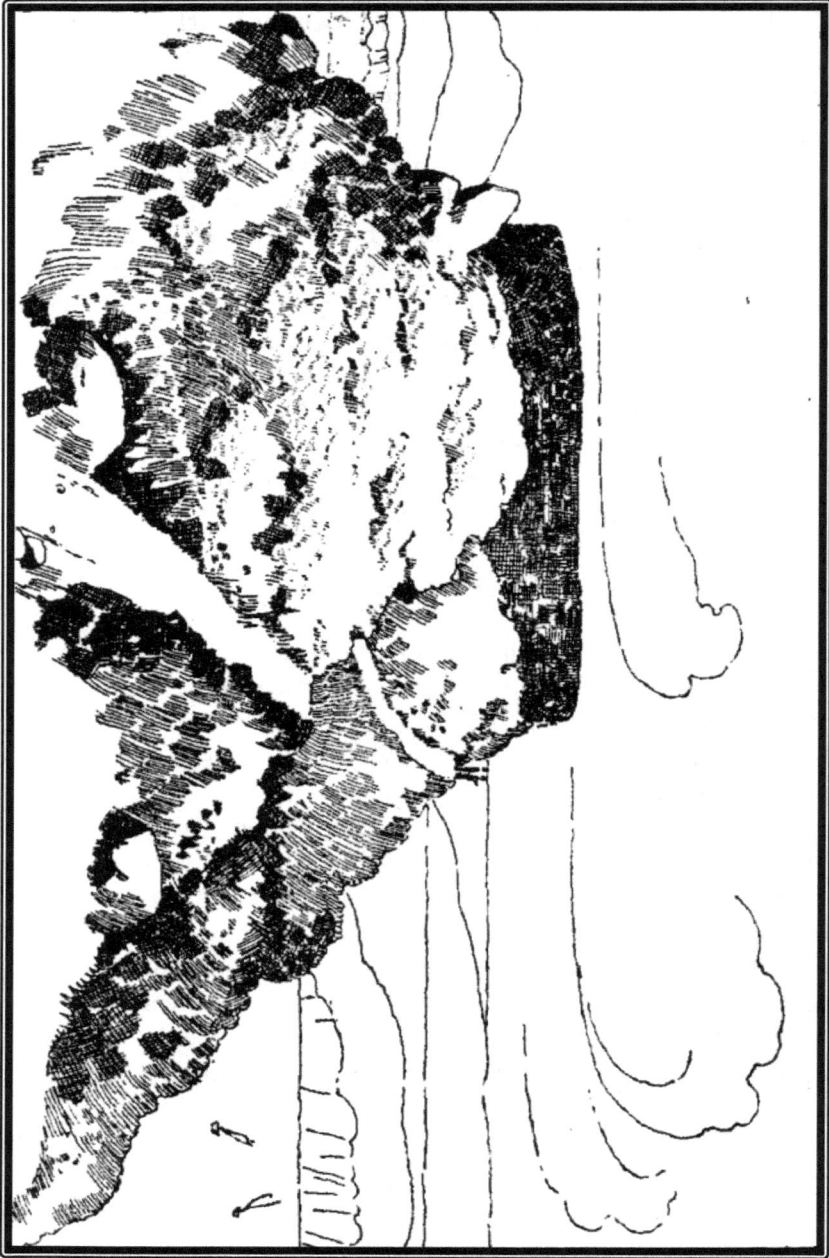

Figure 9. The Cashel on Knockdrum Hill near Drishane, Castletownshend, from John Brougham, Syrian Remains in County Cork in *Journal of the Cork Historical and Archaeological Society*, vol. 2 (Cork: Guy & Co., 1893), p.154.

Figure 10. Pillar stone with cross, entrance to Knockdrum Cashel, from
John Brougham, Syrian Remains in County Cork in *Journal of the Cork
Historical and Archaeological Society*, vol. 2 (Cork: Guy & Co., 1893), p.155.

Figure 11. Pillar stones north-east of Knockdrum Hill, from John Brougham, Syrian Remains in County Cork in *Journal of the Cork Historical and Archaeological Society*, vol. 2 (Cork: Guy & Co., 1893), p.155.

# CONVENT OF MERCY

Co. Chorcaighe
Bar: Cairbre Thiar
Par: Abbeystrowry
Scoil:  Clochar Na Trócaire
Oide: Na Siúracha

Figure 12. Convent of Mercy, Skibbereen (top), ref. L_IMP_2131. Convent of Mercy (bottom), ref L_IMP_2132), Skibbereen, spinning room. Photos by Robert French (1841-1917), used with the kind permission of The National Library of Ireland.

# CONVENT OF MERCY
# Local Folklore and Stories

# The Serpent of Lough Clougher

Long ago, at the time O'Donovan lived in Castle Ibor, there was a serpent in Lough Clougher. This serpent was very destructive as sometimes he would come up on the bank, and if there were any cattle, there he would eat them and go to the bottom of the lake again. This carried on for a long time. At last O'Donovan invited all the people to come to a feast to see could he get anyone to kill the serpent, but no one would venture. At that time there were two Burkes from Tipperary on the run. They heard the story and offered to venture. So, they went to the wood and cut a long pole, and got it forged with iron spikes on the one side and ropes and chains on the other and tied them to a big tree. They went down to the lake. They were not long there when the serpent came up one of them stuck the spike down his throat and then began slashing him with his sword. After a long struggle, the serpent broke the chains and went into the lake and was never seen again. O'Donovan was overjoyed and gave them money and a large piece of land in Cooldorough.[79]

Collected by Breeda O' Mahony
From Jerry O'Donovan, aged 55, Raheen

# The Treasure of Athach Mór

Under a huge stone on the slope of a hill in my father's farm, there is said to be hidden treasure. It is said that one day Athach Mór, a great giant, was challenged to throw this huge stone (at least one ton and a half weight) from Mount Gabriel to that spot on the hill. First the giant seemed unwilling to try this feat, but when he began to lift the stone it seemed of no weight, and he succeeded in landing it exactly on the spot. Under it there is said to be an unusual thing, a nest containing seven golden eggs, each seven inches in diameter and filled with sovereigns. About four perches due west of this stone is another stone, under which a similar treasure is hidden. An old man of the vicinity recently revealed that in order to find the treasure one must draw a straight line from one stone to another, then standing near the middle of the line, hold a cord in the hand and lift it an eastward direction, so that it will cross the stone and a light will be seen over the spot where the treasure is. My uncle, having heard the story, decided to prove this, so he set to work at the mysterious stone. Having drawn the line, he stood near the centre and cast the string eastward. Then to his astonishment he noticed a ray of light over a small portion of the stone. He tried to split the stone but failed. Though still engaged at the work he finds it impossible to do.[80]

Collected by Caitlín Ní Árnéidig, Highfield
From John Connolly, aged 71 years

## Hidden Treasure

There are many stories told about treasure which was hidden in ancient Ireland by the olden people. These treasures were chiefly hidden in lonely valleys and islands where people used not travel. It is supposed that they are protected by animals and such things. I have heard from my father, Denis McCarthy, about some treasure which has been hidden in my district. It is said to have been put there by a little man who got it from a rich gentleman. This gentleman it seems was in dread that his treasure would be stolen from him, so he got the little man to take care of it.

The latter had a son who knew nothing about the treasure or where it was. The little man was to bring the gold with him if he lived, and if he died, he should tell his son where it was. It happened that he was dying, and he told the son as follows: 'There was a large flag standing the height of a man facing south-east, between three freshwater lakes. He would find this stone where the first rays of morning sun would shine on the longest day of the year. It would not remain shining on it but for three minutes, and it is under the end of the shadow of this flag the gold is hidden.' The boy never found the gold, so he told the secret to everybody in the end.

There is also another treasure hidden in Lough Ine island. It is hidden under a huge, big stone, and it is of very rich value. Many people have made attempts to go and look for it, but nobody has ever succeeded. One poor fisherman named Liam Báróid set out one bright moonlight night, armed with a pickaxe and crowbar. He took his boat and made for the spot.

No sooner had he anchored his boat, when he looked about him and saw an enormous cat sitting on top of the stone under which the gold is hidden. His eyes were like two lights in his head, and his legs were like big barrels. He fled in terror, and he never tried the same again, neither would he dare pass the island or do any more fishing.

There is a man in my district by the name of Florence O'Donovan who, as he was one day cutting turf in a bog, found a casket. It was about the size of a bucket and made of timber on the outside. Inside this it was lined with strong leather, and enclosed in the leather was another little leather purse, fastened at each end by strong thongs. This purse contained parchment which was as safe as the first day it was put there. It was a bit soiled from the bog-water and it is thought to have been there for some hundreds of years.[81]

Collected by Eibhlín Ní Chárthaigh
From Donnchadh Mac Cárthaigh, aged 40 years

# The Legend of Lough Ine Castle

In the centre of Lough Ine lake there is an island and on its eastern side stand the ruins of an old castle known as Labhra Ó Leencha's castle. As the story goes it was supposed that the king who lived there had two ears as large as those of a donkey, and to conceal this fact he stopped not even at murder. Once in twelve months he got his hair cut and the lot fell on one of the neighbours to cut it. It happened at one time that the lot fell on a widow's only son and it was also known that the barber would be put to death lest he should betray the secret, but this widow pleaded so earnestly with the King that her son was allowed to live on condition that he would never reveal the secret to anybody.

The boy was ailing, and he went to a priest and told him he had a secret which he could not let out. Then the priest told to dig a sod and tell the secret to the ground and the boy carried out his order. The sod was dug near the shore of a lake and when the reeds grew up and the first gust of wind blew them, they commenced to sing, "Tá dhá chluais capaill ag Labhar Ó Loingsigh [Labhar Ó Loingsigh has two horse ears]". So when the king heard this, he took his boat and was last seen sailing over the ocean.

It is supposed that there is a crock of gold hidden under this castle. At one time an old fisherman was so firmly convinced that it was there, he went with pick and bar to search for it, but to his surprise what did he find there but a black cat minding the castle, so he fled in terror and never since did anyone search for it.

Another version of the above is that the boy went to a druid for advice and was told to ease his mind by telling the secret to a hazel tree. Later a harper made a harp from the wood of this tree, and the instrument could be got to play nothing but the refrain, "Tá dhá chluais capaill ag Labhar Ó Loingsigh".[82]

Collected by Eibhlín Ní Chárthaigh

# A Legend of Myross

In the centre of the parish of Myross is a small lake known as Loch Clúthmhar, or the 'sheltered lake'. The people of the parish have many legends concerning the lake.

Long ago there lived a poor labourer and his wife nearby. One day, when her husband had departed for his days' work, the woman heard a knock at the door. On opening it she saw a lady whom she had never seen before standing there. This stranger asked the woman could she lend him a pot. After hesitating for some moments, the woman gave the pot. It happened this pot was the only one the couple possessed, and it took the part of a saucepan where necessary. When her husband returned, he reproached her for giving their most useful possession to an unknown woman. When supper time arrived, there was nothing in which to boil their frugal meal.

Again, the stranger presented herself in the tiny cottage. She bade the labourer's wife come out and gave her a beautiful cow, telling here if ever she struck this cow with the fetters she would disappear. Years passed and the cow had calves which soon grew, and they, in their turn, had calves until at length the woman had seven cows which were the pride of the old couple, and which surpassed all other cows in their yield of milk. The woman grew more prosperous each year but never broke her promise to the lady. At length, one night when the woman was milking one of the cows, a neighbour came into her and asked for milk. This woman owed the labourer's wife a sum of money for milk which she had previously taken, but she refused to pay it. This angered the woman, and she struck the cow. At once, the cow followed by her calves, ran into the lake and was never seen since.[83]

Collected by Maighréád Ni Síthe, Reen
From Michael Hallihan, aged 64 years

# CONVENT OF MERCY
# Farming, Trade and Crafts

# Local Crafts

Soap was made from tallow mixed with paraffin oil and pot ash. The tallow was first boiled then the oil was poured on it, and the potash was used for drying it, it was then placed in shapes.

Thatching was practised in olden times. A large wooden needle was used for thatching. The straw was first got and made into little fists. These were placed on the roof, and they were sewed with the wooden needle and a cord to the rafters, this was done till the roof was finished.

Dying was done in various ways. Log wood was used for dying, this could be obtained in several colours. Furze blossoms, ivy, and onions were used for dying.

In olden times the people made butter in a small wooden churn, with a staff attached from the inside of it and a hole in the churn through which the staff came out. When the butter was made it was then made up in firkins.

Ropes were made out of oakum, and hemp. The hemp was twisted by two men, one man wound it on a stick, and another twisted it.

Whips were made out of thin leather which was platted. Coopers were also famous tradesmen. These made churns, tubs, and barrels of wood.[84]

Candles were made by means of a mould. The people put the wick which was made of rushes into a mould and they made fat or tallow into a liquid, and they poured it all round the wick and left it there for a few days till it was hard, and they then took it out and the candle was made.

The baskets were made of twigs. The people who were making them stuck the strong twigs in the ground and wound the weaker ones around them. They bent the ones in the bottom, and they also wound the small ones through them, and that was how baskets were made.

Hides were put into a tan hole and they covered them with the bark of a tree. They left it there for a certain length of time and then it was taken out and dried and then the leather was made.

The limestone was put into the kiln and also some colum into it, and they lit it and put fire to it and left it there for several days to let the lime burn. The old people had spinning wheels and the women of the house spun the wool into thread.

Some people made spades of steel to dig the land in the spring and they were called spring spades. The ploughs were all made of timber.[85]

Collected by Séosaimhín Ní Chochláin and Maigread Nic Gearailt
From Pádraig Ó Chochláin and Ristéard Mac Gearailt (aged 52)

# Convent of Mercy
## Local Customs

## St John's Night

On the night of 23rd June (Saint John's night) it is customary in this district to light bonfires on the hills and in the fields. It is believed that this practice was handed down to us from pre-Christian Ireland. Baal or the Sun being one of the deities adored by our Pagan ancestors, they lighted a fire in his honour in mid-Summer. After the coming of Saint Patrick, the fires were still lighted in honour of the birthday of Saint John the Baptist, to whom the Irish have always shown great devotion. In this locality it was the custom for each farmer to go to a stream or river where three townlands met. He brought home a bottle of the water with which he sprinkled the cattle and prevented disease among them during the coming year. Sometimes the boys of the district went to a nearby wood which they set on fire. Bonfires are still lighted in each farm. A lighting bush is brought from the fire to each tillage field and a drink of water is given to the cattle from a stream where three townlands meet.[86]

Collected by Séosaimhín Ní Chochláin
from Pádraig Ó Cochláin, Lichnavar

## Marriage Customs

Near the north end of the island of Cleire, a pillar-stone (gallaun) may be seen standing upright and about four feet high. In the centre there is a circular opening; there is an ancient tradition connected with it. In former times, this was a marriage stone where lovers met and became engaged. As no jeweller flourished on the island and engagement rings were not to be obtained, the lovers adopted the custom of plighting their troth by shaking hands through the circular opening. The mutual vows made on such occasions were strictly observed. This gallaun is looked upon as a venerable relic connected in some way or another with the worship of the Druids.[87]

Collected by Máire Ní Chéadagáin, Skibbereen
From Eibhlís Ní Chéadagáin

# Shrove: Marriage Customs

Shrove begins on the 6th of January and ends on Ash Wednesday. It was during this period in former years most of the marriages were celebrated in the rural districts. It was the custom for a man to go to any house where there was a girl of marriageable age and suggest the name of a certain man. This was known as matchmaking and the man who went to the house was known as a matchmaker. A few days after, the parents of the suggested man and girl met in a public house in the neighbouring town and discussed the fortune and the future home of the girl. If they all agreed they went to a solicitor and the bindings were drawn and the date of the marriage fixed. Very often it was at the altar-rails that the future husband and wife met and saw each other for the first time.

On the morning of the wedding all the friends and neighbours gathered at the bride's house and she was 'conveyed' in procession to the church. The bride rode on horseback behind the bridegroom at the head of the procession and they were followed by several others, also on horseback. When the ceremony was over, rice and oatmeal were showered over the newly married pair as a sign of plenty in the future. Then they returned to the bride's home in the manner they went, and the day and night were spent in feasting and enjoyment.

The bride remained at her home for a few days and then she went to her future home. She was also conveyed there in procession, and the day and night were spent in sport and feasting as on the wedding-day. Then the people returned home well delighted with themselves and they all expressed the opinion that the newly married pair were not slender-hearted for in that particular time if they did not give a big wedding, they were looked upon as very mean and slender-hearted in the eyes of the people.[88]

Collected by Nora Ní Airtnéadaigh, Aghills
From Nora Ní Airtnéadaigh, aged 60 years

# St Bridgid's Day

St Brigid's Day or (Biddy's Day) comes on the 1st of February. The name of St Brigid is held with great reverence around this district as tradition tells us that she paid a visit when travelling through Ireland. There is a well on the southern shores of Lough Ine known as St Brigid's Well, and today the print of her knees and fingers can be plainly seen on the rock where she knelt to drink out of the well.

It is handed down from the penal days that the English Soldiers tried to shame the saint by making a ring around her, and on that account any farmer would not start ploughing or redden the earth on that day, neither would any woman spin on that day. It's many a person discarded their spinning-wheel and I dare say would give her life if compelled to spin lest she would insult that saint.

The following day is called Lá Naomh Mhuire. On that day candles are blessed by the church. [89]

Collected by Eibhlín Ní Cárthaigh
from Donncadh Mac Cárthaigh, aged 40 years

# St Bridgid's Day Customs

Sometimes a piece of cloth is hung over the door on the outside on Saint Brigid's night, and it is said that Saint Brigid comes to the door on that night and blesses the piece of cloth. It is said there is a cure for certain diseases in that piece of cloth.

In another custom, the youngest girl or boy of the family goes out and gathers a bundle of rushes. He or she then kneels on the threshold bearing the green glossy burthen; knocks thrice on the door and cries aloud in Irish: "Down on your knees and humble yourself and let Brigid in." Those inside answer, "Brigid is welcome" and the rushes are carried in and laid on the kitchen table. Each member of the family makes a share of the crosses and puts them aside to be blessed on All Saints' Day. Finally, all partake of a plentiful supper of rice speckled with raisins and served with melted butter before going to bed on that night.[90]

Collected by Maire Ní Mhurchadha

# Clothes Worn by the People

Some of the clothes worn by the people long ago were greatly prized and even if they could be got now, they would be counted very valuable. The old people made all their clothes in their homes. The sheep were reared on the mountains and each year before they were shorn, the wool was brought home where it was combed, carded and spun into wool by the women. This was done with a spinning wheel. Then they sent it to the weaver who either wove it into flannel or frieze. It was then dyed, generally red, and worn by the women as skirts, or it was left white and worn by the men as coats called wrappers. It was the boast as to who had the whitest wrapper.

The quilts were made at home and it often took a fortnight to make one. A large wooden frame was laid on four chairs and the quilt was bound on to this. The design was drawn on the material with chalk and the sewing was done along these lines, generally in diamonds. These quilts took great trouble and time because they consisted of a lot of sewings crossing one another. The quilts were generally lined with white frieze and covered with red frieze.

The people rarely wore shoes and whenever they did the shoes were made by a shoemaker. The shoes were carried in their hands to Mass because the people thought they would wear too quickly if they wore them all the way. The people got special clothes for their marriage which lasted them while they lived. At a girl's marriage she wore a cloak which was very expensive, often costing about ten pounds. This was supposed to be a great luxury. The caps they wore were of white linen shaped like a fan, with face frills which had to be starched frequently. The cloak was made of very heavy material while the hood was of satin.

Everything they wore was of linen or frieze. It was a contest to know who had the whitest and the stiffest linen. The starch was also made in the home. It was made by grating potatoes on a tin with several holes. This tin was called a grater.

When the potatoes were broken up very fine, they were put into water and allowed rest in it for a few days. The starch sank to the bottom, the water was strained, and nothing was left but the starch. This was used to stiffen the linen.[91]

Collected by Cáit Ní Shúilleabháin, Coomnageehy

## Ancient Ideas on Death

It is ill when going with a funeral to meet a man with a white horse. No matter how high the rank of the rider may be, the people must seize the reins and force him to turn back and join the procession at least for a few yards. If a short cut should be taken while carrying a corpse to the grave the dead will be disturbed in the coffin, for it is an insult to the corpse.

If two funerals meet at the same Churchyard, the last corpse that enters will have to supply the dead with water till the next corpse arrives.

When a death was expected, it was usual to have a good deal of bread ready, baked in the house, in order that the evil spirits might be employed eating it, and so let the soul of the dying depart in peace. Twelve candles stuck in clay were also placed round the dying.

Never take a child in your arms after being at a wake, unless you first dip your hands in holy water.[92]

Collcted by Bríghid Ní Mhathúna, Maulicarrane
From Seán Ó Mathúna, aged 58

## CONVENT OF MERCY
# The Natural World and Weather Lore

# Signs of the Weather

Our forefathers had many and true indications of foretelling good and bad weather. Here are some of their signs of foretelling bad weather which are firmly believed to the present day as they seldom go wrong. The first oldest and truest sign is a star following close to the moon with the moon thrown on its back which indicates a very wet period for that moon. A bright circle around the moon is also another very bad sign. A south-easterly rainbow which does not reach the earth was looked on as a fearful sign. It was known by the name of madra gaoithe; the old men used to say, "the dog will soon bark".

The women themselves had their own signs. A cat sitting close to the fire, soot falling from the chimney, a blue flame in the fire, a dog biting grass, the fowl scratching late at evening before they retire to bed, the crows not flying far from the rookery, the seagull soaring high over the hills, the seal coming close to the shore, sniffing water in the air, shoals of fish schooling in the harbour, the swallows flying close to the ground, spring wells drying up, and the sea getting an ashen colour were all indications of coming rain. They depended on the wind as signs of good weather. If the wind follows the sun all day through and goes to rest where the sun sets at night, it's a sure sign the following day will be fine. Rays from the sun shooting skywards are another good sign. The way the harbour sounds along the shore also indicate fine weather, as did the Jack snipe bleating loudly over the bogs in the evening. Another bird, Siobhan a tuírne, plying her wheel after the sun has gone to rest also indicated fine weather. Those signs may look strange to present day astronomers as to weather forecasters, but if a keen interest is taken in those, you will find that they are as accurate as any glass.[93]

Collected by Eibhlín Ní Chárthaigh, Ballyisland
From Donncadh Mac Cárthaigh, aged 40 years

# Ancient Ideas on Weather

It is said that a thick fog on an August morning betokens rain, and if a cool August follows a hot July, it betokens a hard Winter, and a warm dry August betokens a snowy Winter. It is said also that if the milky way in December shows clear, you may safely count on a fruitful year. If the hare wares a thick coat in October, lay in a good store of fuel. It is said that October had always twenty-one fine days. If a part of the sky is starry and a part of it cloudy, it is said to be a sign of rain. It is said that January 14th will be either the coldest or the wettest day of the year. When oak trees bend with snow in January, good crops may be expected. A January spring is worth nothing. All the months of the year will curse a fair February. As sure as the sunlight comes in on Brigid's Day, the snow comes before May Day. If the cat lies on the sun in February, she will creep to the hearthstone in March. If February brings no rain, there will be neither hay nor grain. A dry March never begs its bread. If March comes in like a lion it goes out like a lamb, and if it comes in like a lamb it goes out like a lion. A wet March makes a bad harvest. March winds and April showers bring forth May flowers. The worst blast comes on the 'Borrowed Days'.[94]

Collected by Síle Ní hAirthnéadaigh, Cloghboola

# CONVENT OF MERCY
## Local Cures

# Cures

A bunch of mint tied round the wrist is a remedy for disorders of the stomach. Nettles gathered in a church-yard and boiled down for a drink cure dropsy. The touch from the hand of a seventh son cures the bite of a mad dog. When a family has been carried off by fever, the house where they died may be again inhabited with safety if a certain number of sheep are driven in there to sleep for three nights. Clippings of the hair and nails of a child tied up in a linen cloth and placed under the cradle will cure convulsions. When children are pining away, the juice of twelve leaves of foxglove to be given. When the seventh son is born, if a worm is put into his hand and kept there until it dies, the child will have power to cure all diseases. A child born after the death of his father has power over fever. Wild Sage boiled down and the water used as a drink is good for broken ribs. Wildfire, as it was called, was cured by means of the blood of a pure black cat. If a child had the whooping cough, it could be cured by bringing a donkey into the house and passing the child under the donkey three times.

Fairy Thimble - cure for the heart.[xii]
Adams Blanket - cure for consumption.[xiii]
Coltsfoot - cure for Asthma.[xiv]

Collected by Bríd Ní Mhathúna, Maulicarrane
From Seán Ó Mathúna, aged 58 years

---

[xii] Fairy thimble is a folk name for the foxglove. Pat's Apology (London: Wertheim & MacIntosh, 1850), p. 56. In modern times, fairy thimble refers to the campanula.
[xiii] Adam's blanket is probably a folk name for the common mullein.
[xiv] Coltsfoot is a member of the daisy family.

# CONVENT OF MERCY
## Songs

# A Local Fox Chase

For Cahirmore hilltops the red fox is facing,
Every hound running true, every horse running game,
O'er Bugatia's green hillside the hunters are racing,
Every man in the saddle is riding for fame.

A check in the laurels! but Burns has found it,
As for'rd away rings the veteran's voice.
Thro' the lawn, thro' the yard, thro' the house and around it
Ride hard and ride fast, all are open for choice.

Man! who could forget that wild-ringing chorus,
Re-echoed from Ardagh thro' Milleen's lone glen.
Now, who could forget that cheer so uproarious,
As Harry the Master rides past the Froe men.

Thro' the boulders of Benduff the veteran is leading,
With gallant old "Peacock" going free in his stride,
While for Cononagh's big wood the red fox is heading
As he dips down the vale to the thick covert's side.

See the Hurleys and Roches making clear the approaches,
No poacher or lurcher dare stop a game fox,
'Tis the run of the season, and for that very reason
Make way for bold Reynard o'er hills, dales or rocks.

Thro' the covert the music grows fainter and fainter,
Has Callaghan failed to stop all the earths?
By Jove! if he has, but this veteran wood-ranger,
Will lose a nice job and the easiest of berths.

No! hark to that shout from the greatest of horsemen,
   As Townsend of Myross sings out tally-ho,
   And listen again to Burn's answering horn,
Saying he's gone far away on the coach-road below.

   Over Leap's craggy hillside the music is thrilling
   With huntsmen and hounds going gallantly on,
And past Shepperton Lakes, oh! the pace it is killing,
With Miss Smyth of Downeen closing up in the van.

How oft' by those waters she has met and beat them
   And shall we today forget Auld Lang Syne,
   When gallant Maria led the bravest of horsemen,
And captured the brush on the banks of Lough Ine.[95]

Collected by Nóra Ní Airtnéadaigh, Aghills
From Nóra Ní Airtneadaigh, aged 60 years

# Convent of Mercy
# History and Archaeology

# The Corran

The Corran is situated in the land of Mr. Patrick O'Driscoll in the townland of Skeagh, which is in the Parish of Aughadown. The Corran is a large circular mound of stones, of an area of about a hundred square yards, and the centre of it is about twelve feet high. It is said that a chieftain was buried there about three hundred years ago, and that everyone who attended the funeral put a stone on top of the grave, and that was how they raised the big mound of stones there. Years after he was buried there, it is said he was seen there riding a white horse around the Corran. Standing on top of the Corran you could see the Atlantic Ocean, the Fastnet Rock light-house, Kilcoe Castle, Cape Clear, Sherkin, Hare Island and a number of smaller islands in the Atlantic Ocean. You could also see seven schools and churches from it.[96]

Collected by Máire Ní Chéadagáin, Skibbereen
From Eibhlís Ní Chéadagáin

# CORRAVOLEY

Co. Chorcaighe
Bar: Cairbre Thiar
Par: Cill Cua
Scoil: Corravoley, Achadh Dúin
Oide: Eileen Read

## CORRAVOLEY
# Local Folklore and Stories

# A Hidden Treasure

In the district of Rossard in County Cork, near to where I live, and about a mile from Corravolley school, there is an old cowlac or ruin. It is said that long ago, a crock of gold, a crock of silver and a crock of brass were buried underneath this old cowlac. This cowlac was supposed to have been occupied by giants long ago. These ruins are still to be seen. It is stated that anybody who would take away these crocks would be spirited up in the air. Some men at one time were determined to find the treasure, so one day they set off to dig for it. When they tried to dig, the handles of their spades got broken and their hands were getting terribly cut when trying to lift the stones. They had to return home then, greatly disappointed, and feared to ever seek for the treasure again. Nobody has ever dug for it since, but it is said to be lying buried there still.[97]

Collected by Betty Connell, Ardura Beg
From R. Connell, aged 50, Ardura Beg

# Forts

There is a large fort near my home in the townland of Lissydonnell. It is said that once, long ago, there was a man called Seán MacCarthy who lived near the place. One day, he saw a door at the side of the fort and entered. When inside he walked, he came to what seemed to be a fine large room. He then went on til he came to another, but it was rather dim, and he could not see clearly. He suddenly found the dimness very trying. He became very frightened and rushed out forgetting to close the door after him. Next day, one of his cows was grazing near the fort, and seeing the open door, she entered. Seán just happened to come along and seeing the cow disappear he made a dash to catch her; but she disappeared and suddenly Seán heard a voice saying. "Let the cow along and you will be rewarded by the price of ten cows". Seán ran home more frightened than ever. Next morning, he found a great sum of money in gold under his door. The cow has never been seen from that day to this.[98]

Collected by Chrissie Berry, Cappagh Beg
From J.J. Berry, aged 55, CappaghBeg

## CORRAVOLEY
# People, Places and Property

# The Leimawaddera River

In the district of Kilcoe at the back of the school which I attend, there is a beautiful little river called the Leimawaddera. It means the Dog's Leap because it is so narrow that a dog is considered able to leap across it in some places. It rises at the foot of Mount Kid in Constable Lake. This lake covers over four acres of land. It is so called because a policeman was drowned in it a very long time ago. After leaving the lake, the Leimawaddera comes winding down through marshy land till it reaches Ballybawn, which means the white townland, because in summer when the hawthorn is in bloom the place looks like a mass of white. The river next runs through Glounakillena, which means the glen of the church, then on through Rossard near to the old ruin underneath which it is said there was a treasure consisting of gold, silver and brass buried by giants long ago. The Leimawaddera then wends its way through Lishenacreahig, divides Ardura from Corravolley, and on it goes till it reaches our school. In summer, at play time, the school children love to run down and paddle in its cool waters. It next runs under a tramway bridge, and after that under the Crooked Bridge, and it enters the sea at Poolgorm Bay which means the Blue Hole. Lisheenacreahig means the fort of the fairy kings.[99]

Collected by Betty Connell, Ardura Beg, Skibbereen

# Local Place Names

There are a great many places with Irish names round my district. One field is called Carraige Tuerna, which means the rock of the wheel. It is said that long ago, people used to see a fairy wheel there at night, and a fairy was supposed to have been seen turning it. At the foot of Mount Kid there is a huge stone called Clocoir, which means the stone of gold. It is said that long ago a large quantity of gold was buried there.

There is a crossroads in the townland of Cooranuller called Carraige Hapall, which means the rock of the horse. The people around that district take their horses for a drink there. In the townland of Cappabeg there is a large stone which is called the Baleick which means a stone. This stone is lying flat on the ground. It is said that this huge stone was laid there by a giant a long time ago.[100]

Collected by Chrissie Berry, Cappagh Beg, Skibbereen
Information known locally

# Copper Mines

Long ago, there was a splendid copper mine at Roaring Water Bay. A great many men were employed in this mine. The blacksmith who used to do all the iron moulding on his anvil for the mines was a man called Driscoll. His grandson is the present Station Master in Hollyhill where the Light Railway runs from Schull to Skibbereen. There are two large caves in Roaring Water Bay to be seen still from which the copper has been extracted. These caves are very broad and lofty which show that an immense quantity of copper was taken away. It was taken from Roaring Water Bay to England. One of these caves reaches as far as Hollyhill where O'Driscoll still lives. Roaring Water is a very pretty place, and many tourists visit it during the summer months. The old castle of Kilcoe is not far distant.[101]

Collected by Chrissie Berry, Cappagh Beg
From J. Lynch, aged 40, Hollyhill

# Illustrated London News

Saturday 30 May 1863

## CORK AND KINSALE AND WEST CORK RAILWAYS

Saturday, the 16th inst., was marked by an of great importance to the western part of the county of Cork – the cutting of the first turf on the projected line from Bandon to Skibbereen. [...] It is intended to construct the railway in three sections – the first undertaking being that between Bandon and Ballineen. The works on this section will be commenced simultaneously at both ends, and it is expected that they will be completed in less than twelve months. In that case it is contemplated to carry the line up to Dunmanway within the year – thus opening seventeen miles instead of ten. It is also in contemplation to at once make a short section out from Skibbereen, so that no time may be lost in completing the whole line between the two terminal points (Figure 13).

Figure 13. Lord Carbery raising the first turf of the West Cork Railway (top Illustrated London News, 30 May 1863. Skibbereen Station, view from sign box (bottom), photo by James P. O'Dea, used with the kind permission of The National Library of Ireland.

## CORRAVOLEY
# Farming, Trade and Crafts

# Querns

Long ago, people used querns instead of mills for grinding wheat. Those querns were like round flags with a hole in the middle of each. They were usually made of cement or stone and were about five or six stone in weight. Before the wheat was ground, it was heated in a pit in order to make it soft. The quern was composed of two of these flagstones joined together and turned by a handle. The person who threw in the wheat between the stone had also to keep turning the handle until the wheat was ground. When the wheat was ground in the querns, it was then fit for use. To prepare the food, it was mixed with milk, and it was considered the healthiest food among the poorer classes. It was also the most commonly used.[102]

Collected by Chrissie Berry, Cappagh Beg
From J. Berry, aged 81, Cappagh Beg

# Weeds

There are some very harmful weeds in this district such as the thistle, the dock, the phmphmroughmwee,[xv] the nettle, and many others. The thistle is very injurious, for when it blossoms and the seeds come on, they are blown about and get rooted very quickly, and soon fill the field with thistles. People are very careful to dig them before the seeds come on. The dock is the most harmful weed of all, for once it grows in a field it is very difficult to get rid of it. If it is allowed to grow till the seed come on, it is almost impossible to get rid of it at all. The phmphmroughmwee grows mostly in cornfields and meadows and in gardens. It destroys corn if it is not pulled in time. Some people destroy this weed by spraying it with bluestone and lime. The nettle seldom grows in crops. It chiefly grows in kitchen gardens or hedges and is easily banished by cutting it down.[103]

Collected by Sammy Sweetnam, Murrahin

---

[xv] It has not been possible to identify this particular plant.

# Candle-making

Long ago, when people wanted candles, instead of going to the shop to buy them, they made them at home from the fat of cows. When the cow was killed, the fat was taken and melted in a pan over the fire. A mould was then ready, and the hot grease was poured into it. For the wick they used a thread which was held in the centre of the mould while the grease was being poured in. Then these liquid candles were put away in a cool place to harden. When well set the candles came out quite easily from the mould and were then fit for use.

There was also another way by which candles were made. A large vat of melted fat of the cow or sheep was made in readiness. A large wire was then taken to which were extended many lengths of thread or string which were intended for the wicks. To the end of each wick a weight was attached so as to keep the threads straight. These wicks were then dipped in the fat and as a quantity of fat adhered to each wick, the whole row of wicks was taken out of the fat and then suspended to dry. As these dried, they were dipped again and again, and more and more fat adhered each time. The process of dipping was carried on till the wicks became the size required for use. The greater the number of wicks dipped each time, the greater the number of candles made. These candles, when ready, were called dips.[104]

Collected by Sammy Sweetnam, Murrahin
From Mrs S. Sweetnam, aged 48 years, Murrahin

# Basket-making

I know a certain man called Tommy Kearney. He lives in Ardralla in the parish of Aughadown, and he earns his living by making baskets. In the winter months he gathers sally-rods which grow along the brinks of rivers or streams, and he takes them home and saves them. Then he weaves them into baskets. On fair or market days, he takes them to the local towns in his donkey cart and sells them at about half-a-crown or three shillings each.

Collected by Betty Connell, Ardura Beg
From R. Connell, aged 50, Ardura Beg

# Spinning

There is an old cowlac[xvi] near my home in the townland of Cappaghbeg, about two miles from Mount Kid, in which a weaver used to live long ago. All the people round the district in which I live used to cut the wool off the sheep and wash it carefully. They used to then card it and spin it into thread and take it to this weaver who used to manufacture it into cloth. The name of this weaver was Goggin. He died about thirty years ago. There is no sign to show that weaving was ever carried on in the district except the old ruins that still remain there. My grandfather, who is eighty-one years of age and who is very active, still remembers the weaver very distinctly. He says that many a time he used to go and sit in his cottage and watch the weaver at work.[105]

Collected by Chrissie Berry, Cappagh Beg
From J. Berry, aged 81, Cappagh Beg

---

[xvi] A ruin.

## CORRAVOLEY
# Leisure

# Bowling

There was a great bowling match held one Sunday about Easter of this year 1938 not far from our school on the public road. The score was thrown between two good bowlers, namely MacCarthy from Skibbereen and Whooley from Lissaclarig. The score was thrown from Aughadown station to the Cross House, a distance of about four miles. A large crowd attended this score from both sides. It was thrown for twenty pounds a man, and the money was given to Mrs Michael O'Neill to hold, while the score was being thrown. The score was very interesting, and the people all cheered the two bowlers. After tremendous excitement, in the end Whooley won the score with over a bowl of odds. He was cheered and cheered, and all his friends crowded round him to try and shake his hand and congratulate him. He then invited his followers into the local public house called the Brass House. Here they all partook of refreshments and spent a jolly evening. While the man who was beaten reluctantly turned his steps homewards.[106]

Collected by Sammy Sweetnam, Murrahin

## CORRAVOLEY
# Local Customs

# The Wren Boys

It is the usual custom in this district, and in many other districts in Ireland, for groups of boys and young men to go round from door to door on Saint Stephen's Day. These are called the Wren boys. If possible, they procure a wren to take with them, if not, they pretend they have one. They then tie the dead wren to a holly bush, which is decorated with festoons of coloured paper. They disguise themselves, blacken their faces, and wear all sorts of peculiar garments and go from house to house playing a melodeon or a mouth organ and singing the following lines:

> The wren, the wren, the king of all birds,
> Saint Stephen's Day she is caught in the furze.
> Although she is little, her family is great,
> Rise up me old lady and give us a treat.
> Off with the kettle, and on with the pan.
> Give us our answer and let us be gone.

And they usually say, "give us all silver and no brass". If the people of the house are kindly disposed towards those wren boys, they usually give them a few pence. At the end of the round the proceeds are counted up and the takings are evenly distributed among the party of wren boys.[107]

Collected by Sammy Sweetnam, Murrahin
Told locally

# Christmas Candles

It is a great custom among the people of West Cork, or Carbery, to have a lighted Christmas candle in every window of the house on the nights of Christmas Eve, Christmas Day, New Year's Eve and Epiphany, the latter which is called Little or Women's Christmas. The Women's Christmas is so called because the men try to make everything as pleasant as possible for the women so that they can enjoy a peaceful and happy time, the women having worked so hard to make the real Christmas day a happy one for everyone else. The reason why the candles are lighted is because the child Jesus is supposed to be passing by and the lights are to guide him on his way. It is the custom in every house that the youngest is supposed to light the candles and the oldest to put them out in the morning. They are left burning all night. These candles are not like the ordinary ones. They are long and thick and each one weighs a pound. Candle sticks for these candles are made from turnips. At first a good-sized turnip is procured and both ends are cut off so as to make it stand steadily. Then a hold the width of the candle is scooped out of the centre in which the candle is put standing. This improvised candlestick is then beautifully decorated with coloured paper, holly, and berries and is put in the window. On any of these special occasions it is a beautiful sight when going 'round the country to see every window lighted up.[108]

# Herbs

There are delicious wines made from herbs and some are taken as medicine. The wine made from dandelions is counted excellent for kidney trouble. Blackberry or blackcurrant wine is said to cure a cold if taken before going to bed at night.

Long ago people used to dye their curtains and clothes with the blossoms of the furze or gorse. They used to gather the blossoms and leave them soaking in water over night. Then they used to strain off the leaves and the water was ready for use. There is a plant called the milk wort and it is said to cure warts if it is applied every day for a few weeks.[109]

Collected by Betty Connell, Ardura Beg
From J. Connell, aged 42, Ardura Beg

## Wake Customs

It is usual when anyone is dead for his people to get a quantity of pipes, tobacco, and whiskey to be used at the wake. The owner of the house usually gets one or two of those who are present at the wake to cut up the tobacco into small pieces, and with it to fill the pipes. Then everyone present is asked and expected to take a pipe, no matter whether he smokes or not. It is considered an insult to refuse to accept one. The pipes are usually white clay pipes made in Ireland, especially in Knockerockery. After some time, all those who can take intoxicating liquid are presented with a glass of whiskey while everyone else is treated with tea and cake. Another custom is to give a band of crepe to all the relations and friends of the dead. These are tied loosely round their hats. All ther clergymen who attend the funeral, as well as the drivers of the hearse, wear a very large band of pure white linen across the right shoulder and tied under the left arm at the waist. These pieces of linen are new and bought specially for each funeral and are never used at a funeral again, but are afterwards given away, usually in charity.[110]

Collected by Sammy Sweetnam, Murrahin

## Wines

People make delicious wines from sloes, blackberries, dandelions, elderberries, rhubarb and many others. Cider is also made from apples. My mother makes a delicious wine from sloes. At first, a large earthenware jar is procured, then a layer of sloes is placed in the bottom of the jar. These are then covered with sugar. Next, a second layer of sloes and sugar on these again, and so on till the jar is about three quarters full. The jar is then covered with a piece of muslin and left in a cool place for about seven or eight weeks. At the end of this time the wine is fit for use. The liquid is strained out of the jar and bottled. When required, a little is taken, and water is added as desired. This makes a delicious summer or even winter drink. It is called Sloe Gin.[111]

Collected by Betty Connell, Ardura Beg
From J. Connell, aged 42, Ardura Beg

# Cloaks

Among the women of West Cork or Carbery a particular kind of cloak is worn, especially among some of the farming classes, although many women in the towns wear them also. These cloaks, which are especially peculiar to West Cork, are rather expensive. The material is of beautiful texture. It is a kind of thick, soft black face cloth and gives very lasting wear. A cloak often being in the same family for many years, was worn for generations having been handed down from mother to daughter and so on. When one of these cloaks is about to be purchased, the principal members of the family all come to town and spend the day over the buying of the material. Selecting the material is the first thing to be accomplished, then a lining of rich satin and also ribbon for trimming the hood are purchased. These are then given to a cloak-maker to be fashioned into the proper shape. The cloak, when finished, is of a voluminous nature. From the neck to the shoulders there is a beautiful gathered or pleated yoke, and the folds hang gracefully to the hem of the skirt. The hood which is attached to the neck of the cloak is also beautifully worked and trimmed with the ribbon round the bonnet part over the head. In cold, wet, or stormy weather this hood comprises a complete covering for the head.[112]

Collected by Betty Connell, Ardura Beg
From J. Connell, aged 42 years, Ardura Beg

# CORRAVOLEY
# Local Cures

# Old Cures

Old people in this district long ago had many cures. It is known for a fact that when a person wanted to have a thorn taken out of his hands or feet, he used to get the tongue of a fox and put it up to the thorn and it used to come out quite easily. For rheumatism, they used to gather some parts of a plant called the Devil's Bit, and they used to pour boiling water over it and leave it in a pot near the fire to simmer for a few hours. After that, they used to bottle it and drink it as required. This was considered an excellent cure for rheumatism. To purify the blood, they used to gather some sprats of bisom and treat it in the same way. The liquid, thus procured, was considered a splendid blood purifier. The pain caused by the sting of a nettle is supposed to be eased immediately by applying a dock leaf to the effected parts.[113]

Collected by Betty Connell, Ardura Beg
From R. Connell, aged 50, Ardura Beg

# CREAGH

Co. Chorcaighe
Bar: Cairbre Thiar
Par: Creagh, Ráth
Scoil: Creagh, An Sciobairín
Oide: Pádraigh Ó Donnabháin

CREAGH, a parish in the barony of West Carbery, in the county of Cork, province of Munster, Ireland. The parish extends along the right shore of the mouth of the Ilen, and includes part of Skibbereen, and some minor islands. It is mountainous, with bog and slate. The church adjoins the ruins of the former one. It is neatly built and has a square ornamental tower. The expense of its erection was met by means of loan and gift from the late Board of First Fruits. There are private and parochial schools. Lough Hyne runs up into the interior for a considerable distance; in it are beds of very fine oysters. On an islet with this gulf stand the ruins of Cloghan Castle, the ancient seat of the O'Driscolls.

*The National Gazetteer: A Topographical Dictionary of the British Isles*, vol. 1 (London: Virtue, 1868), p.682.

# CREAGH
# Local Folklore and Stories

## Wishes for the end to fighting

In the year 1920, Sinn Féin were fighting the Black and Tans. This was then going on about four years since the Easter week rebellion in Dublin. People were tired of fighting and war. Every change they hoped for would make peace. That year the first Catholic Lord Lieutenant was appointed in Dublin by the English. The country people around here heard it in town one Saturday. They were heard talking of it and the hopes of peace. Several in the crowd agreed that the Catholic man would please the people. But one was heard to say, "If Our Lord himself came he would not please everyone."

"That is very true", said another, "for did he not come on earth once, stay amongst people for 33 years, and only a small crowd was pleased with him.[114]

Collected by Lizzie Minihane, Creagh, Skibbereen
From Mr Minihane, Creagh, Skibbereen

# CREAGH
# People, Places and Property

# Old Chapels

On the shores of Lough Ine lake, about a mile from Creagh school, there stands the ruin of two old chapels where mass was said about the year 1700. Of the oldest one very little remains except a small part of one wall and a heap of stones, where the other walls have crumbled down. It is called Skourer Chapel. Skourer means a saucer-shaped hollow between hills. This ruin is in a small hollow between three very steep hills, each about 400 feet high. Four different roads meet there. There is a great spring of ice-cold water from a well underneath where the floor of this chapel was. This spring never runs dry. The people around there never use the water except for blessed purposes. There is an old tradition that the water could not be boiled for household purposes. People still go to visit it and pray on May eve, 30th of April. They pray while walking in a circle around the church and well.[115]

About four hundred years ago, St Bridget lived in Lough Ine, about a mile from Creagh School. The last church used by her for prayers stands on the west side of the current one, by which the salt-water flows in and out of Lough Ine with the tide. The ruins stand on top of a small hill; it can be seen about a ½ a mile away. The church is about 20 feet by 10 feet in size. About twenty yards from the east gable, and a little to the south of it, stands a small blessed well in a high rocky place. The prints of St Bridget's hands are to be seen in the rocks, and also her knees, made by her drinking without a drinking vessel from the well. Beside the well is a big flag or stone which was taken out of some part of the church and taken about a half a mile away to build a cottage, but it used to be back again next morning so that this cottage was never finished. The slates were taken off about 50 years ago. The tradition about this stone places the time about 1800. The land around this well, church and stone was then owned by a Protestant called Atkins. He was a landlord and is buried inside the ruins of Creagh Catholic graveyard. It is said that no grass grew on his grave although grass seed was tried on it.

As a Protestant Coast Guard Station was then at Lough Ine, about 400 yards distant, the Coastguard heard of the stone so often returning. So, one of the Guards broke the stone in two parts and took it away in a boat and threw it overboard, but the stone was back again next morning. It is there to be seen still, and no Coast-Guard Station is now on the West Cork seaboard. Tradition also had it that a safe harbour or anchorage was in Barlogue Bay in St Bridget's time. A fleet of fishing boats and other merchant ships were often in there for shelter. The foreign sailors so much disturbed St Bridget's time of prayer with drunken shouting and heaving of chains that she prayed to heavens to prevent it. So, one night, as if by a miracle, a big hill toppled over and so blocked the best part of Barlogue Bay in a way that no big ships can come in since to Lough Ine Bay. This obstructing rock is called Bullocks Island. I expect it had some old Irish name.[116]

Collected by Jeremiah Minihane, Creagh
From Mr Minihane, Creagh

## Sir Henry Beecher's Birds

About the year 1850, a landlord named Sir Henry Beecher lived at
Creagh demesne near Creagh school. He planted a lot of trees
and shrubs to form woods to rear game in, principally pheasants; birds
about the size of a common hen. He had a gamekeeper to rear and
feed them. When they got plentiful, they strayed out to the farms
around as far as two or three miles. As the owners of those farms
were Beecher's tenants, they were not allowed to keep any dog or gun
for fear of disturbing the birds. The gamekeeper paid about one
shilling each for the old birds, if taken to him alive, also about a half-
crown for a nest of eggs or young birds (pheasants). If a dog was
found with any farmer those years, he would be evicted from his farm.
If a gamekeeper found a next of pheasant's eggs anywhere near, he
forced the farmer to hatch them with hens for him. In those years a
farmer would be evicted for the least reason. If they offended the
gamekeeper or bailiffs or agent of a landlord in any way, even if they
attempted to pass them on their horses on the road going or coming
on a journey, they would be evicted from the farm or the good horse
taken from them.[117]

Collected by Lizzie Minihane, Creagh
From Mr Minihane, Creagh

Figure 14. Creagh Church (top), ref. L_ROY_08937, photo by R. French,
used with the kind permission of The National Library of Ireland.
Old Court Castle, near Creagh (bottom).
The Illustrated London News, 27 August 1887.

# CREAGH
# Farming, Trade and Crafts

## Potatoes

Potatoes are about the strangest crop grown on the farm as the people must generally plant old ones in the ground to produce new ones. They do not grow from seeds like mangolds or turnips, or other root crops. They cannot produce seeds, although they can produce blossoms. The reason the blossoms cannot produce seeds is because there is not any pollen in them. They cannot be fertilised to produce seed. It is the only flower grown that the bees cannot get honey from. The flower is of a neuter gender.[118]

Collected by Jeremiah Minihane, Creagh
From Mr Minihane, Creagh

# CREAGH
# Local Customs

# St John's Night

It is right to light a bonfire on St Johns Night in the potato garden to keep away disease and blight from the potatoes. It should be lit at the side the wind is from so as to let the smoke go over the garden.

A priest named Rev. John Power was buried in Rosscarbery about 70 years ago. He used to cure a lot of people as if by miracle. He promised the people he would cure them even after he was dead. Since then, a lot of people visit his grave on St Johns night to get cured. There are a lot of sticks and crutches left on his tombstone by people who were cured.

The old people say that the fires lit on St John's night commemorate the lighting fires on the Hill of Tara, which St Patrick lit to defy the king of pagans who forbade fires to be lit on the night until the king had lit the first fire. The people had no fires for three nights at that time until the pagan king lit the first one. Around that fire they had special pagan adorations as it was a sacrifice for their pagan religion.

The old people used always dig the new potatoes on St Johns night for the first meal.[119]

Collected by Lizzie Minihane, Creagh
From Mr Minihane, Creagh

# The Roofs of Old Houses

The roofs of the old houses were made of fir or bogwood, dug up when cutting turf. The rafters made from it were joined together by timber pegs of oak. As no iron bolts were then made, slates were also held on with timber pegs, about two inches long, and as thick as a lead pencil.

All the horseshoe nails were made by the blacksmith in the forge. Very thin easily bent nails were made by the smith and used for pig rings. Long splinters of fir were used in the houses in-stead of candles, held by special holders made by the black smith.[120]

Collected by Lizzie Minihane, Creagh
From Mr Minihane, Creagh

# Butter-making

Everybody who came to the house while the butter was making was expected to help to turn the barrel, or at least put his or her hand on the barrel for luck. When doing so, they would say 'God bless us.' Any person who came to the house for a message would wait until the butter was made for fear of carrying away the luck or the butter. A piece of butter, made a week before, was sometimes thrown into the barrel. Also, money would sometimes be thrown in for luck.

In those times, matches were scarce, and a man would sometimes go to a neighbour's house to light his pipe. In some houses, if the butter was making, he would stay and turn the barrel before being allowed to light his pipe, and then after he was not allowed to go away while smoking his pipe, but he should smoke enough there in the house. The people were extra superstitious about taking out fire from the house on churning day. The fire was supposed to keep away any misfortune from the barrel. In winter, if the butter was extra slow in making, the people of the house would redden the shovel in the fire to drive out the badness, or for a very slow butter-barrel in making, a coulter of a plough, or some bit of steel, was reddened in the fire to frighten away the evil spirit. Sometimes, even a sod of red-lit turf was placed on the floor underneath the barrel. Butter was always made in the kitchen.[121]

In old times it was remarked that no butter could be made from the cream of the milk on some farms from the first of May until the cows calve again the following year, as the butter was taken by witchcraft. To prevent this, about 50 or 60 years ago, nearly all the people would make the sign of the cross on the back of every cow with a burning stick on May eve. Some people stayed all night in the field with the cows to mind them from the witch, as it was not believed lucky to keep the cows in the stall on May eve. Sometimes they would see the person trying to carry the milk or butter, but they could not capture them. The man who makes the churn is called a cooper.[122]

Collected by Lizzie and Jeremiah Minihane, Creagh
From Mr Minihane, Creagh

# Local Traditions

People in the old times in this part of the country would not sow seeds on St Bridget's day, the 1ˢᵗ of February, [and] also on St Facthna's day, 14ᵗʰ August. St Facthna is the patron saint of the diocese of Ross. He was born about a mile from Creagh school. Good Friday was also a day on which seeds were not sown, and no ploughing took place.

People would not remove furniture to a new residence on any Friday of the year. Against the rule of this tradition the British law made all R.I.C men remove on Fridays. The Irish government are carrying on the same rule always. Nobody would remove during the Lenten season.

If people got married on Shrove Tuesday away from home and did not return before 12 o'clock on that night, they should remain away for seven weeks of lent.

Up to the present-day people would not dig a grave on Monday unless a few sods were dug the day before. In digging a grave, people are always careful to throw the earth in the direction away from the nearest water or river, and if a wrong grave is opened and some people claim it as their property, before closing it in again, a kitchen broom was got from some house and covered over in the grave.

Weddings do not take place on Fridays or during Lent. But in every parish one couple was allowed to be married during Lent.[123]

Collected by Lizzie Minihane, Creagh
From Mr Minihane, Creagh

# CREAGH
# Sea and Shipwrecks

# A Shipwreck

About a dozen years ago, a small ship loaded with about 150 tonnes of coal for Old Court, arrived in the river near Innisbeg Island, about a mile from our school. It arrived late on Christmas eve. It was dark where the crew had her anchored. They came ashore to Old Court for provisions or messages leaving no one on watch. After two hours, when the men returned, the ship and cargo of coal were on fire. The part of the ship over water was burned, also the top part of the cargo. Some man bought what remained of the wreck for a small price and tried to bring ashore some coal out of it. A part of the wrecked schooner can still be seen in the Ilen River near Innisbeg.[124]

Collected by Lizzie Minihane, Creagh
From Mr Minihane, Creagh

# CREAGH
# History and Archaeology

# Lioses

A lios is a circular mound of earth surrounded by a high fence. At the outside of the fence there is generally a big, wide drain full of water. This big hole of water was a help to protect the lios people when attacked by enemies or robbers. The lioses all have several underground rooms. About 50 years ago, a person could walk around in a stooping position in the rooms, but they have all sunk in these late years so that no person could even creep around in them now.

Tradition has it that these lioses were built by the Danes when they invaded Ireland about the year 1014. These rooms were first roofed with timbers, on top of which was placed about two and a half feet of white earth which hardened like cement. It was supported by pillars of stone about six to eight feet apart. It is said that another timber shed was erected over ground on the lios. The underground rooms were used for stores.[125]

Collected by Lizzie Minihane, Creagh
From Mr Minihane, Creagh

# DOONEEN

Co. Chorcaighe
Bar: Cairbre Thiar
Par: Castlehaven
Scoil: An Dúinín
Oide: R Ó Motharua

## DOONEEN
# Local Folklore and Stories

## The Shoemaker and the Spirit

There was once a shoemaker who lived in the country and he was short of stuff for making shoes. He went into town one evening for material. Being anxious for a pint, he had a drink in town remaining there until it was late. On his way home he had to go by the road where a spirit used to be seen. He met the spirit in the shape of a woman dressed in white. It was said that the spirit could easily kill a person by coming between him and the wind. The shoemaker asked the spirit to leave him go and he would come again the following night. "What security will you give me", said the spirit.

"I will give you Almighty God" said the shoemaker.

"Be sure and come tomorrow night or I will have you," said the spirit. The shoemaker went to the priest next day and told him about it. He asked the priest to go to meet the spirit the following night. After great persuasion, the priest consented to go. When they came to the place, the priest made a circle with holy water. The spirit came at midnight and advanced towards the spot where the shoemaker and the priest were standing. When she came to where the holy water was sprinkled, she could go no further. The priest asked her, "What condemned you?"

"I stole a sock off a plough", she answered.

"That did not condemn you", said the priest.

"I killed an illegitimate and stole my hire", she replied.

"That did not condemn you", said the priest.

"I killed three of them altogether."

"That condemned you", said the priest. "You'll be here no longer." She went up in the air in a blazing fire and was never there again. She was supposed to be from the neighbourhood and was called Máire an Bhóthair because her house was beside the road. She was supposed to be a bad character and her people never agreed.[126]

Collected from Padraig Ó Donnabháin, Bawnishall

# The Fianna in this locality

Suidhe Fínn means the chair of Fionn. It is a roughly made chair cut out of rock. This rock is on top of a hill between Dooneen and Bluid. Old people say that Fionn Mac Cumhall used to sit on this chair and watch the chase every morning.

The Fianna had a competition in this parish long ago in jumping and Fionn won it because he jumped from a hill called Cnoc na nGabar to the Stags near Toehead.

There is a well near Toehead called Tobhar Pártalan. It got its name from a man called Pártalan because he got his sight restored at this well, and he used to come to it every day to pray.

There is a gap in Ballycahane called Geara na gCorp. Long ago when there a funeral passed, the coffin used to be left down in the gap, and everyone present would pray for the dead person.

Another competition was held once for jumping also, and Fionn also won it. He jumped from Mr M. J. Goggin's field to Mr P. Murphy's field, a distance of one and a half miles. Mr Goggin lives in the townland of Farran Connar and Mr P. Murphy lives in the townland of Dooneen.[127]

# Body Snatching

In the olden days, a good many years ago, there was a custom of stealing the dead bodies of people freshly buried in the graveyards. A man from this part of the country was buried in Castlehaven and that same night the dead body was taken up by a party of men. One of the men was formerly from the neighbourhood and when he called to see his people at home twelve months later, he found his brother had been buried twelve months and that he had helped to steal the body from the grave.[128]

Collected from Mícheál Ó Súilleabháin

# Buried Alive

There was a minister living in Skibbereen. His wife got a fit of convulsions. Four doctors came to the woman and said she was dead. She was about a week in the house, before she was buried. Before the funeral her husband put rings on her fingers and put much valuable jewellery on her. A tramp went to the grave and opened it. He tried to take the rings off her fingers but could not do so because her fingers were swollen. He took out his knife and commenced cutting her fingers. When he started cutting them the dead woman rose up. The tramp ran away terrified, and she ran after him. She went to her own house and knocked at the door. The servant girl of the house woke and told the minister. One of the maids looked out the window and saw her outside and she told the minister that it was his wife. The minister shouted, "clear away or I will shoot you". She called out to him, "do not shoot me because I am your wife". They lived happily together afterwards.[129]

Collected from Dean Uí Ceocháin

# DOONEEN
# People, Places and Property

# Strong Men

Con Driscoll of Gorthbrack was the strongest man in the district about 70 years ago. He challenged another man of strength to lift a large stone. This he failed to do, but Driscoll lifted two such stones quite easily.[130]

# Famous men of this locality

Tim Collins (of Lickowen, Castletownshend) walked to Cork, a distance of about 60 or 70 miles, in twelve hours. Batt Sullivan (of Ballycahane) walked to Cork to pay his rent to Mr French, the landlord. He started at 9pm one night and he was home again at 8pm the following night.

Twenty-five years ago, Dan Dwyer, a sailor who lived in Castletownshend, lifted half a tierce of porter with his teeth by catching a grip on a rope tied around the barrel and put it on a counter in Mr Bob Mahoney's public house in the village.

In the townland of Gorlycrossig, Castletownshend, there is a high, square tower of origin unknown. It now has a dwelling house attached to it occupied by a Maguire family. It has been the custom for many years for local men and boys to assemble beside this tower on Christmas Day after breakfast. Here they indulged in feats of strength, casting, jumping and football etc.

Famous athletes locally popular were the Sheehy bros., Tim Crowley and Mortimer Hourihane. In one epic contest, the last named beat all comers in a hop, step and jump.

Laurence Daly was a remarked mower. Working for Mr Jeh. Mahoney of Dooneen, he mowed 3½ acres in two days. William Hegarty of Toehead was another famous reaper about 30 years go. He cut 1½ acres of corn in one day and made sheaves himself after every swath he cut.[131]

# Travelling Folk

There are many travellers going around the country looking for charity, and we call these people tramps or beggars. It is not right to describe all these people as such, because some of them are decent, respectable people.

The tramps that frequent this parish may be divided into three families: the Hogans, O'Driscolls and the Sheridans. The Hogans are easily recognised because most of them are fair-haired. These people come to the door on the pretext of being chimney sweepers. The Sheridans are the most respectable people. They seldom come round this part of the country. These people follow the big horse fairs as they deal in horses. The Driscolls are the people who come round the oftenest. They live in Chapel Lane in Skibbereen. They are the black-haired tribe. It is amusing to see the Driscolls going along the road hunting a drove of donkeys before them, followed by a car full of children.

Some of them have small goods selling, and they buy these in sales cheaply. They sell laces, tiepins, studs and camphor. They have wicker-work baskets holding their goods. People do not have any welcome for them when they come too often. Some of them are very daring and they ask many alms. In the summer, they sleep in the side of the road but in winter they sleep in their own house.

The principal charity given to tramps in this locality is a few potatoes, a gábhail of hay, a few mangolds, a slice of cake or a basin of flour, or a couple of coppers.

There is a well-known travelling man who goes about the country and his name is Jerh. Lynch. He is very tall, and he wears black glasses. He is getting ten shillings a week blind pension. He was once a well-to-do man but owing to bad sight he could not secure a position and he had to take to the road. He is a very gay-hearted fellow as he is continually singing.

The tramps that come around this part of the country beg for food in the houses. If they get what they ask for, they say, "God increase your store." Many of them have spring carts pulled by a donkey or a pony, and into the cart they put potatoes which they collect.[132]

Colleted by Áine Ní Laogaire, Bawnishall

## DOONEEN
# Local Customs

# Food in olden times

Long ago, the people usually had three meals a day. In the morning they had stirabout, in the middle of the day about one o'clock they had potatoes. At about half-past eight at night they had stirabout again. They used to have butter milk with the potatoes. Yellow meal stirabout was commonly used, and the cakes eaten were made of potatoes or yellow meal.

During summer months, many went fishing and caught as much mackerel as would last the winter. These were pickled and eaten two or three times a week. When tea was introduced, a quantity of it was put in a pot of water and boiled, being stirred often. It was then strained into a shallow pan, sweetened, and milk was added. Black tea was always drunk during lent. Three meals of nettles (boiled) in March were considered necessary by old people to avoid sickness.[133]

# Stampy Cakes

Mrs Kate Collins of Gortbrack described how stampy cakes were made when she was a girl.

When making stampy cakes long ago, potatoes were scraped into shreds with a grater. To make this, a tin box was opened, and holes put in it with a nail, and it was then nailed to a board. There was no fixed number of potatoes grated. It depended on the size of the stone on which the cake was baked. They used to wash the potatoes. They never peeled the new potatoes, but they always peeled the old ones. They used grate them onto an earthenware pan, and then they used put them into a small bag with a fist of flour to toughen them, and salt was also put to taste. The bag was made of calico and there was a running string on top of it. They then put it down on the table and pressed it with their hands. They greased the flat stone with butter or fat, and then spread the cake on it, and then it was pressed. They faced the stone with the cake on it to the fire. When the bottom of the cake was baked, the stone was reversed. When baked, it loosened from the stone, and it was turned.[134]

# Piseóga

When a cow had calved, the first drop of milk from her should be thrown behind the fireplace. This ensured rich creamy milk for the year. A basin of milk should be set out on the dairy window on May eve for the fairies. Cows 'ran away' if this was omitted. When butter was made on May eve, a small piece of it was rubbed to a rafter in the dairy, also to the handle of the butter barrel. Bad luck followed neglect of this practise. One meal of meat on St Stephen's day prevented sickness during the year. Three meals of nettles (boiled) in May ensured health for the year following.[135]

Collected from Pádraig Ó Donnabháin, Dónal Ó Duibhir,
Tomás Sáltar, and Bean Seáin Uí Mhurchadha

# Querns

Long ago, grain was ground in this locality (Toehead, Skibbereen) with querns made of two stones, one being place on top of the other. The under stone was somewhat saucer shaped and the upper one fitted into it. On the side, about half-way between the centre and the rim of the under stone, was a hole to allow the crushed corn to escape. A tubular hole was bored through the upper stone where the corn to be ground was poured in. Near the edge of the upper stone, a third hole was made to hold a short wooden handle by which the upper stone was whirled around. When grinding, a vessel was placed under the edge of the lower hole to receive the crushed corn. Some under stones contained two holes.[136]

Collected from Jack Murphy, Bawnishall

# DOONEEN
# Local Cures

# Cures

A sore throat was treated by boiling potatoes and then roasting them in hot ashes. They were then put in a stocking which was tied around the neck.

A 'wisp' was cured by one's fasting spit or by rubbing it with a gold wedding ring and making the sign of the cross three times.

A stye could be cured by bathing it with cold tea.

A burn could be quickly cured by rubbing a lizard to it. A poultice of cowdung was also effective.

Measles could be cured by drinking milk left over by a ferret.

A red-hot needle placed on a tooth soon relieved the toothache. Salt put in the tooth also helped.

A hot plate was used to cure mumps.

To cure a boil, fill a bottle with very hot water. Empty it and apply the mouth of the bottle over the boil. A poultice of soap and sugar was very effective for this complaint.

A growth was cured by applying a fox's tongue.

Garlic was a cure for consumption.

By making the sign of the cross nine times on the door before sunrise, whooping cough was cured.

People born on Good Friday and baptised on Easter Sunday had healing powers.

A posthumous person had wonderful healing powers. The seventh son of a seventh son was gifted in a similar manner.[137]

# DOONEEN
# Sea and Shipwrecks

# A Shipwreck

One harvest day about fifty years ago a company of four men and two women set out from Tragharta strand to a regatta which was to be held in Ross. The men's names were Tom Taylor and Richard Taylor, who were brothers who lived in Scobawn, and another was a sailor from Ross by the name of Collins. The fourth was a brother to the two girls whose names were Patrick, Mary and Johanna Hegarty from Tragharta. On their homeward journey when they were near High Island, a dispute arose between them, and as the men were drunk, they had some struggling in the boat. The boat capsized, pitching its occupants into the water. While struggling in the water, one of the girls caught Tom Taylor and he could not loosen her grip, so he pulled out his pocketknife and severed the fingers from her hand. This he did to save himself. He was the only one to survive as he was a good swimmer. The others were all drowned.[138]

Collected from Mairéad de Barra, aged 52, Glasheenaulin

# DOONEEN
## Songs

# The Mermaid

One morning in May as thro' care I rambled along,
Viewing the sea being so neat and smooth as the glass,
The porpoise, the whale, the hake, the sunfish and shark,
And they having their play and hailing the coming of sol.

Contemplating the seas, I deemed a pleading to stop.
For it is over the deep I freely stretched on the grass,
A damsel, nearby I had spied with a rack in her hand,
And she combing her hair so neat as her ringlets did hang.

Being alarmed and amazed I gazed with my heart in a trap.
The seeing of her face being so fair and her neck like the swan.
Her fine golden hair being so fair and blazing eyes like the stars.
Her figure and frame so neat and her lily-white arms.

If in Asia she had been at the time the apple was cast.
Between Russia and Greece,
I'm sure there would have been no war.
But I said with an air that gave best tact to my heart,
Pray tell me your name or else the heaven you've lost.

And that's your mistake I'm sure you're certainly mad
And that you may gain I pray you quickly dispatch.
Oh, hurry you rake and play with some other lass.

And if God would implore who knows the secrets of hearts
They will banish those rogues, those foes and shepherds of flocks.
He will banish I hope, for the summer is nearly past,
Those winter rogues who at home of heaven at once.[139]

Recited by Mrs Keohane of Toehead

# The Sweetest and Fairest that ever you know

When first in this country I came as a stranger
I place my affections on a maid that was fair
She being young and tender her waist it was slender
Kind nature had placed her to my overthrow.

On the banks of the river 'tis there I beheld her
She appeared to me like Juno or a Grecian queen
Her eyes shone like diamonds, her face brightly gleaming
Her cheeks blooming roses or blood upon snow.

It was her cruel parents that first caused my variance
Because they were rich and above my degree
I'll do my endeavours my darling to gain her
Although she was born of a rich family.

If I had all the riches that's in East or West Indies
Or if I had all the gold that's in the queen's store
I would give it to you, unto you my nice darling girl
For there's no other creature on the earth I adore.

And now since I gained her, I'm content for ever
I'll put rings on her fingers and rings on her ears,
With diamonds and pearls I'll adorn my brown girl
She's the sweetest and fairest that ever you know.[140]

Contributed by Mrs P.Cahalane, Lickowen

## DOONEEN
# History and Archaeology

# Fortified Headlands

According to Westropp (Fortified Headlands, pt. 1):- Along the seaboard of this parish is a number of promontory ring forts, such as Dooneendermotmore, Coosdergardoona and Poertadoona.

In Tudor times, the proprietors of this parish were O'Driscoll, McCarthy Reagh, Clandermot McCarthys, Clanteighilen McCarthys and O'Donovan.  O'Donovan had come in as a refugee from Limerick, where he was driven out of his territory, Cairbre.  On his succeeding in establishing himself in the barony of Corcalee (Corca Laidhe) he drove the O'Driscolls to the south-western coast and renamed the barony 'Carbery'.[141]

# DRISHANEMORE

Co. Chorcaighe
Bar: Cairbre Thiar
Par: Abbeystrowry (An Sciobairín)
Scoil: Tráigh Omna
Oide: Ml Ó Dálaigh
27.1.1938 – 16.12.1938

# DRISHANEMORE
# Local Folklore and Stories

# The Kidnapped Boy

Once there was a boy who went out to see if his brother was coming home from town. He went on top of a hill, and he sat down on a rock so that he could see his brother coming down the road. When he did not see or hear his brother coming, he blew a whistle so his brother could hear. He was not long there when two men came upon him, took him away up the hill, and carried him into a cave. They took him in all the ways until they came to a room. In the room there was a foxy lady sitting by the fire. The men put the boy at the fire and went away. Then the red lady said that the men would get supper, and said not to eat it, and there would come a black dog under the table, and to give him the food if he could. If he did not, he would remain inside the cave and get enchanted, because she herself ate the food and was kept inside. Also, she said, "For twelve months, if you are let go, do not tell the story to any person for your life." The meal was ready, and the men told the boy to eat the food. When he got the chance, he slipped the food to the black dog under the table. When he got up from the table, the two men caught him and put him outside the cave. He went home, but he never told his own people where he had been.

One day, there was a flax meithal in a neighbour's house, and the boy was asked to help. The meithal stopped for a rest and the men began to tell stories. The boy was tempted to tell his own story, so he said, "You all have fine stories, but I have a better one than you all." He began to tell his story and was only half-way when he got suddenly sick. One of the boys went for the priest on horse-back, but before the priest came, the boy was dead.[142]

This story was told to John Joe Driscoll by his grandfather, Jeremiah Collins of Drishanebeg. The latter, a farmer, was told the story sixty years ago by his own father.

# A Strange Sight

A farmer and his wife were going home late one night from Skibbereen. They lived in Currabeg in the parish of Castlehaven. It was the custom of the time for both husband and wife to ride on the one horse, the wife behind the husband. The farmer and his wife were riding along peacefully until they came to a steep hill in the road. Here it was said that a hound as big as a calf used show himself. The woman spoke to her husband and asked him, "Where is the hound seen?" No sooner were the words out of her mouth when she saw a large animal by her on the road. His eyes were flashing fire, and the man also saw the animal. He spurred the horse, but as fast as the horse galloped, the hound kept by their side until they reached their home.

The two old people lived to a ripe age and the man, named Patrick McCarthy, told the story to my grandfather, John McCarthy of Lettertinlish, Skibbereen, who in turn handed it down to his daughter, Ellen McCarthy, now 86 years of age, and who is my aunt, and to whom she told it.[143]

Collected by Mícheál S. Ó Dálaigh, from Patrick McCarthy, Curranbeg

# Gollán an Óir

In the townland of Gleann na gCill in the parish of Castlehaven, Barony of West Carbery, there is still to be seen a gollán called gollán an óir. One story relates that a giant in olden times buried a croc of gold beneath this stone where it still lies buried. Another story relates that pirates were chased into Tragumna Bay where they came ashore and buried two large boots filled with gold. It is said that one boot was found by a man named Sweeny, while the other boot with its treasure was never found. The common belief is that his boot is buried under Gollán an Óir.

Recorded by Miss Mary Hegarty who heard this account from an old man named Tadgh Hegarty of Laherdanemore in the parish of Castlehaven

Gollán an Óir is to be seen on a hill called An Garbh Leaca, about 200 yards east of Tragumna school, Skibbereen, Co. Cork.[144]

# A Strange Story

I heard of a woman who was coming from a market in Skibbereen. She had sold her eggs and butter at a fair price, and was taking the road home, and she was singing for herself because she was happy. When she came to the fairies' gap, she could go no farther, and her legs got stiff. A woman rose up out of the ground before her and asked her to come to a land where she would never grow old. The woman who was coming from market said that she would not, as she preferred her own home. The next minute, her basket and her shawl lay on the ground, and she found herself in a big mansion. Every night from that one she used be riding with the good people. So, one night when the woman's brother was coming home late from Castletownshend, and a very wild night it was too, he stopped to light his pipe. At that minute he heard the galloping of horses coming towards him. They galloped past him, and while they were galloping past, he could not get his pipe to draw. All but one horse passed, and on this last horse road a pale, sad, forlorn woman. She stopped her horse and said, "John, will you carry a message for me to my husband?"

"I will", said he "and welcome."

"Tell my husband," she said, "that I am out riding with the sídhe each night. Let him come and claim me about Hallow Eve, because after that there will be no good in trying.

Next morning, he went to the husband's house. When he went in, he met the husband and said, "Good morning. I have queer news for you."

"Is it about Julia?" cried the husband.

"I was coming home from Castletownshend late last night", said John. "As I was coming along, I stopped to light my pipe for company. I heard a sound of galloping horses behind me. I could not get my pipe to draw until they were after passing. The last horse stopped, and on it was a pale, sad, forlorn woman, and that woman was Julia, your wife. She told me to ask you to claim her before Hallow Eve, for it would be no good trying after."

Then the man of the house said, "Sure it wasn't Julia at all. She could not sit on an old cart and horse without falling off."

"It was Julia." Said John. "Didn't I see the salt tears streaming down her cheeks?" John was going away, and he turned back to the husband

and said, "May the Lord forgive you if you forget Julia." Then John went on his way home.

Hallow Eve came, and there was the husband sitting at home by the fire, crying for his Julia in the strange country. At the same time, Julia was riding in through the Fairies Gap, and when she did not see her husband there, she fell in a weakness. The good people lifted her and placed her on a silver bed in the mansion. Then she started to cry once more. The fairy woman asked her what she was crying for. Julia said that she was lonesome for her husband. "Why should you weep for that good for nothing fellow?" said the fairy woman. Then the fairy woman asked Julia how old was her youngest child, and if he was walking when she left her home. She asked her so many questions that Julia stopped crying. "Now", said the fairy woman, "do not cry any more, but let you call your youngest baby, and he will answer it." So, Julia cried out, "Come my honey pot, come, oh! Come, my darling. I can't do without you." She fell into a deep sleep, and when she woke, she had her baby in her arms. The little one pulled at her hair and crowed with delight. Then the good people sent the woman and her baby to live in a little cottage, and she never went home to her husband.[145]

James Nagle, a pupil at Tragumna National School got this story from his mother who heard it told by her father, James Scully of Laherdane (in the parish of Castlehaven, Co. Cork). James Scully is now eighty years of age and is a fluent Irish speaker.

## Stories Told at Wakes

One night, fishermen were out on the sea when they noticed a large seaworm following the boat. The worm came near and was trying to overturn the boat, so the crew threw out a stool which the monster swallowed. As he was still following, they threw him a bucket. This also disappeared. The third time they threw him a goat which he also swallowed. Still, he was after the boat, and he came under it and capsized it, and a woman, who was on board, was swallowed by the worm, and then he disappeared.

Sometime after as fishermen were hauling in their trawl nets, they caught the worm. They killed him, and when they cut him open, there inside was the woman sitting on a stool milking the goat into the bucket.[146]

There was once a boy who went to a wake one night. He wore a hard hat, and after saying his prayers he went up and sat on a stool by the fire. Before the dawn, the poor boy fell fast asleep, and when he was snoring, some other young lads rubbed soot on his face, and when he woke up later, he couldn't understand what the others were laughing at. So, he knelt down, and said his prayers, and home he went. He went upstairs to bed and soon was sound asleep. Later in the day, his mother went into his bedroom to rouse him. On looking at the sleeping boy, she gave a loud scream which woke her son. He thought his poor mother had gone mad when he saw her crying that her own son was gone, and that a black man had come home instead. The boy quickly dressed himself, went downstairs, and looking in the glass, he jumped when he saw his sooty face. Then he knew why his mother was frightened, and also the young men who had played the trick on him while he was asleep in the wake-house.[147]

Story heard and told by Denis O'Sullivan (aged 50 years), Bawnlahan

## DRISHANEMORE
# People, Places and Property

# Local Place Names

Near Tragumna School there is a field called Pairc an Teampaill. It is said that Mass was offered here in the Penal Days. The field is in the townland of Bawnlahan in the parish of Castlehaven, Barony of Carbery.

Separating two townlands of Drishanemore and Ballyally there is a cave or cuas called Cuas an Teorann. Near Cuas an Teorann there is a strand called Tráigh na mbó. Many old people still living in the locality tell the story of a fight between Fionn Mac Cumhail and Diarmuid O'Duibhne on this strand.

*From John O'Driscoll, aged 85, Drishanemore, Co. Cork*

# Tráighomna

Tráighomna is supposed to get its name from the stumps of oak trees dug up out of the strand. Others say that the name should be Tráigh na móna, as turf is to be seen in patches on this strand, and even local farmers draw this home for fuel at the present day.

*From Patrick Geaney, aged 50, Drishanebeg, Skibbereen, Co. Cork*

# An Cúl Tráigh

There is a small strand south of Tragumna called the Cúl Tráigh. In this sheltered strand, fishermen of the district in bye-gone days used keep their small boats and spread out their nets.[148]

## DRISHANEMORE
# Farming, Trade and Crafts

# Tithes

In the past, the protestant minister had to get a tenth of a sheaf of corn, the length of a spade of potatoes, and £2 a year for wine for the church from each household. This was paid twice a year. The people also had to pay window tax, hearth tax, and tithe money. Those who could not pay the window tax were allowed no windows, and instead of windows they put 'poll a beds'. These were red slates and were supposed to be brought from Tráighomna. There were six or seven round holes in them.

When tithes were due, there was usually great trouble. If the total amount of tithe money could not be collected, the bailiffs used take the cattle to a pound. There is a pool in High Street, Skibbereen called the Pound Pool. Also, there is a field in Boulibawn, a townland in the parish of Skibbereen, two miles north of Tráighmna School, called Páirc an Phóna.

Father Jeremiah Crowley, the Roman Catholic administrator of Castlehaven parish, went to law with the Protestant Minister of Castlehaven, named Morritt. The priest had two lawyers from Cork at great fee to fight his case against Rev. Morritt. The court was held in a small house in the Still Meadow, in Market Street, Skibbereen, near the Boys School. The case lasted from Monday morning until Saturday morning. Morritt (Morritteen grádha coach as he is named in the local poem called Tpáigh Leagach) swore that Father Crowley was the Captain of the Whiteboys, but the priest won his case. Then the priest wrote to Dublin Castle, and Morritt got three days to quit the country. The Somervilles of Castletownshend were kindly disposed to Father Crowley, as they were to those farmers who supplied them with hay potatoes and oats.[149]

Collected from Miss Ellen McCarthy (aged 87 years) of
North Street, Skibbereen

# Trouble over tithes

In July 1823, the payment of tithes to Rev. Morritt had indeed caused trouble. Morritt, having heard of growing unrest, returned to Skibbereen from London just two days before the uprising. It had apparently been a long time coming. Indeed, *The New Times* acknowledged that catholic tenant farmers, being required to pay tithes to the 'Clergymen of the Established Church', namely a protestant one, felt honour-bound to resist.[xvii] The incident resulted in the death of four men; Cowen (a policeman), Driscoll (Morritt's driver), and two 'countrymen'. Ten or twelve farmers were wounded, five dangerously so. That the names of the countrymen were not initially reported, but the newspapers were quick to note that Lieutenant Hawkshaw had lost his cap in retreat, indicates bias in favour of the protestant church and state.[xviii]

Although details were at first unclear, two subsequent inquests were held to establish the facts. The first, convened to ascertain how the four men had died, was presided over by James Daltera, Esq., at Glashmanlin, and later at Lakemount. It found that John Cowen and Patrick Driscoll died as a result of head-wounds inflicted by the stones of the protestors. Denis McCarthy died as a result of a gunshot to his body, and John Regan, to his head.[xix]

A full inquest opened on 10th September. Jeremiah Conolly, giving evidence on the part of the 'country people', recalled that he'd risen before sunrise on the morning of the incident, and his attention being drawn by gunshots, he'd encountered an armed party at Reendickinson where he saw McCarthy fall. Half-an-hour later he heard further shots fired by the constables. Cross examined by the Rev. Morritt, who proposed that the fracas actually took place after sunrise, Conolly insisted that it had not. Morritt then proceeded to question him about another incident that had taken place the previous year, but this met with objections, it not being relevant to the inquiry. Trying to justify his line of questioning, Morritt explained that he was referring to an organised parish plan which had been put in place to 'rescue any distress he may make' as a result of tithes. His entreaties

xvii *New Times*, 08 July 1823, p. 2
xviii *Dublin Mercantile Advertiser*, 07 July 1823, p.2
xix *Dublin Mercantile Advertiser*, 14 July 1823, p. 3.

fell on deaf ears. Exasperated, he demanded to know if 'a solitary Englishman was to be despoiled of his property amongst strangers.' At this point, Rev. James Crowley, the Catholic priest, asked if he might intervene on behalf of his parishioners, and was given permission to do so. Conolly, questioned by Crowley, stated that he'd 'not the least inclination to riot or to resist the law' until after he'd heard the gunshots. Examined by Mr Blacker, Conolly reported that around forty country people assembled, drawn by the sound of the shots, and that the police then opened fire on them. He admitted that stones were thrown, but that the men had been unarmed. Morritt intervened, stating that Conolly was a parishioner of Castlehaven and that there were things he could say about him, but that he'd prefer not to. He commenced a story about an incident related to tithes in 1815, but those present were unable to follow his argument.

Next, Denis McCarthy was sworn in and examined by Counsellor O'Driscoll. McCarthy, like Conolly, stated that he had risen before sunrise. On hearing that the police and Morritt's men had confiscated cattle, he was climbing over a ditch to see what could be done when he was shot at. He ran into his potato garden where he was confronted by Timothy Sullivan who cocked a pistol at him. McCarthy told him to take the cattle but to kill nobody. A Police Officer then arrived and knocked McCarthy to the ground with the butt of his gun, where he remained for a considerable time before his senses returned. He then saw the police fire at Denis McCarthy who immediately fell. Morritt cross-examined the witness. McCarthy reported that his tithe was outstanding against his will, and that he owed nothing. He had offered Morritt payment, but the minister had refused it. Instead, he paid Mr Triphook what was due. "I always paid double what the Rector was entitled to," he stated. McCarthy had paid him 18s two or three weeks before the murder; he claimed that Morritt was actually in his debt.

On 11 September 1823, presided over by Lord Carbery and Mr Blacker,[xx] the enquiry continued. Mr Hawkshaw, one of Morritt's men, was examined by Blacker for three-and-a-half hours. The witness stated that he may not have reached Castlehaven until after sunrise. However, he revealed that he'd not received a 'legal warrant, nor written paper' from Mr Morritt, but that he had received a letter from him. A warrant had been requested of Morritt, and he'd 'been

---

[xx] Southern Reporter and Cork Commercial Courier, 11 September 1823. pp. 2-3

expressly told by Major Wilcocks not to go on any business of the kind improvided with a legal authority.' Morritt then stated that Sullivan, one of his drivers, had the warrant, but when examined, it was found to authorise the distraining of cattle, not the action taken. Lord Carberry here intervened, and turning to Hawkshaw asked, "Mr Hawkshaw am I to understand you went out that morning unprovided with a legal authority?" Morritt rose to speak but was told by Carberry that he wished to hear only from the witness. "So it appears my Lord?" replied Hawkshaw. Morritt, produced three or four law authorities, and proceeded to justify Sullivan's actions, before claiming personal responsibility. Hawkshaw, realising his error, arose and stated that his part in the action was taken with the 'purest and most conscientious' motives. Lord Carbery reassured the witness: "We do believe you acted with the strictest purity throughout."

Serjeants Strong and Donald, and John Lovell of the police, were questioned next, their testimony corroborating that of their Chief's, and Rev Crowley responded to questions from Mr Morritt. Crowley was unaware of any organised system to resist the payment of tithes, and was prepared to swear an oath to the effect. He wished to address the court and was given the bible to swear upon, but his request was declined by Blacker. However, Morritt again handed the bible to Crowley, wishing to hear his competitor's words, before desisting on the advice of friends.

James Driscoll (one of Morritt's drivers) was then sworn in. Driscoll had a warrant of authority to distrain but, being unable to read, couldn't confirm the contents of the document he'd handed over; he had proceeded to action in accordance with the evidence given by Sullivan. Driscoll claimed that two months before the incident, he'd been warned by Daniel Kean of Lickowen 'not to go south or he may as well provide coffins for himself and party.' He had also been told that the parishioners had been ordered not to pay a farthing in tithes. He added that he'd heard that the north side [presumably of the Parish] was ready to join the south. Of the incident, Driscoll stated that he was stood within 2 yards of Michael Driscoll when he fired the first shots, and that the country people were at that time running away.

As the day ended, Jeremiah Sheehan was questioned. He recalled hearing the Rev. Crowley offer to murder Mr Morritt or his men for a weight of potatoes from each house in the parish, though apparently the potatoes were not forthcoming. Here, the inquiry was adjourned to the next day.

The following morning, Counsellor Flemming rose to address the court.[xxi] Referring to a statement made by Morritt, who 'in the most sweeping manner asserted that the reason why he did not apply to many of the Magistrates of Skibbereen and its neighbourhood, was that he conceived them prejudiced against him, and that he could not expect they would administer justice [...].' Flemming asked Morritt to name the Magistrates, but the clergyman replied that he had not selected any particular men, claiming that they were all hostile towards him. He added that Mr Kenny, a Magistrate who stood at his tithe adjudication, was unqualified, but Kenny rose to refute the clergyman's claim. Townsend now stood asserting that he considered Morritt's words as a personal attack, demanding time to defend himself, but Blacker drew the vexatious discussion to a close, it being a distraction from the case in question. The meeting had become stormy and Blacker threatened to dissolve it unless the subject was dropped immediately.

On the fourth day, the case rumbled on. Jermyn Lynch's evidence was incendiary. He claimed to have travelled in a coach with Mr Morritt and heard the man say, 'there would be blood spilled in the Parish', and that he would provide twelve men with blunderbusses. Morritt, by now sounding rather like a modern-day politician, replied, '[I] am not conscious of having made use of any such expressions.' The investigation closed at half-past two and the Magistrates consulted for two hours. On returning. it was announced that Mr Blacker would deliver the verdict. He stated that despite differing during the investigation, the Magistrates were now unanimous. Morritt was acquitted, having 'acted on the authority which the Act of Parliament had invested him.' The actions of the Police were criticised; 'the Chief should have acted with more circumspection; he should have been more cautious how he went on such an errand unprovided with a legal warrant, and he should have applied to Mr Wilcocks.' However, the judges believed that the action had started after sunrise, not before as stated by the peasantry, and so the transaction was legal. Turning to the death of Mr Leary, the Magistrates had disagreed and chose not to publish their opinions. Morritt was found to have conformed with the law when collecting payment of tithes. The judges suggested that the

xxi Southern Reporter and Cork Commercial Courier, 13 September 1823, pp. 2-4.

system was at fault, 'rendering the Clergyman obnoxious to the people', and that Morritt should consider acting in accordance with the wishes of the community. Speaking publicly afterwards, Morritt declared that he would seek reconciliation, treat the peasantry with the utmost leniency, and establish good feeling.

## Flax

The flax was sown in May, and when ripe, it was pulled and made into bundles, placed in a pond, and left there for 21 days. Then it was taken out and spread to dry and to bleach. It was again made into bundles and taken home, and táithíní made of it. It was then pounded with a 'forgaire' and drawn with 'tlú'. The hulls were taken out of it by 'smid'ing. It was hackled with a 'tairdil'. A 'cuigeál' was got, and the flax spread around it and tied. The 'maide' was then put on the 'Dutch' wheel and the flax was spun.

Hanks were made and wound up. Ashes were got and placed in a pot of water. The hanks were placed in the water to boil. They were then taken out, and taken to the 'caol', or the river, and washed. Then it was taken home, spread out, and bleached. Then when bleached it was taken to the Fígheadóip.[150]

Collected from Ellen McCarthy, formerly of Letterlinlish, Castlehaven. Ellen used spin flax and wool and used the linen and frieze cloth. In 1938, aged 87 years, she lived in the town of Skibbereen.

## DRISHANEMORE
# Local Customs

## Old Customs of Shrove Tuesday in Skibbereen 30 Years Ago

O n that night, crackers (made of lead piping with powder and fuse) were exploded in the streets of the town. Sometimes, these were thrown into shops where they exploded with great noise. The townspeople gathered on the square, and there a fireball, made of rags and soaked in paraffin oil, was kicked by the young men and boys. The crackers were exploded there also. A donkey would run madly down North Street followed by yelling youngsters who had tied an old tin can to his tail. It was the usual custom that many couples were married on this day. There were often nine or ten weddings in the Catholic church. The Sceilg List was composed by the local wits on this night and copies sent to parties who had not changed their state during the Shrove.[151]

Collected by Mícheál S. Ó Dálaigh

## Visitors in the old times

W hen people went visiting in the country about sixty years ago, instead of tea, they were given a mixture of oatmeal and cream or milk. The cream or milk was poured over the raw meal, and this was a great treat for young and old. This was called Ríbiúin. Yellow meal cake was also used, and in the famine years it was the common food of people in this locality. The yellow meal was boiled in fresh buttermilk or with spring water. It was then allowed to cool and made into scones, and fried on a frying pan.[152]

Collected from Ellen McCarthy (87 years), North Street, Skibbereen

# Catching Birds

An old custom was to take a lantern in the wintertime and go into a wood or place where birds were sleeping. The light of the lantern dazzled the birds and they were easily caught.[153]

Boys and girls in wintertime used make a small hole in a field over which they placed a flat stone or portion of slate in a slanting position. Food was placed on a twig so that when the bird perched on the twig, the slate fell and covered her in the hole.[154]

# The Stations Party

In the locality of Drishanemore, Skibbereen, and in Bawnlahan, Castlehaven, it is at present the custom on the occasion of the stations, that the man in whose house they are held invites all those who have come to remain for breakfast. Several old men and women remain, and the day is spent in eating and drinking, in song, and in dance. The oldest men and women must dance the reel and jig, while in the evening the young people who are invited favour the sets or quadrilles. Songs are sung between the dances usually in English, but occasionally an Irish song is sung by some of the old people. This station party is sometimes on as grand a scale as a wedding feast, and the dancing may last into the early hours of the morning. Everybody, both old and young, are in the gayest of spirits. Old stories are told, and the most marked feature of the party is the air of friendship and peacefulness. No arguments are allowed at the station party that might lead to hot words or blows. It is a notable day for the people of the above-mentioned townlands.

At Stations held in farm-houses, the priests hear confessions, mass is offered, holy communion given, and offerings are paid to the parish priest. The priests then take breakfast.[155]

Collected by Michael J. Daly, Tragumna

# DRISHANEMORE
# Local Songs

# A Poem – Casey of Drishane

As the boys of '67 sought to right the Isle of Green
Up rose a youthful Fenian band round dear old Skibbereen
Amongst them was a leader true, a fair haired buachall bán
The daring youth, the soul of truth, Tom Casey of Drishane.

As master of a country school well known for miles around
The greatest problem of the day, his pupils could expound
Beloved by every Fenian from _____ to Sullane
As truer Celt ne'er wore a belt than Casey of Drishane.

His patriotic fervour won his every pupils' heart
As the story of their injured land to them he did impart
The older boys indignant grew, each Pádraig, Séamus, Seán
With Tade and Mike all grasp the pike with Casey of Drishane.

Above old Coomnageehy's crest the midnight moon doth shine
Reflecting _____ and the waters of Loughine
The heart of every Burchill youth in Gurteenalomane
Throbs high with pride to march beside Tom Casey of Drishane

Long years have gone, the country school is a weed-grown place today
The master and his pupils, ah where, ah where are they?
The flowery bloom of Carbery's youth, the men of brain and brawn
The true and tried who stood beside Tom Casey of Drishane.

The Master Captain paid the toll at death's mysterious gate
He's sleeping 'neath Northampton soil in Massachusetts State
Were he within his native land waiting judgement's dawn
In Sherkin's shade would friends have laid the captain of Drishane

God rest you Captain Casey, you've not lived nor worked in vain
Your teaching finds expression in the movement of Sinn Féin
Where 'ere fair Carbery's cloud capped hills the shades of night have drawn
Fond tales are told of Casey bold, and the Fenians of Drishane.[156]

Tom Casey was school master in Drishanemore School at the time of the Fenian rising. Drishane school was abandoned when the present school, Tragumna, was opened in September 1871.

Collected from Mrs Daniel Regan, Drishanebeg

# DRISHANEMORE
# History and Archaeology

## An Altar Stone in the Townland of Ballyally

A large flat slab of stone, said to have been used as an altar in the penal times, is to be still seen in the townland of Ballyally, in a field belonging to Mr John O'Donovan who lives in a portion of the former coastguard station of Ballyally, Skibbereen. Mr O'Donovan informs me that very few people in the locality are aware of the existence of the altar stone. He cuts the briars, rushes, and grasses that surround it every year, and it is easy to approach and shows signs of being carefully preserved by the man in whose ground it is situated.[157]

Collected from John O'Donovan, Ballyally

## The Battle of Trá Leagach

There is a strand in Castlehaven parish called Tráighleagach where a battle was fought in the nineteenth century. In this locality there were seizures go leór and pounds at every crossroads. The Battle of Tráighleagach was fought between farmers and mounted policemen. The farmers struck against paying the tithes to the Protestant minister, and the policemen came to put the law in force. The farmers and their wives gathered near Toe Head (Ceann na Tuaithe) to fight and defend their stock from the policemen and soldiers. The battle lasted all day, and women were seen with their red petticoats in the thick of the battle. In the evening a widow's son was shot on the farmers' side, and a policeman named Cowhig was killed in the Crown forces. Cowhig had been firing all day in the air. When he was dead, the women got a stone and stuck it down his throat. The Crown forces then withdrew, and when they were coming back in the direction of Tráighomna, they saw and old man named Connolly. They shot Connolly dead as a reprisal.[158]

Collected by Patrick Geaney, Skibbereen

# The Famine of 1847

My grandfather at the time lived in Lettertinlish, two miles east of the town of Skibbereen. He and his family were fairly comfortable, but other farmers had to boil swedes and praiseach bhuidhe when the potatoes had failed. Cormac MacCarthaigh, had 15 bags of wheat in his barn which he sold in November for 30 shillings a bag, and in the following year in February it had risen to £3 a bag. One day, as the dinner was being prepared, a poor starving woman came into the kitchen and asked for food. The woman of the house had a pot of potatoes boiled, and she gave her the contents of the pot in an apron, and then turned round to boil another pot. So, not everyone ate donkeys around Skibbereen (as this nickname lives to the present day). The corpses in the Skibbereen district were all buried in one large plot in the Abbey grave yard. When Queen Victoria paid a visit to Cobh, on stepping ashore a large inscription met her gaze:

Arise ye dead from Skibbereen,
And come to cork to welcome your queen

Turning on her heel, she boarded the vessel and never fulfilled her engagements in Cork City. So, Cobh became Queenstown to the Gaill.[159]

# Turned Away from School

My Grandfather, John McCarthy, with his brothers, attended a School in Townshend Street, Skibbereen, conducted by a teacher named Brickley. They knew no English, so the master catching them speaking to each other in their native language, ordered them out of his School, and not to return until they were able to speak English.[160]

Collected by Michael J. Daly from his Aunt, Ellen McCarthy, (87 years) North St., Skibbereen, eldest daughter of the above-named John McCarthy (RIP). Lettertinlish

# A Holy Well in Boulibawn

In a glen called Gleann Doirin in the townland of Boulibawn, there is a holy well at which people used make rounds on May morning. The well is now known as Tobar na gCapall. Young boys who did not understand cut some trees near the well one time, and soon afterwards they died. The well is in a valley on the hillside, and above is the cave called Cúm. The water of the well was weighed by Father Beausang and Dr Dan O'Donovan, and it was found to be two ounces lighter per gallon than the water in the Holy Well in Loughine.[161]

Collected from Mr Patrick Geaney (aged 48), Boulibawn

# Ruins of an Old Chapel in Boulibawn

West of the well, there are the ruins of an old chapel. About thirty years ago when Father Kearney (R.I.P.) and Father Daley (R.I.P.) were in Skibbereen parish, stations were held in Boulibawn, and Father Kearney ordered an old man named Burchill to make the Jubilee in Skibbereen. The old man answered that he would make the Jubilee in the old chapel. Father Kearney asked him where that was, and the old man pointed out the ruins. The two priests went to it and knelt down and prayed, and Father Kearney gave orders that the stones were never to be removed.[162]

Collected from Patrick Gearney, Boulibawn

# The Year of the Big Snow

Morning, in this part of West Cork, was calm and sunny. When the snow came, it went into the smallest crevices, keyholes, windows, and joints of the doors. It fell in February and some of it did not melt until July.[163]

From Ellen McCarthy (aged 87 years), North Street, Skibbereen

# HEIR ISLAND

Co. Chorcaighe
Bar: Cairbre Thiar
Par: Achadh Dúin
Scoil: Inis Uí Dhrisceoil
Oide: Donnacha Ó Donnabháin

# FOREWORD

I regret to state that this island is relatively poor in folklore; and though I went from house to house, I was successful in collecting only the small amount which I have written into this book.[xxii]

## D. O'Donovan, N. T.
## December 1938

As we ramble along, observing the various points of interest, we obtain some fine views of the adjoining coast. The hundred isles of Carbery are seen, the entire cluster dotting the surface of Roaring Water Bay (Lough Trasnagh), a very turbulent expanse of water, too, during the prevalence of a south-east or southerly gale. The names of the islands are familiar to our readers, such as the Skeams (St Keam's), Hare Island (Inish O'Driscoll), the Three Calves, so called on the *lucus a non lucendo* principal, because they raise no cattle there, whilst there are no hares on Hare Island.

Daniel Donovan, Sketches in Carbery (Dublin: McGlashan, 1876), p.63.

---

[xxii] In Irish, Hare Island (Heir Island) is known as Inis Uí Drisceoil.

# HEIR ISLAND
# Local Folklore and Stories

# A Story

I took down the following story as 'twas told to me. About ninety years ago, the people of the island were very, very poor. A good number of families were also almost starving. At this time a minister by the name of Spring came to the island. He was a Kerry man and he had plenty of money. He built a school on the Island. There is no trace of this building today, but the site on which 'twas built is still pointed out by the old people. He also built a house which he used as a church. He went around among the people and offered them money and food if they would send their children to his school and attend service in his church on Sundays. Most of the inhabitants were forced, through poverty, to accept this money and food. Those who attended his church got plenty of money and food and clothes. Others would not take either food or money and many of them died of hunger. He gave employment too to those who were willing to work, and a rough road in the midland is still known as boithrín Spring. There was a Song made about him but I have only a couple of verses of it.

> Spring was a Kerryman born.
> He took his departure of late;
> He steered his course for Baltimore Harbour,
> And bid adieu to his old mother Kate.
> Tis there he met Carthy the Preacher,
> Michael Donovan, Jerry Shea then also,
> Young Harry and old Harry Casey
> And a man who they call him Joe.

'Twas hard to blame the old people for turning with him, as God only knows how badly off they were; and 'twas hunger and nothing else made them do it. But plenty food came after to them.

During Spring's time, a ship laden with wheat ran ashore at Rinn Point on the southern point of the island. It was on a Christmas Night, and at the dawn on Christmas morning the people went towards the wreck and drew home the corn in strong home-made linen sheets. They ground the corn with querns, and so they had plenty to eat then, every one of them, except the family of McCarthy Mór Spáinneach who turned away from Spring, and so he left the Island in disgust. This McCarthy Mór died a Protestant, and one of his sons remained a Protestant, afterwards joining the Police Force. I met this same man when he was in the Force. His family are Protestants to this day.[164]

Collected from Michael McCarthy (aged 74 years), Hare Island West

# Lutharagans

I was about eleven years of age and I was one day minding the cow in a field called Gort Bráthair, which is in the western end of the Island. About twelve o'clock I was looking towards the southern ditch of the field, and there resting on the ditch I saw a lutharagan.[xxiii] He wore a claw-hammer jacket, long black trousers and a black beaver hat. He looked at me, and I got afraid. I ran back home, and I didn't go back to the field again that day. This was the only occasion on which I saw a lutharagan. I often heard the old people saying that this field was full of lutharagans. I heard my grandmother saying that a man named Charles McCarthy followed a lutharagan one day in the same field. He had his hand just over the lutharagan's shoulder to catch him, when the lutharagan said to him, "féach ar na caoirigh sa gort [Look at the sheep in the field]". Charles looked east but he saw no sheep, and when he turned again the lutharagan was gone. I often heard the old people saying that the lutharagan had a purse, and that if you could get this purse, you would have a shilling every time you opened it. They used to call this purse sparán na sgcillinge.

There was a big flat stone in the middle of Gort Bráthair and the old people said that lutharagans used to live under this stone. The old people wouldn't touch this stone because they believed the lutharagans would harm them if they interfered with the stone in any way. A neighbour and myself lifted this stone about 33 years ago, and we found a heap of different shells under it. The shells were all empty and the underside of the stone was as black as soot, just like a hob stone. No harm came to me or my neighbour.[165]

Collected from John McCarthy (aged 73 years), Hare Island West

---

xxiii Lutharagan is another term for leprechaun.

# Story of a Spirit

My mother told me that she and her brother, Peter Cotter, were going home one night from a neighbour's house. They had to pass by a big strand, and a spirit in the form of a dog used to be seen there. Just as they were passing, they saw the dog. Peter stood and told him to leave the road in the name of God three times. But the dog got bigger and bigger until he was as big as a cow. Peter then put his hand in his pocket and took out his pocketknife. He asked the dog if he wouldn't leave in the name of God, to leave in the name of the Devil, at the same time he made a drive of the knife at the dog. As he did, the dog leaped west over the ditch. They then went home, and as soon as my mother went inside the door she fell in a weakness. They told their experience to the parish priest, Fr O'Sullivan, Aughadown, and he was supposed to have banished the spirit. He told them that the spirit would not be seen again for 60 years. This incident happened about forty years ago.

In the same strand, and a short while before the above story, a man by the name of Mike Harte was coming home from Skibbereen. As he was passing about nine o'clock that night, the spirit, in the form of a man, stood before him and asked him where he was going. He told the spirit that he was going home. The spirit then attacked him and he was found almost dead by his aunt, Nony Minihane, who was going home from the Northland about 10 p.m. She brought him home, but he never again left the bed, and he died about six months after.[166]

Collected from Kate Murphy (28 years) and Daniel Murphy (77 years),
Heir Island Middle

N.B. The Strand mentioned is situated on southern side of the island and is known as the Tráigh Mhór. The people believe that Fr O'Sullivan banished the spirit, as it has not been seen since. Fr. O'Sullivan was parish priest at Aughadown in the Diocese of Ross. He died about 10 years ago and is buried in the churchyard, Kilcoe. He was close on 90 years when he died.

# HEIR ISLAND
# People, Places and Property

# The Old Houses

When I was a young boy all the houses on this island were thatched (Figure 15). The cupboard and dresser made a partition between the kitchen and little room. The fireplace was always at the gable-end, and turf was used in every house. There was no chimney or flue, and the only escape for the smoke was through a hole in the thatch by the gable. On a calm day the house used to be filled with smoke, and often the smoke was so thick that we failed to see one another. I remember, sometime after this, seeing flues built. A strong beam was fixed across the house from one sidewall to the other. This beam was about four to five feet from the floor and from three to four feet from gable. Strong sticks were driven into the gable. The lower sticks were driven at the level of the crossbeam, and as they reached the top of the gable, they became shorter. Through these sticks briars and twigs were woven, and thus closed up the flue. They were plastered with cow dung in my father's house. The bottom crossbeam was called mada clúir. This type of flue was later replaced by a stone one. The space on each side of flue was called the cúloir. This was planked from the crossbeam to gable, and cured dry fish was stored there. Every house used to have the two cúloir filled with fish for winter. The loft over the kitchen was called the main loft. Here, the beds were on the ground. The loft over the room was about a foot or so lower, and here a standing bed was kept. About sixty years ago there were no standing tables. Tables consisted of two nine-inch planks, about three feet long, nailed together with treasnáins. They had ledges about an inch-and-a-half high to prevent potatoes from rolling off. When in use they were placed on top of boxes. After every meal they were scrubbed and placed against the side wall of the house. Afterwards the tables were hinged to the back of the settle, and when not in use were held upright against the wall by a clamp.[167]

Collected from Michael Neill (aged 73 years), Heir Island Middle

Figure 15. Old, thatched cottage, from Emily Lawless, *The Story of Ireland*
(New York: Putnam, 1888), p.272.

# HEIR ISLAND
## Local Customs

# Food

When I was a young boy, the inhabitants of this island used to have yellow-meal stir-about for breakfast and supper. The dinner consisted of potatoes and fish. Though a lot of wheat used to be grown, it was sold in the town of Skibbereen. The money thus obtained used to pay the rent, and a good number of the old people were supposed to possess a lot of money at that time. To cook the stir-about, a pot of water was boiled and then thickened with yellow meal. Salt was added to taste. It was served in deep plates. Each member of the family was given milk into which the spoon of gruel was dipped before eaten. Up to forty years ago, querns were in use in every house on the island. The grinding was usually done by night. A linen sheet was spread on the table and the quern placed on it. The wheat was heated in a pot sat over the fire and thus hardened before being ground. Some of the ground flour was eaten as réabún. Sometimes it was boiled with water and used as gruel for supper.[168]

Collected from John McCarthy (aged 73 years, Hare Island West

# Lights

When I was about ten years old, bog-deal splinters were used as lights. They were sold in the town of Skibbereen, and on Saturdays the people used to go to town and bring home a week's or a fortnight's supply. The sticks of bog-deal were split into splinters about the thickness of wheaten straw. The splinters were stuck in the gable wall near the fire. They used to be lit while the supper was being prepared and eaten. When I was about fifteen or sixteen years of age, I saw the old people melting the livers of skate, codfish, or ling, and the oil thus obtained used to be kept in an old jar. They used to buy shallow vessels called slighthe at that time. These vessels were filled with the fish oil, and a strip of calico or an old rag soaked in the oil was placed in the slighthe. One end hung out over top of it, and this end was lit. Sometimes rushes were used instead. The outside skin was peeled off, and the soft spongy inside used as a wick. Instead of the sligthe, pieces of broken pots were often used. The oil was called geataire caol tréanach.[169]

Collected from John McCarthy (aged 73 years), Hare Island West

# Funerals

Up to sixty years ago, no Priest used to visit a wake-house on the Island. An old man named Stephen Neill used to say certain prayers over the corpse on the day of the funeral. He was called on at all deaths on the Island to perform these rites. No one on the Island could repeat the prayer or prayers said by him. Three sticks, usually spade handles, were lashed underneath the coffin, and the protruding ends of the sticks were gripped by the six men who carried the coffin. Coffins were not borne on the shoulders at the time because it was impossible to do so as there were no roads then on the Island, and so they had to be carried over rough paths. Six men of the same name were the first to carry the coffin, and the same six men used to bear the coffin into the graveyard. There is no graveyard on the island. On the day of funeral, the coffin is borne (now on shoulders) to Cúisín na gCorp which is situated at the eastern end of the Island. Here the coffin is laid on the ground before it is put on board a boat. Here in the exact spot on which coffin is laid, a clump of rushes, roughly about the length and breadth of a coffin, grows. The ground around is quite clear of rushes, and during the lifetime of the oldest inhabitants, corpses have been rested on this clump of rushes. Though there is a fine slip at eastern end of Island and within twenty yards of Cúisín na gCorp, under no circumstances would the inhabitants dream of boarding a coffin at the slip. The boat carrying the coffin leads, all other boats following, one tied to the other by painters. The corpse is landed at a point on the mainland called the Tobacco Point.[170]

Collected from John McCarthy, Hare Island West

## Old Substitute for Baby Powder

When I was a little girl baby powder, also known as Fullers' Earth, was unknown on this Island, but I saw my own mother and the other old women using the following. They used to strike the old moth-eaten beams and rafters of the outhouses and the dry powder, thus obtained, used to be shaken on the babies after being washed, in the same manner as baby powder is used today. The old women had a very high opinion of this powder.[171]

Collected from Mrs Kate Burke (aged 65 years), Heir Island Middle

## Heir Island
# Local Cures

# Cure for Evils

I was born on Good Friday and baptised on Easter Monday, and when I grew the old people told me that I had a cure for evils. I was eventually persuaded to use my supposed power. On six occasions people were brought to me. They were suffering from sores which the old people told me were a form of consumption. I blew my breath nine times on the sores on nine successive mornings. The patients, as well as myself, had to be fasting. After each breath I made the sign of the cross over the sore. The people brought to me were of both sexes, and to my knowledge they were all cured. The sores went, and these people lived to be old men and women. I have not practised this for the past twenty-five years for the following reason. I was lobster fishing in Ballycotton about twenty-five years ago, and I met a man named John O'Brien who warned me never to use this cure again because he told me that I would one day suffer from a sore myself which could not be cured. So not for all the gold in the world would I practise this now, and I have made up my mind never again to do it.[172]

Collected from Richard Cotter (aged 72 years), Heir Island South
Occupation: Small farmer & fisherman

# Tobar a' Lúibín

Tobar a' Lúibín, is a well, situated on the south side of Cnoc-a-trágha-bháin. It overlooks Tráigh bán. I remember when I was a young man people suffering from sore eyes used to visit this well. There was no fixed day for those visits. They used to go there three mornings, early, in succession, and on each visit they used to recite a decade of the rosary and then bathe the eyes with the water from well. People suffering from pains and other sickness used also visit the well. The custom no longer prevails on the island.[173]

Collected from John McCarthy, Heir Island

# HEIR ISLAND
# The Natural World and Weather Lore

## Signs of Weather

When rooks fly high 'tis a sign of bad weather. When black divers go south beyond the bridge, 'tis a sign of bad weather. When they are seen flying from the south over the land - a sign of southerly wind and rain. When they fly from the north - a sign of breezy strong northerly wind. When Mount Gabriel is capped with white fog coming from the east, 'tis a sign of fine weather. When covered with black fog 'tis a sign of bad weather. When there are beams from the rising moon 'tis a sure sign of a gale or strong wind. A ring round the moon portends bad weather. But if the ring is open, 'tis sure to get a breeze from that point. When ducks or geese go to the bog and dive madly 'tis a sign of rain. When the sun goes down glaring and red - out with wind and rain. Seagulls well in on the land a sign of bad weather. Rays from the sun in the evening are a sign of good weather, but rays from the sun in the morning are a sign of bad weather.[174]

Collected from John McCarthy (aged 73 years), Heir Island West,
Michael Cahalane (aged 71 years), Heir Island South

# KILCOE

Co. Chorcaighe
Bar: Cairbre Thiar
Par: (Achadh Dúin) Kilcoe
Scoil: Cill Chothrach
Oide: Tadhg Ó Spealáin
December 1938

KILCOE, in the Barony of Carbery, county of Cork, and province of Munster, is 6 miles from Skibbereen. It is situated upon Roaring Water Bay. One rectory is impropriated in the representatives of Lord Castlehaven; and one rectory belongs to the Archdeacon of Ross.

Nicholas Carlisle, *A Topographical Dictionary of Ireland* (London: Miller, 1810)

# KILCOE
# Local Folklore and Stories

# The Building of Lisheen Church

In former years, there was no priest allowed to live in Aughadown and for this reason they had to live in a small house in Coolbawn. The parish priest who was in Coolbawn at the time happened to go on a sick call to Lisheen. He went there on horseback, and he took a near way across fields because very few roads were made at the time. It happened, however, that it was across a landlord's fields the priest went, and as he was approaching the landlord's house, he happened to come out and he forced the priest to go back again. A great argument arose between them, and the priest had to return back, and when the priest arrived at the sick person's house, the patient had died. The following morning when the servants of the landlord's house arose, they noticed the house full of every kind of creeping animals. When the breakfast was prepared for his lordship, he could not taste any-thing as the insects tormented him in every way possible. The landlord begged his butler to send at once for the priest. When the priest arrived, the landlord promised anything he would wish so long as he would banish the animals from the house. The priest said all I wish for is sufficient ground to enable me to build a Church. The landlord gave him enough land to build Lisheen Church. The Church, which is in Lisheen at the present time, stands in memory of this great mystery the priest worked.

Collected by Sighle Sexton
From Mrs Ellen Sexton, 56 years, Foherlagh

# The Nurse and the Good People

In olden times there lived a man and his wife who was a nurse, near the townland of Caheragh. At that time women rode on side saddle behind their husbands as it was the only mode of conveyance. It happened one night that a handsome young man came on a call for the nurse. She got ready, and as was her usual habit, she went behind him on the saddle. The man drove off across a broad country, the night being so dark, that the nurse could not recognise what part of the country she was in. They were travelling on for a few hours until they came to a house, the man stopped the horse, and told the nurse that this was the house. He opened the door to leave her in, and when she was just inside the door there was a woman coming out against her who told her not to take anything she would be offered there, not even money, but when they would say that they would like to pay you in some way, to ask for the spancel which is hanging on the door.

The woman took the nurse to the room where the patient was. This room was full of the finest women the nurse had ever seen before, some of them eating and others singing. There were several in the crowd whom the nurse knew had died, particularly the patient she had attended who was a near-relative of her own. Then she was offered some refreshments and money but would not of course take any after the orders she got from the woman, so she asked for the spancel, which she got.

The man took the nurse home again, and the next morning she related to her husband all that had happened. On that day, she went to the house where the meat was kept, and she found that the meat had disappeared. The nurse got a great fright, and when she was returning in to call her husband, she saw in the field a cow feeding grass which had died previously. This was a still greater surprise to her husband.

Sometime afterwards, the two of them went to Skibbereen to buy a cow, and after arriving at the fair, they saw the very same man that took the nurse on the sick call. He was buying cattle. After a while the man bought a cow, and when they were coming home, they stopped for some refreshments at Bauraville Public House. When they went into the snug they noticed a very large crowd at the counter, and amongst them was the strange young man. The nurse remained looking at him for some time and at length she arose and went to the barmaid to ask her what was the boy's name. The maid began to sneeze, and sneeze, "Oh said," the nurse "God Bless us All. And may the Lord have mercy on all the poor souls who died belonging to us". At that moment the young man suddenly disappeared amidst the crowd. All the people ran to the door to know where he was gone, but nobody could see him, he disappeared like a ghost. The nurse fell on the floor in a weakness, and the Priest was sent for. After he had arrived, she told him the story and he blessed her. He also blessed the magic cow, and she disappeared, and he blessed the spancel, and that too disappeared. The priest went home and after a few days he found out that the nurse died.

Collected by Sighle Sexton
From Jermiagh Sexton, 28 years, Foherlagh

## Forty gold sovereigns

Long ago, an old man and his wife lived in a small little house in a field in my father's farm (John Donovan) now known as Pickeys field. He was called Pickey. He had the grass of one cow, and he was very poor. One day, when he was minding his cow, he saw a rat come out of a hole in the fence. He looked around him and then he disappeared again into the hole. After a few minutes he returned again with a gold sovereign in his mouth and placed it on a flat stone close to where the old man was sitting. He looked around him and again disappeared. Soon he returned with another sovereign, placed it on the stone, looked around him and disappeared. He continued like that until he had forty sovereigns on the stone. Then the old man could have patience no longer but when the rat went in again, he ran and took the forty sovereigns. When the rat returned and saw that all his gold had disappeared, he fell dead on the ground. The man took the money home to his wife and they lived happily ever after.

Collected by Mary O'Donovan
From Mrs Mary O Donovan, aged 84 years, Skeagh

# A Dream of Gold

In the townland of Skeaghanore there lived a young man named Michael Burke. On three successive nights he dreamt that a pot of gold was hidden under a whitethorn bush near a bridge in the Co. Limerick. One day he set out to find the gold. He came to the bridge the very same as he had pictured in his dreams and a few yards farther up on he could see the whitethorn bush. As he was walking over the bridge, he met a man who stood and spoke to him. In the course of their conversation, he told Burke that on three successive nights he had the same dream. "I have dreamt" he said, "that there is a little house in Skeahanore, and opposite that house there is a whitethorn bush and under the bush is gold hidden." Burke knew that this was his own house, and without making himself known to the stranger he immediately turned round and went home again.

The next day he got all his men to cut down the tree and dig up the roots. At last, they met a big flat stone on which was written. these words, "Turn me over and you shall see." When Burke read this, he was delighted as he thought he had come to the gold at last. But alas, after much difficulty they at least raised the stone only to read on it, "Turn me back again." That is how Burke was paid for all his labour.

Collected by Mary O' Donovan
From John O Donovan, aged 54 years, Skeagh

# The big black dog on the road

A man was cycling home on a moonlit night. He saw a large parcel on the road. He came off his bicycle and stopped to pick it up. As he was about to do so it changed into a big black dog. He was seized with fear and quickly mounted on his bicycle. The dog followed him to his house. The man fell sick, and he was very bad for a few weeks afterwards.

Collected by Bridie Goggin
From Mrs Bridget Goggin, aged 50 years, Corravoley

# Galloping Horses

A man named Jim Mac Carthy of Corravoley was accustomed to go "sgoruigheacting" to Mr Whites houses, about a half a mile from his own. One night, as he was returning alone about eleven o'clock along the by road leading to his own house, he heard a great number of horses galloping after him. He walked along quickly to his own gate with the intention of reaching it before they passed. As the horses came very near to him, he looked back to see who they were. To his amazement he did not know anybody. When he went in, nobody was in the kitchen. They were all assembled in his mother's room because she was dying. When he went upstairs the galloping continued around the house. That night his mother died.

Collected by Bridie Goggin
From Thomas Goggin, aged 54 years, Aghadown

# The ghostly trap

Two men were accustomed to go for a walk every night about seven o'clock after their days work. One night, they went out for their accustomed walk as far as was usual for them. Before they parted after the walk, they rested near a bridge. They heard the noise of hoofs of horses coming towards them. After a few minutes they saw a trap coming towards them, and there were two men sitting in it. The two men appeared to be asleep, and the pony was not driven by any of them. As the trap was passing, the two passengers suddenly disappeared leaving the men staring into space. They returned home and they were never seen going for their accustomed walk again.

Collected by Bridie Goggin
From Mrs Bridget Goggin, aged 50 years, Corravoley

# The ghostly boat

Long ago, a boat left Baltimore for Schull on her maiden trip with eleven hands on board, including passengers and crew. She went well until she ran on a rock outside Horse Island sound. The skipper and six passengers were lost. One Baltimore survivor rescued his sister and placed her on a rock while he was returning to rescue others. The waves washed her off the rocks and she was swept out to sea and drowned. After a few days, the bodies were recovered and buried, and to this day it is said by fishermen that the boat and her lights can be seen on the same course which she made when she was lost.

Collected by Bessie
From Mrs O'Connor, aged 54 years, Kilcoe

# An Ancient Fort in Gurteenroe

In the lands of Gurteenroe there is an ancient fort. People came from all places to travel through it. People passing or working near it usually heard noise. One day, two men made up their minds to make a search in this old fort. As they went along, the first thing they met was a door. They travelled along through it and they saw all kinds of household furniture. The two men went astray in such a way that more of the neighbours went in search of them. The neighbours had to take lights with them. When they arrived at the door, the lights were quenched. Then they had to call the lost men, and after a long time they arrived out as far as the door. Those men died shortly afterwards, and their cry was heard around that fort, for a long time, and it was said that the Danes had lived there.

Collected by Josephine
Told by John Hickey Ardura Aged 54 years

## Help from the good people

Long ago, a man was returning home from his days work. He was in a great hurry to get home to see his son who was dying of pneumonia. The man was walking along the road. Someone stopped him and settled his hat on his head, and he was lifted off the road. He did not know where he was until he was placed down on the road outside his own house. When he went in home, he was surprised to find his son had just died. He said afterwards it must be the good people who hurried him home before the boy died.

Collected by Bessie O'Connor
From Mrs O'Connor, aged 54 years, Kilcoe

## Ghostly passengers

Long ago, there were no motor cars on the road for taking the mail to Cork, and it was a horse and side car that took them from Schull. They went by night and returned in the morning. It was one man who always took the mail. One night, as they were travelling on their journey, the horse was not able to pull the load. They did not know what was wrong with the horse because he had only the usual load. The man looked back in the car, and he was surprised to see a number of people sitting in the car near him. He did not know who they were, and he spoke to them, but they never answered him. They remained in the car until they came as far as the Abbey gate. They left the car and disappeared.

Collected by Bessie O'Connor
From Mrs O'Connor, aged 54 years, Kilcoe

# A haunted house

Long ago, in a certain house, many servants were employed from time to time, but none of them would give constant service owing to the fact that the house was haunted. Many servants came and went after a few days service. Every night, the haunting started at a certain hour. They ventured to remain in a room nearby, one night, with the intention of seeing what was going on. At the usual hour they heard the noise of work in the kitchen, one of them asked the other would they go and see who was in the kitchen. When they arrived in the kitchen, they were surprised to see nobody there, and it was in the same condition as when they left it.

Collected by Betty O'Connor
From Mrs O'Connor, aged 54 years, Kilcoe

## Delayed by the good people

Long ago, a man came for a priest for a relative of his who was ill at home. The priest was in a great hurry to reach the house before the person died. He went to the house by bicycle and as he was travelling along, he was surprised to hear a beautiful song, Cailín deas cruidie na mbó,[xxiv] being sung on the side of the road. He came off of his bicycle to find out who was singing and was surprised to find a hound on the side of the road. He went on his bicycle again and when he reached the house the person had died. The priest said afterwards that it was the good people who delayed him on the road so that the person would be dead before he would reach the home.

Collected by Jeremiah Twomey
From William Twomey, aged 50 years, Ardura Beg

---

xxiv An Cailín deas cruidie na mbó is a traditional Irish song, the name of which translates as *The Pretty Maid Milking her Cow*.

# The ghostly house

One night, a man started out for the fair about 9 o'clock with a cow. When he had gone a short distance, he took out his pipe to light it. He had no matches and he thought it was too far to go back again. He walked along until he came to a house and he saw a light in it. He went in to light his pipe. He saw a crowd of people dancing. When he stood at the door, they beckoned him up to the fire where he lighted his pipe. They gave him the hat and he put a sixpence into it. He arrived at the fair in the morning and sold his cow. He came back the same road and looked in at the house, and he saw nothing but an old ruin consisting of four walls and no roof on it. His sixpence was on a stone in the middle of it. He left it there and returned home.

Collected by Jeremiah Twomey
From William Twomey, aged 50 years, Ardura Beg

# Buried gold

In the town land of Rossard there was a castle long ago, and the remains of it are to be seen there still. They say that there is gold buried in it, and that there is a dead man minding it. Whoever goes digging for this gold is sure to lose his life. His brother was living in Kilcoe Castle. They buried it in a straight line between the two castles. The great O'Donovans found one crock of gold when making a drain in their land.

Collected by Jeremiah Twomey
From William Twomey, aged 50 years, Ardura Beg

# A fairy funeral

Once upon a time, in a place called Leap, there were two old men named Patrick O'Driscoll and William Collins. They were coming home from town late in the night. It was said that Patrick O'Driscoll lived with the fairies, and he knew all about them. As they parted, he told the other man to hurry home, for it was as much as he could do if he were in home or near it before a funeral came along and overtook him on the road. It was true for Patrick because he was only just inside his door when it passed by. It was a great big one with many people walking and some on saddle horses with women riding behind them. He went in home then and never saw them again.

Collected by Kathleen Keating
From Mary Keating, aged 50 years, Hollyhill, Aughadown

## Never fool the Good People

There lived nearby a man who had a cow which got sick and died. In his land there was a fort. The cow came out feeding in it every day. One day he went to watch her and caught her by the tail. Then she ran into the fort, and he followed her. There were two grey old men sitting by the fire and they asked him what he wanted. He told them he wanted his cow that had come in here just then. They asked what the price of her was, and he said £20. Then one of them went to a big box and counted out £20 in notes. He went home very happy for he knew he had twice the value of his cow. He gave the money to his wife and he said he was very sorry as he had not asked more for if he had he would have got it. There was a fair next morning in Skibbereen and he said he would go there to buy a new cow. In the morning he went to get the money but there was nothing there before him only twenty leaves of briars. He was very angry, and he never saw the money again.

Collected by Kathleen Keating
From Denis Keating, aged 74 years, Hollyhill, Aughadown

# Stories from Hollyhill

In the townland of Hollyhill there is a hill where in olden times they buried children who were not baptised. One day, a poor man was coming home from a bog and he had a basket of turf on his back. There was a resting place near the hill, and he left his load down on a stone, and as he did, he was thinking how he would feed his family of ten children. He was there for some length of time and just as he was going to go home, out came a little rabbit with a yellow sovereign in his mouth. He washed it in a pool of water and he put it upon a stone. He went back and brought out another and kept doing so until he had twenty-one out. The old man was looking on and was wondering how many more the rabbit was going to bring out. The next time he came out he brought nothing but took one back. When he went in, the man took the twenty remaining sovereigns and went home. When he went home, he told his wife and children, and they lived happily afterwards.

Collected by Kathleen Keating
From Denis Keating, aged 74 years, Hollyhill, Aughadown

Long ago there lived in the townland of Hollyhill a family who held a dance in their house on November night. About midnight they were dancing and thought of nothing only their own fun. All of a sudden, they heard a knock at the door and a mournful cry. Somebody went to open the door, but they could see nothing. The old man of the house told them to stop the dancing and say the rosary, but they would not, and danced on. The same noise came to the door again. The old man then said, "The Lord have mercy on the souls", and he insisted on their saying the rosary. They did, and after that they had no more dances, and they were not again disturbed.

Collected by Kathleen Keating
From Mary Keating, aged 50 years, Hollyhill, Aughadown

# A Dream of Gold

Long ago, in the district of Dunmanway, there lived a family who were very poor, but they had a farm where a servant boy slept in the kitchen every night. One night, he dreamt that there was gold hidden under a tree. The next night he dreamt it again, and for three nights more the dream reoccurred. The man of the house was astonished to hear him so restless, and he asked him what the matter was. The boy said he was dreaming about a crock of gold. In the morning, the man asked the boy to show it to him. He took him to the place where it was hidden, and when they were about to come upon it the man sent the boy to get more tools. With the boy gone, the man got attendants to take it out. When the boy returned, he told him he had not seen the hidden gold yet. So it was that the boy got nothing, and he never dreamt of it again.

# The Unbaptised Child

Not very long ago there lived a family of six, a father, mother and four children. The father got sick and died. The night of the wake, one of the children asked her aunt to take her down the stairs of the cellar. As they opened the cellar door, a round, black ball bumped step-by-step down the stairs until it disappeared. They were very frightened and did not know what to do. A few days after, as the aunt was speaking to the priest, he asked her if any child had died without baptism. She said she did not know. She went back and asked the mother who replied that there was one. When she came back, she told him. The priest said, "Ah, that was the child coming to meet its father but couldn't see its way. If you had had the presence of mind to make the sign of the cross, you'd have seen a bright light shine. It would have saved the child's soul. But you'll probably never get the chance again."

Collected by Kathleen Keating
From Denis Keating, aged 74 years, Hollyhill, Aughadown

# New York and back in time for dinner

Long ago in Skeaghanore there lived an old man who worked very hard. One evening, when he returned home from work, he wanted to have a smoke but had no tobacco. He said he would go to Ballydehob for some while his daughter was preparing the supper. The village was only about a mile away, and as he lived near the water's edge, he could easily travel a path at the edge of the water. When he went out the door, he saw a little boat come into the bay. In the boat there sat a little man. He thought the man was a neighbour so he went down to the boat and told the man he was going to Ballydehob and asked if he would row him over. The little man in the boat agreed, so in he went. Off went the boat, and the old man was so amazed at its swiftness that he thought he was in a dream until he saw a beautiful city, all lit up with electricity. He asked the little man where he was. The man replied that this was the city of New York and asked him if he had any friends there. The old man told him that his brother lived there and that he knew his address, but he could not find him. The little man asked him for the address, and when the old man told him, he led him to the end of a beautiful street and told him to go to the fourth house and he would wait there until he returned. The old man did, and there in the fourth house he met his brother who of course was more than surprised to see his brother in his old clothes in the beautiful city. When the old man had related his tale to his brother, he enquired about all his old friends in Ireland. Then he gave him presents of every description for those at home, and he gave him as much tobacco as he wouldn't use in a whole year. He then said he wouldn't delay him any longer in case the boatman would be gone. They went down to the boat and the little boatman, and when he saw the boat going off, he returned home. The boat went back as quickly as it had come and before the old man knew where he was, the little boat was stopped in the bay outside his own door. He then thanked the little man and left the boat. When he went in, his daughter was surprised to see him so soon, and when she saw all the parcels, she asked him where he had got them. He then told his story, but she would not believe him until she got a letter a few days afterwards from her uncle asking if his brother had reached home safely.

Collected by Mary O'Donovan, Skeagh, Skibbereen
Told by John O'Donovan, aged 54 years, Skeagh, Skibbereen

# KILKOE
# Local Customs

## Local Marriage Customs

Marriages take place in shrove. Wednesdays and Fridays are thought unlucky for marriages. Matches are made in my district. Money is given as dowry and sometimes goods are given. Music and dancing take place on the wedding day. The straw-boys visit the house. They dress up in women's clothes. They sing and dance around the house. A Wedding procession is held. The guests stay a few hours in the bride's old home and then they go with her to her new home. They race against each other on the way home. Wives sat on the horses with their husbands in former times on the way home from the wedding, about two o'clock in the morning.

Collected by William Twomey

# Kilkoe
# History and Archaeology

# Fairy Forts

There is one fairy fort in my district. It is called a rath. There are other forts in the neighbouring district, and they are in view of each other. They are round in shape. There is a fence of earth and trees around them. There is no entrance hole in the centre of them. No one ever went down into the fairy forts to find out what was there. When the Danes were in Ireland long ago, the people built these forts to protect themselves.

Collected by Jeremiah Twomey
From William Twomey, aged 50 years, Ardura Beg

# Kilcoe Castle

The Clan Dermod is descended from Dermod Donn, a sone of Donal Gott MacCarthy, Lord of Carbery (1205 to 1251). They possessed an extensive district in Carbery, and the castles of Kilcoe and Cloghane. Kilcoe Castle was situated on a point of land at the head of Roaring Water Bay (Figure 16), not far from Ballydehob; and extensive ruins of it consisting principally of a large, massive square tower, with a small turret, are described by Lewis as being in existance at the time he wrote – upwards of sixty years ago.

S. T. McCarthy, 'The Clan Dermod', in *Kerry Archaeological Magazine*, vol. 1. Oct. 1908-April 1912, pp.18-19.

Figure 16. Kilcoe Castle. J. S. Flemming (1834), ref. PD 1974 TX 10 (14), used with the kind permission of the National Library of Ireland.

# LISHEEN

Co. Chorcaighe
Bar: Cairbre Thiar
Par: Achadh Dúin
Scoil: Lisín Upper
Oide: Seán Ó Riagáin

# Lisheen
# Local Folklore and Stories

# The Enchanted Lake

The people say there is some enchantment connected with every lake in Ireland, and there is some legend or old story told about every one of them. There is a lake in the neighbourhood and a very strange story told about it. In old times, there was a family living near this lake, and they were so poor that they had scarcely any furniture. only a pot in which they boiled stirabout, their only food. One day a strange woman came into the house and asked for the loan of the pot. The woman of the house gave it to her without asking for her name or where she came from. That evening when the time came for boiling the stirrabout, there was no pot to boil in in, and the woman of the house had great trouble in preparing the meal. Next day, about the same hour, the strange woman walked in again and she told the woman of the house she had brought her a cow, and she warned her never to be angry with the cow nor to curse her, nor to beat her with the spancel. The strange woman said to her that if she did what she had directed her to do the cow would never leave her, but she would feed from the house down to the lake and she would give her plenty milk for the use of her family. Then the strange woman departed. Her words came true. The cow was a good one and she yielded daily a good flow of milk, more than sufficient for the needs of the family. In the course of time, the cow had a calf and this calf grew to be a cow, and after five or so years the poor family had a little herd of five or so cattle in their possession, and they began to feel very independent. All went well for some time, until one morning while the woman was milking the cow, she got angry with the it, and she cursed her and beat her with the spancel. When she let her out after milking, the cow waited until the others were let out, and she led them down towards the lake, and she and the other cows disappeared in its depth and were seen no more. The day after the cows disappeared, the strange woman came in again and told the woman of the house that she had brought her back the pot which she got on loan. She also said that she was very sorry for what had happened to her, but she explained to her that it was her own fault because she did not fulfil the conditions which she had laid down for her when she gave her the cow. The strange woman also told her that she could not keep the pot a moment longer after the cows had left her possession, and that owing to her impatience she was reduced to poverty again.[175]

# The Sale of a Dead Cow

Once upon a time there was a farmer. One of his cows became sick and pined for a few days, and then died. He was a very early riser, and short time after the loss of his cow he was out one morning before sunrise seeing if his crops were uninjured as he sometimes suffered from trespassers. It happened he had to pass by the rath (fort) and when he turned round the corner, what did see but the cow that had died, feeding greedily. As he drew nearer, the cow raised her head and looked at him. The all at once she started to run towards the gap in the high fence that surrounded the rath. The farmer ran towards the gap also, and as the cow arrived at the entrance, he succeeded in catching her by the tail, and being a very strong man, he was able to stop her, though she struggled hard to get away. All at once a strange man stood by him and ordered him to loose his grip on the cow's tail. The farmer stoutly said he would not, for he claimed the cow was his. As the strange man saw the farmer was determined to hold the cow, he soon changed his attitude, and asked the farmer the price he wanted for the cow. The farmer demanded a high price, but the strange man did not haggle or try to reduce the sum. He only said to the farmer to come again at the same hour the following morning, and that the money would be in a certain spot inside the fort which he showed him, and on these conditions the farmer released the cow. When the cow found herself free, she rushed off into the rath and disappeared in a big opening which led to an underground passage that explorers could not find an end to. Before parting, the strange man gave him a strict warning that the money he would find ready for him in the fort the morning after should not be kept in his possession after sunset that evening.

The farmer came as agreed and found the exact sum bargained for in the very spot the strange man had pointed out. He went immediately and paid his rent and all the debts he owed, and he had the last penny of it disposed of before sunset, and he never heard any more about it afterwards.[176]

## An old story told by a man who died
## about twenty years ago

This man was living in a place which in years gone by had been famous for fox-hunting by gentry on horseback. Joined to the house in which he lived was a small end in which he kept his horse. It came to pass that he used to hear at the dead of night, as it were, a horse walking out of the yard, and he used rise early every morning to see if his horse were in the stable. Finding his horse always there, he tried to persuade himself that he was merely dreaming and imagining that he heard the steps of a horse. But at work during the day, he began to notice that his fine strong horse has less and less energy, and he began to suspect that perhaps some roguish person was nightly taking his horse away to do some sort of work or night travelling. He resolved to be wary, and to listen again for the steps of the horse leaving his premises.

Next night, he was awakened by the steps of a horse passing his window. He jumped out of bed and drew on his pants and hastily made for the door. It was custom in those days to keep the cock inside the door of the kitchen, perched over it on a stick driven into the wall. This was done perhaps for a superstitious belief in the cock, or perhaps to rouse the household at a certain hour before clocks came into general use. When the man was going to the door, the cock crew and blew in his face and drove him back. Again, he tried to open the door but the cock again crew and blew against him and prevented him from opening the door. Then it became a fight between the man and the cock, so that the household were all awakened and came to see what was the cause of the great commotion. The man explained to them what had happened, and they persuaded him to go back to bed, and all returned quietly.

Next day, the cock began to shed his feathers and the day after he was stark naked having lost his last feather, and then he died. The man concluded that it was the Good People who were taking his horse away at night to the hunting field, and that his cock knew this and sacrificed his life to save the man of the house, preventing him from going out to thwart the Good People who would kill him for doing so.[177]

# A halfpenny worth of lies

Last night I received the news of an old hag's death. I was overjoyed with the glad news and every tear that fell from the back of my head would split six fathoms of turf and set a mill turning. Off I went and the first thing I saw was children playing hide and go seek under a hack-cock made of stones. Then I saw a man and his eldest son threshing tobacco leaves into pears. One of the pears jumped over the ditch and began to bark at a tomcat which was followed by three blind pensioners who had lost their heads, legs and bodies in the battle of Waterloo. I said myself I could run as well as any of them. I took my head under my arms and my shinbones in my pocket and away I went through sloughs of stirrabout and bog holes of buttermilk until I reached Kildare. There I met a coach-driver who was driving fifteen blind donkeys. He asked me did I know anything about old John Fox. I said he was to the north of three blind mice where the wind never blew, the clock never crew, where the cow passed a hatchet next week. There was an old woman who had fallen into the Liffey. She was burned in a blaze of cold water and came out of it at the North Pole.[178]

Told by Jerry Horrigan, Church Cross, Skibbereen.

# LISHEEN
# People, Places and Property

# Cnoc Osta

The highest mountain which can be seen from this place is called Mount Gabriel. It is not known how it got its name. The name the old people had for it was Cnoc Osta. There is an old story told among the people about it. It is said that when St Patrick was banishing paganism out of Ireland, the devil was in such a rage that he pulled a piece of rock out of Mount Gabriel and flung it into the Atlantic Ocean some miles west of Cape Clear. This lone rock had been many years there and several ships were wrecked on it until close on one hundred years ago a big lighthouse was built on it. This rock was called the Fastnet Rock, and the lighthouse got the same name. In Irish it is called Carraig Aonair. This lighthouse is situated on one of the greatest trade routes in the world. It is said that on every May morning the Fastnet Rock leaves its place and sails around Cape Clear and northwards to three rocks called the Bull, Cow and Calf, and returns to the place again before sunrise.[179]

# Local weight-lifting heroes

Mr Gaeney (deceased), North Marsh, Church Cross, Skibbereen, was seen to carry a twenty stone bag of meal from the main road to the top of the rock – about 200 yards. Jim Evans (37 years) Ardralla, Church Cross, Skibbereen took three cwt. bags of coal, tied in one rope, from the strand to his home – uphill – about 400 yards. Patrick Hickey (27 years), New Court, Skibbereen, took a two cwt. bag of artificial manure from the car, threw it over his shoulder, and carried it to a field on the farm. Bob Swanton, Ardalla, Church Cross, Skibbereen, can still lift two half cwts. on his two little fingers and put them over his head.[180]

# Old Houses

Old houses were all very small. Most of them had only one room serving for kitchen and bedroom. The fireplace was at the gable-wall in all of them, the fire on the hearth. The fireplace extended from side wall to side wall. The front of the fireplace was closed down within four feet of the ground. The oldest pair in the house usually sat up in the corner at either side of the fire. There was usually only one tiny window, one pane of glass immovable or else the 12-inch space was open during the day and stuffed with a bag of hay for the night. The floor was made of white clay (blue till) put in very wet and packed as hard as possible. There was only one door in the front and many of them had a half door, or half hatch as it is still called. The coop for the hens was usually at the side wall inside the door. Hence the cock crow call in the morning. Often the cow and calf fitted in at the end of the kitchen. The settle bed took the place of the ordinary bed or else they had straw pallets on the floor around the fire. The roof was of thatch. There were professional thatchers in every locality. Wheaten straw after slashing, or reed cut in boggy, marshy places, was used for thatching. Spars made from strong old briar stems, pointed at both ends and about two or two-and-a-half feet long were cut to bind the thatch. The reed was first laid down evenly on the part to be repaired. It was then sewn through with a needle (like a poker). White cord was used for the sewing. A second person inside fastened the cord around the toabhán.[xxv] The spars were then driven in at even intervals around each sheaf. The thatching always began at the eaves and finished at the ridge of the roof above.[181]

---

[xxv] Taobhán – a longitudinal beam

# Townlands

Gurteenroe - Goirtín Ruadh - red earth - poor land for crops

Ardralla - árd-roilig - reilig

Marsh - Corach - a inlet of the Ilen river - ground marshy at both sides

Droumnacara - Drom na caróg - A big stone on the farm

Collatrum - Colla Ririm

Lisaree - Lios an Riogh - a fort on farm

Poulnacallee - Poll na Caillighe - a huge hole near Michael Driscoll's house

Ardagh - Árdach - a height

Fasagh - Fásach - a wilderness - this townland is rough and rocky

Ardnagroghery - Árd-na-Gcrocaire - The hangman's height - where anybody who earned the landlord's displeasure was hanged

White Hall - The landlord's residence - the name extended to the townland

Turk Head - Ceann Tuirc - A turk was buried there at the Sack of Baltimore

Cunnamore - cuan na muir, cúl na muir

Kilkileen - Cill-cillín - Ruins of an old monastery

Aughadown - Acadh Dúin.[182]

# LISHEEN
# Farming, Trade and Crafts

# Making butter and local crafts

Some years ago, there were no creameries in the country and the farmers made their butter in their own dairies. When the cows were milked, the people used to put the milk into earthenware pans of similar material to our flowerpots. Those pans were glazed inside to keep the milk from soaking into them and from getting sour. The milk was left two or three days in the pans and by this time all the cream had risen to the top. Then it was skimmed off and put into a cream crock, and when there was enough cream for a churning it was put into a churn and butter was made of it.

Any person not of the household who happened to come in while the churning was in progress should take the handle of the churn and do a few turns saying at the same time, 'God bless us.'

Long ago the people had their own crafts for making all the things they needed for household use. There is an old mould in the house nearest the school. They had their own tallow which they melted and put into the mould and then they had candles made. They had their own wool which they spun into thread. This thread was made up in big balls and given to the weaver to weave it into a very warm cloth called frieze. There were very clever linen weavers in Skibbereen and the country around it. Some women have tablecloths woven by them many years ago. Into these were woven patterns of a cup and saucer, knife and fork, spoon and egg stand. These cloths are carefully preserved as precious heirlooms in the family.[183]

# LISHEEN
# Local Customs

# Peculiar beliefs about certain days of the year

The people have special ideas about certain days of the year. On Little Christmas night it is believed that the water is turned into wine at midnight, and one night long ago a girl remained up to drink the wine, and she was dead in the morning. It is also told about three men who stayed up on another Little Christmas night to drink the wine. In the morning, one was found dead, the other blind, and the other sleeping.

The women long ago said Saint Brigid's Day was a holiday for wheels, and they used not spin at all on that day.

On St Patrick's Day the head of the house brought in a branch of withy and burnt one end of it in the fire. Then he took it out and spat on it to quench it and made the sign of the cross on the left shoulder of every person with the charred end of it.

On Good Friday the farmers do not like to plough or to redden earth, but they always like to keep a bucketful of seed to plant on that day, because it is said that every seed which would be planted on that day was sure to grow.

It is regarded as wrong to go to see a sick person for the first time on Friday, or to give away money on Monday. People also do not like to get married on Mondays, Wednesdays, or Fridays, or to go out at night spreading clothes which have been washed.

Every May morning, the people usually get up early, and they vie with each other to have the first of the water from the well. The people go out to wash their faces in the dew, and it is said by doing this they got no sickness for twelve months after. People who are suffering from warts go out before sunrise on May morning and look for a stone on which the dew drops are. They rub the dew drops to the warts in order to banish them. It is usual that young boys and girls pull nettles on May Day, and they slash each other with them causing stings to each other. Sometimes grownup people indulge in the practice and many lively scenes occur.[184]

# Fishing Lore

There are many strange stories told about fishing. It is said they would not allow a woman to go with them because if they did, they would not catch any fish that night. It is also said that anyone on board would not be allowed whistle or sing or curse because it is not lucky.

# Life in the Days of
# our Great Grand People in West Cork

In the old days, the women did not wear boots or shoes when in their homes and engaged in their ordinary household duties. They simply went barefoot. But when going to Mass or to the market in the hometown, they carried boots and stockings with them, not on their feet but slung on their arms. When they had come near the journey's end, they washed their feet, and put on the stockings and boots, and on the return journey they took them off again and travelled homewards barefoot. There is a stream on the western side of Skibbereen flowing into the Ilen on the left bank of which the town is built. This tributary stream is known as Sruthánín na mBan for the reason above stated.[185]

# Meals in olden days

The men, and often the women, went out to work at dawn. They had no time but god's, they tell us. Breakfast was at nine, or after a couple of hours work. The meal consisted of griddle cake and sour skimmed milk. Dinner was late in the evening. Potatoes (and all partook of many of them) were emptied into a scitheóg which was placed in the middle of the floor, and all sat around.[xxvi] They had as well home-cured salt mackerel or herrings and sour milk. Supper at bedtime was griddle cake and fish roasted on the red coals with sour milk or gruel (Indian meal boiled for hours with sour milk).[186]

---

[xxvi] Scitheóg: a shield-shaped basket.

## Proverbs heard locally

Habits in youth become nature with age.
As the old cock crows, the young ones learn.
Once a man and twice a child.
A stitch in time saves nine.
'Tis late to spare when all is spent.
You never miss the water 'till the well runs dry.
A fool and his money soon part.
Have money in your pocket and you will always have a friend.
A thing done right is done twice.
A straw shows how the wind blows.
Show me your company and I'll tell you what you are.
Empty vessels make most sound.
Early to bed and early to rise makes a man healthy, wealthy and wise.
Miss an hour in the morning and you'll hunt it all day.
A bird in the hand is better than two in the bush.
A friend in need is a friend indeed.
Laugh, and all laugh with you.  Weep, and you weep alone.
The longest way round is the shortest way home.
You can mind yourself on a thief but not on a liar.
There is nothing on earth as certain as death.
What's bred in the marrow comes out in the bone.
Breeding beats feeding.
You must not expect from a pig but a grunt.
As you live so you'll die.
Don't like the book by the cover.
Bend the twig while young.
Children and chickens are always picking.
A watched pot never boils.
Whenever there's smoke, there's fire.
Two heads are better than one if only cabbage heads.[187]

# LISHEEN
# Local Cures

# Herb Cures

The dock-leaf is used to remove a nettle sting. The leaf is rolled, and the injured spot rubbed with it, repeating at the same time:

Nettle out, dock in, dock remove the nettle sting,
In dock, nettle out, don't let the blood settle.

The celandine, which has yellow juice, was used to cure yellow jaundice.
The liverwort was used for liver complaints.
The wood-sorrel was in great demand as a cordial or pick-me-up.
Catseye and birdseye was used as remedy for weak eyes. People bathed their eyes in eye-bright lotion as we do now in boracic lotion.
The root of Solomon's seal was boiled, and the water used to bathe bruises caused by a fall.
Nettle rash was cured with nettle tea, which was made from ordinary nettles gathered from hedges.
There were three cures for warts, the husk of the broad bean, the ash and the elder. In the first case the soft downy part of the husk was rubbed across the warts saying three times.

As this bean-shell rots away,
So soon shall all my warts decay

Any person who licked the lizard was supposed to be able to cure cuts, sores and toothache.
Food left behind by the ferret was taken to cure whooping cough.
Agrimony: (boiled) drank to cure weak stomach.
Wild sage: boiled and drank for hurts and for stomach troubles.
Garlic: for worms in cattle and for rheumatism.
Besom: for pains in the bones.
Jack of the bush: a small yellow flower – a single root like parsnip – grows under the furze bush – used for kidney trouble.
A plant in a boggy place (resembling a twig – the name forgotten) to cure animals passing blood.
Rosemary: boiled and drank for lung trouble.
Holly: the skin off holly – enough to go right round the leg – to cure farcy in horses.[188]

# Lisheen
# The Natural World and Weather Lore

# Weather Lore

A red sky in the early morning is sure to bring rain before night. A circle close round the moon tells of rain near at hand while a broader circle foretells a storm. If fluffy white clouds rise to the west, we may expect a raining spell. A rainbow in the morning is looked upon as a sign of showers, while one seen in the evening is taken to mean finer weather may be expected.

The sea is about the best weather guide in these parts. Any stir or heave in the water is a sign that there is bad weather outside which will soon draw nearer. Particular notice is taken of what is called 'a draw on the rocks.' If the surface of the water has a glossy appearance – say in early summer – sultry weather may be expected. South-south-west or west winds bring rain. East winds – dry and cold.

If the wind in changing follows the sun, the weather is expected to get finer. If the wind howls through the house, storm and rain are not far away. If gulls fly out to sea or the swallows fly high, a period of fine weather may follow.

If the cat sits with its back to the fire or the dog eats blades of green grass, rain is sure to come within twelve hours.

Should the smallest fog appear on Mt Gabriel, rain is expected any moment. Seamen consider that the fog of Mt Gabriel, if it goes out to sea in the morning, is a sure sign of a fine spell.

Much notice is not now taken of the chimney smoke but older people tell us that if the line of smoke is over the chimney-level, fine weather is to come. Should any blue flame appear in the fire, a storm is brewing.

The Fastnet light is watched by all. If it throws a broad, bright flare, bad weather is sure at hand.[189]

# Signs of Rain

The climate in this country is very changeable. The people have many signs by which they know when rain is coming. At night a circle comes round the moon. In the daytime the crows fly fast and caw and also do somersaults in the air. The wind whirls round and raises the dust in clouds up in the air. There is a little river in the neighbourhood with a little waterfall, and when rain is coming there is heard a great booming noise, but when the weather is settled this noise is not heard a lot. In like manner, the ocean makes a noise moving in and out among the rocks which is heard only by the people living near the shore. But when rain is coming, there is a loud booming noise heard a great distance inland.[190]

# LISHEEN
# Local Songs

# Roger the Miller

Roger the Miller came courting of late
A rich farmer's daughter called beautiful Kate,
She had for her fortune a store of fine things,
She had for her fortune bright parcels and rings,
She had for her fortune broad acres of ground
She had for her fortune five hundred pounds.

When the match it was made there was joy beyond bounds
About Kate and her fortune of five hundred pounds
To her father, said Roger, "although Kate is fair
Indeed, I won't marry her without the great mare."

Then Roger the Miller was put out the door
And told he should never come there anymore.
In despair then he tore at his fine yellow hair
And grieved that he ever spoke of the grey mare.

A couple of months after or something above
He chanced for to meet with Miss Kitty, his love.
Said Roger – all smiling – "now don't you know me?"
"If I'm not mistaken, I've seen you", said she,
"For a man of your likeness with fine yellow hair
One time he came courting my father's grey mare."

"Indeed then", said Roger, 'tis you are to blame,
For sure 'twas a courting of you that I came.
I thought that your father would make no dispute,
To give with his daughter the grey mare to boot.
The price of the grey mare was not all too great,
To give as a present with beautiful Kate".

"Your sorrow", said Kitty, "I value it not,
There are many young men in this place to be got,
If you got the grey mare you would not marry me,
But now you have neither the grey mare nor me
I'm done with you now, for your love came too late,
So fare you well Roger, no more about Kate."[191]

# Batty Hegarty's Bit of Moonshine

Batty Hegarty's Bit of Moonshine was published recently (a second time) in the issue of 'The Southern Star', 24-12-30. It is a newspaper published weekly in Skibbereen. It relates to an incident that occurred about 90 to 100 years ago. The remnants of the old park wall are still to be seen, as well as the ruins of Squire Beechers residence. He was a kinsman of Sir John Beecher, Mallow, Co. Cork. Batty Hegarty's descendants are to be found in the parish of Achadh Dúin.[192]

(Reproduced from the issue of "Cork Co. Eagle and Munster Advertiser of April 30, 1910)

When the springtime tints the hedgerows,
or the autumn leaves are brown,
'Tis a pleasant thing to wander through the fields of Aughadown,
And to gossip with the husbandmen of matters grave and gay,
Reminiscent of the times and folks that long have passed away.
By the roadway, in the meadow, relic of the past is shown,
Hoary pile of crumbling ruins all dismantled, ivy-grown,
Round which circles a quaint stone wall, work of crafty hands,
And the background of a story passing current in the land.

Have you ever heard the tale, then? Well, 'tis true, beyond a doubt,
That this stone wall, on one occasion tricked the bailiffs out-and-out.
'Twas the park wall of Beecher, and a man well known was he,
In the fox-hunt and the steeplechase and old-time chivalry;
And he lorded in his hey-day o'er that smiling countryside,
Riding down hills and pasture to the Roarwingwater tide.

'Mongst his goodly host of tenants Batty Hegarty was one,
Whom it would be hard to rival for pure Irish wit and fun;
But the pity was that hard times came to peep in at his door.
And his cares and disappointment seemed to deepen more and more.
As the rent day drew nigh quickly, in the stealthy flight of time,
And he lacked the landlord's money, then, as now, a heinous crime.
He was upright and hardworking; his intentions were all bent
To be fair and square in dealing; but intentions are not rent.
Let that fail to be forthcoming on the next accounting day
And adieu to merry Batty; he must bundle and away.

Now, was every man's resourcefulness so sorely tried as that?
Straight-way must he shoot the landlord?
Must he rob a bank? – or what?
Yerra no; behold that twinkle brightening up his roguish eye;
And how cleverly he'll manage it you'll learn by and by.
For a ride used go his landlord every morning just at nine
With the circumstance and moment, Batty's plot must fall in line,
Out-of-doors betimes he sallied, and he slyly took his stand,
By the landlord's flanking stone wall, with a crowbar in his hand.
There he waits expectation, whether will he win or fail?
Meeting with opposing forces, Batty ne'er was known to quail.
Hark! At last it is the landlord! Hear his horse's hoofs to ring.
Up jumps Batty, grips his crowbar, wields it with a mighty swing,
Brings it clanging on the stone wall, raising sparks that madly flashed,
Just as round the bend the great man on his prancing hunter dashed.

"Ho! There, rascal! What the deuce, then, are you doing to my wall?"
Feigning wonderment, the schemer quickly let his crowbar fall.
"Top o' the mornin' to yer honour, sir, and faith! Yer looking fine,
"There's no gentleman in Cork, sir, that could cut so grand a shine."
"And," said Batty, "by yer lave, sir, all about it I will tell,
How I went to Skibbereen yesterday a thing or two to sell;"
"For the rent is due today, sir, and I know I'm duty bound,
to square matters with yer honour for that little bit o'ground."
"And last night when steppin' home'ard faith!
A thought came to my mind, that if Peggy touched my guineas
they would scatter with the wind."
"And I stopped here thinkin' of it, and for fear such would befall,
I found out a secret crevice, and I hid 'em in this wall,
And the moon was shining brightly, and the shadow of a tree,
Fell across that bit o' roadway that lies just twixt you and me.
But the moon makes people queer sire, and though I were to be shot,
I couldn't say this minute whether this or that's the spot.
But tonight, sir, when the moon shines, I will come again and see,
And I'll surely come a near it by the shadow of the tree;
And I'll search and dig and delve, sir, and my gold I'll surely find,
If I have to fell the wall, sir – a few perches you wont mind.

"Tut! You ruffian!: cried the landlord, "not for those few coins of gold,
"Not for all the farm produce you have every bought or sold,
Would I let you break my stonewall, that I look upon with pride!
So away with you immediately, and from this place keep wide."
"Uille murdher!" whimpered Batty, "what am I to do at all,
Must I starve and be evicted while my money's in this wall,"
Thus went on the wordy warfare, thrust and parry fairly dealt.
Till the soft tone of relenting in the landlord's voice was felt
And he said in kindly accents, as it thus befell on you,
"I'll remit the whole instalment of the rent that's falling due,
But I stringently enjoin on you a clear command from me,
That you daren't touch my wall again, or punished you will be."

Of course, Batty thanked "his honour,"
and straight homeward then he went,
Chuckling how the ancient stone wall
paid the missing half-year's rent.
That's the story as they tell it; as it is, then let it be-
Always Batty's bit of moonshine in the shadow of the tree.

# Lisheen

# History and Archaeology

# Ancient Monuments

About two miles from this school there are two big stones standing perpendicularly, about sixteen feet in height, known as the galans. There are two cromleacs about half a mile from this school, one in Lisheen and the other in Droumnacharough. These consist of big stones, several tonnes in weight, lying horizontally and resting on three smaller stones. Some people used to say that these were altars on which druids used to offer sacrifices when Ireland was pagan. This is not true. It is believed that these were big monuments under which chieftains were buried long ago. There are many strange stories told about the field in which the cromleac in Droumnacharough is. It is said that anyone who ever entered that field after nightfall became bewildered and continued walking round and round the field unable to find a way out until morning. One night a man was coming home from work and he crossed the field, entered the one in which the cromleac is situated. After a time, he found that he was not able to find his way out but all the same he continued walking round and round the field for a couple of hours scarcely knowing what he was doing. At last, he got tired and sat down and he began to think that there was something wrong with him. He remembered that he had heard told about people who became bewildered and what they did to recover themselves from it. So, he took off his coat and turned it inside out, and when he put it on again, he found that his mind cleared. It is also said that a woman was going home from work one night and she entered the same field. After a time, she found that she was not able to find her way out, but all the same she continued walking for hours until she was tired out. Then she sat down in a dazed condition until morning. She had lost her sense of direction and did not know which way to turn to go home, but at daybreak came to herself and was able to leave the field and go home safely.[193]

# Lissalohorig

Co. Chorcaighe
Bar: Cairbre Thiar
Par: Abbeystrowry
Scoil: Lios an Lothraigh
Oide: Seosamh Mac Domhnaill

# LISSALOHORIG
# Local Folklore and Stories

# Going with the Good People

About fifty years ago there were many people who were supposed by the neighbours to go with the good people. Sometimes they went and returned on the same night. On other occasions they remained away for a number of days or maybe a week. There lived in Corran, Leap, at that time a man who was supposed to have much dealings with the fairies, and it was said that he went with them regularly. He was always given some means of getting home. On one occasion he got a plough on which he rode home and then the plough disappeared.

On one particular night he went to a fairy banquet a great distance from home, and when morning drew near, he was given a calf on which to ride, but he was told not to speak under any circumstances until he had reached his journey's end. The calf travelled at great speed, up-hill and down dale, till the man began to wonder if the animal could possibly keep it up. Just then he saw in the valley before him a great wide river, the Bandon. His heart sank as though he thought that the calf could never jump it. But to his surprise the calf took a great spring into the air and landed on the other side without the least bother. Though he had been warned that if he spoke the calf would throw him off and leave him there, he could not contain himself any longer."Wisha good boy calf", he said, "Dá mbéinn-se gan tuille abhaile go brách [If I get home, never again". Immediately the calf threw him off and left him go the remainder of his journey on foot.[194]

From Donnachadh Mac Domhnaill, aged 67, Skibbereen

# The Old Witch

There was an old witch who could turn herself into any shape she wished. One day she was going through the country in the form of a cat. The hounds spied her and gave chase, but she ran into a cabhlach. When the hounds came up, she had turned herself back into the form of a woman, so they had to go away. Soon after, a man was passing by and saw her. She asked him to take her to the shoemaker to get a pair of shoes. "How do you expect me to carry you to the shoemaker?" he asked. "I'll manage that alright", she said, and explained to him telling him that he was to put her in a bag. He did so and set out on the journey. Soon they happened to come near the hounds again. The hounds smelt the cat and began to bark and howl looking for her everywhere about. She gave him a pick of her claw through the bag. "Mind me" she said.
"There!", he said throwing her to the hounds, "Mind yourself ".[195]

From Donnachadh Mac Domhnaill, aged 67 years, Skibbereen

# The Search for Our Saviour

When the Jews were looking for Our Saviour, they were inquiring one day of a crowd of people whether he had passed by that place. The people would not give them any information, but a dara-daol[xxvii] who was near conveyed to them that he had passed on the previous day. Ever since, the dara-daol is looked upon as a traitor, and it is said to be such a good thing to kill one, and that a person who does will have their sins forgiven. When a person kills one, he must say: "Gach aon cheann 'es mo pheacaibh ort, a dhara- daol dubh". Some people say: " Seacht gcinn 'es mo pheacaíbh ort a dhara-daol dubh".[196]

From Donnachadh Mac Domhnaill, aged 67 years, Skibbereen

---

[xxvii] Dara-daol – devil's horse.

# The Giant and the Fianna

There lived in the East a giant of great strength who was famous in every part of the world. He heard of Fionn and his men and decided to come and try himself against them. Cluas le hÉisteacht[xxviii] heard him coming but for some reason the Fianna[xxix] did not wish to meet him, so they made up their minds to be away when he came. Before they left, they told the woman to bake a cake and to put the griddle into it and to give it to the giant to eat when he arrived. There was a big stone in front of the house. It was so big that the strongest of them could barely lift it. She was told to point it out to the giant and to say that the Fianna used it in exercise, that they used to throw it over the house and then run around and catch it before it landed on the ground at the back.

As the giant came near, the baby was taken out of the cradle and Fionn got in. The rest of the Fianna then went away. When the giant arrived, food was set before him. He ate the whole cake that had been baked for him. "Is that the bread the Fianna eats?" he asked, and he was told that it was. "It's fine bread", he said, as he ground the griddle under his teeth.

When the meal was over, he asked the woman if she could show him any of the exercises performed by the Fianna. She showed him the stone they used in weightlifting and the jumps they did. He tried these and various other exercises, and he did them all without any trouble. Then she showed him the big round stone and told him that they used to throw it over the house and then run around and catch it at the back. He took the stone and threw it with a mighty heave right over the house. He rushed around to the back, but he was just too late. He was not in time to catch it as it fell. He tried it again in the other direction, but he did no better. He kept at it till he was too tired to be able to do it anymore. "The Fianna must be mighty smart active men", he said to himself, "to be able to get around that house so quickly. And no wonder, considering the strong bread they use".

---

[xxviii] Cluas le hÉisteacht – This loosely translates a 'all ears'. Perhaps 'Big ears' is a good approximation.
[xxix] Fianna – a mythical band of Irish warriors

On thinking the matter over he decided that he would be no match for the Fianna and made up his mind to go away. But he thought that before going he should have some satisfaction, and he asked the woman to show him the baby. She took him to where the cradle was. He put his thumb into the child's mouth (as he thought) with the intention of breaking his jaw, but instead of that Fionn bit off his thumb. "It's time for me to be going", said the giant. "When the baby in the cradle is so strong, what chance would I have against the men?"[197]

From Donnachadh Mac Domhnaill, aged 67 years, Skibbereen

## The Fianna and the Enchanted Castle

One day Fionn and the Fianna were out hunting. They startled a great deer and gave chase. They followed him all day, and in the evening, they found themselves, tired and worn out, in the heart of a great wood. They did not know where they were as in the excitement of the chase, they had not paid much heed to the way they came. They were completely lost, but they could do nothing only try to get out of the wood in some way, so they travelled on wearily. Suddenly, they came to an open space, and they saw before them a great castle. They were greatly surprised as they had never seen this castle before, nor known of its existence. They went up to the main door, up the steps, and in, and were still more surprised when they saw no sign of life and heard nothing. Soon they came to a great hall. There they saw a long table running from end to end of the room covered with the very best of food and drink. Cluas le h-Cisteacht was sent back to the door to keep guard, and the others sat down without further delay to a meal of which they were in sore need.

All went well until the time came to be going. Then someone discovered that he was stuck to the seat he was sitting on and could not rise. When he mentioned this, each man tried to rise but they all found that they were in the same fix. Somebody asked Fionn what was to be done, so he chewed his thumb for a while and then told them that there was only one thing that would free them - "bounds-water".

Cluas le h-Cisteacht was called in and Fionn directed him to go for the water, giving him full instructions as to where he should get it. Off he went, and the Fianna had nothing to do but to wait patiently till he returned. They had to wait a good while too, for the journey was a long one. However, he returned at length and applied the water to where the first man was stuck. To their delight he was set free. Then each man around the table was set free in turn till they came to Conán. Conán happened to be the very last man and when they came as far as him, they found that they hadn't a drop of water left. They had used it too lavishly it the start.

They were in a great hurry to get out of the place then as they knew it was enchanted, so it would take too long for anyone to go for more bounds-water. And of course, they could not go away and leave Conán behind. Nobody could think of any plan, so Fionn took hold of Conán by the two shoulders and lifted him by force, but in doing this, he left a great piece of Conán's skin behind stuck to where he was sitting. Poor Conán was in a very bad state as his injury was all red raw. They left the castle and the first thing they saw outside was a sheep. The sheep was caught and killed; the skin was taken off and placed over Conán's injured part. The wound soon healed up. The wool was shorn off but in a short time it grew again very plentifully. From that time forward, Conán was able to supply enough wool to keep stockings to the Fianna.[198]

From Donnachadh Mac Domhnaill, aged 67 years, Skibbereen

# LISSALOHORIG
# People, Places and Property

# Droichead na Gamhna

The Lissalohorig bridge is situated about three miles northeast of Skibbbereen. It is spanning the river Caol na Meala and joins the townlands Cill na Claise and Lios-a' lothraigh. It was built about the year 1820 and was broken down again in 1921 by the Irish Republicans so that the Black and Tans would not take their lorries across. In about 1923, a timber bridge was built, and it was left there until it broke under a load of slate. Then in 1925 the bridge was built again. Its name is Droichead na Gamhna[xxx] and an old story follows how it got its name. There used to be a white calf seen there that was said to have human speech. One night a man was going home from a neighbour's house. He spoke to the calf and immediately he fell asleep, and when he awoke, he was on the calf's back. He was taken to the Kerry hills and when he reached there, he said, "well done white calf." He had to walk home but it is said that if he did not praise the calf he would be brought home again on his back.[199]

Collected by Máire Ní Shúlleabháin, Lissalohorig
From Pádraigin Ó Súlleabháin, aged 60, Lissalohorig

# Wells

There are thirteen wells in Lissalohorig. One is blessed and it is called Tobair na Beithe.[xxxi] It is situated in an old boggy field behind the school. There is a stream flowing down from the rocks which supplies water to it. It is supposed to be the best water in the land, and it never dries, summer or winter. Several people from the land get water there for the tea. It is situated in the east of Lissalohorig. The other twelve ones are small ones. One of these is a wart well in the western end of Lissalohorig in Mr. O'Sullivan's field. It is supposed to be blessed. It would cure a wart by visiting it three times and washing your hand in it.[200]

Collected by Siobhán Nic Charthaigh, Lissalohorig
From Domhnall Mac Charthaigh, aged 56, Lissalohorig

---

[xxx] Droichead na Gamhna means Calf Bridge
[xxxi] Birch well

# LISSALOHORIG
# Local Cures

## Piseóg: How to get rid of warts

Put as many stones as you would have warts into a bag and bury them in your neighbour's potato field, and when he would be digging the potatoes, if he found the stones, he would take the warts.[201]

Collected by Siobhán Nic Charthaigh, Lissalohorig
From Domhnall Mac Charthaigh, aged 56, Lissalohorig

# LOUGHINE

Co. Chorcaighe
Bar: Cairbre Thiar
Par: Creagh (Ráth)
Scoil: Loughine
Oide: Dd. Ó Caoimh

From Baltimore to Lough Hyne, about 3½ miles. Leave the town as though bound for Skibbereen, but turn off to the right alongside the telegraph wire. A small fragment of a ruined tower is seen on the left, and from the top of the road there is a good view looking back, while north of the road is the rugged ridge passed on the outward journey. Suddenly Lough Hyne comes into view with a curious embossed hill on its far side. On the shore near its northern end is a private residence of the Beecher family, prettily set in woodland with lawns sloping to the water. The hill down to the lough is very steep but picturesque [a road diverges on the right through the trees to the western side of the lough; there are the remains of an ancient chapel close to the rapids, on the outlet], and at the foot you see almost the entire lough. Turn inland up a fine little glen, with the bold wooded steep of Knockomagh above on your left. At the top of the small pool, left, and, over a bit of desolate country, you soon join the road to Skibbereen.

# LOUGHINE
# Local Folklore and Stories

## The Hidden Treasure of Castle Island

According to an old saying, there was a man lived in Licknavar, Skibbereen, whose name was Bill Barret. He dreamt one night that there was gold concealed at the corner of the castle in Castle Island. The following night he set to work with tools, hoping to find the treasure. When he had a little dug, a big black cat with two heads appeared to him. He left the tools there and went home immediately. It is said ever since that gold is hidden in Castle Island.[202]

Collected by Máire de Búrca
From Randál de Búrca, Ballyoughtera, Skibbereen

## The Hidden Treasure of Lough Ine

There is an old man in this district who told me that there was a highwayman in this place one time whose name was Donnacada Dub. When he was captured and sentenced to death, he said that his gold was hidden between two lakes under a flag facing north. The old person believes that it is between Loch na Ceardhċain, which is situated in Baileuachrarach, and Loch Meilrhíne which is situated in Corravolley. Between two lakes there are a number of flags facing north. Nobody even attempted to find it as they do not know rightly which flag it is hidden under.[203]

Collected by Pádraig de Búrca,
From Randál de Búrca, Ballyoughtera, Skibbereen

# The Hidden Treasure of Lough Ine

Over a hundred years ago their lived in Lick a man named Bill Barret. His principal occupation was fishing. Lough Ine being the nearest and most convenient place, it was from there he went out. Weather permitting, this was his daily routine. On the way from the Quay in Lough Ine he had to pass an Island in the centre of the lake known as Lobar O'Loinnse castle. Tradition says there lived a man by that name on this Island who had ears like a horse. On this Island he built a castle, the ruins of which are to be seen at the present day. Whether Bill Barret ever heard of any hordes of gold being hidden there I have never heard, but on three separate occasions he dreamt it was hidden there, and also the position in which it was concealed.

He determined to put his dreams to a test. With little fear of been seen, he put out for the Island; he had little or no trouble in discovering the spot of his dreams. He started digging, being cheered by discovering things that were in his dreams, until he came to a large stone under which the supposed hoard of gold was concealed. Then something frightened him, probably some wild fowl or beast, but he himself would insist it was something supernatural. Anyway, he fled from the spot, and from that day hence, he left Lobar O'Loinnse castle and treasure alone.[204]

Collected by Maisie Taylor,
From Patrick Fitzgerald, Spain, Baltimore

# Hidden Treasure Beneath a Crooked Hazel Tree

In the townland of Coolnaclehy there is a grove of hazel trees, and among them there is one crooked tree. It is said that a famous thief, named William Crotty, was sentenced to death. He knew he was going to be hanged, and he told an old man in the district that there was gold under the crooked hazel tree. Nobody ever made any attempt to get it, and so it is there from that day, until now.[205]

Collected by Cáit ní Donnachadha, Lahernathee, Skibbereen
From Seán de Búrca, Ballyoughtera, Skibbereen

Figure 17. Lough Hyne, refs. L_ROY_04918 (top) and L_ROY_02634 (bottom). Photos by Robert French, used with the kind permission of The National Library of Ireland.

# LOUGHINE
# People, Places and Property

# Famous People

The old people of sixty and seventy years ago were great for telling stories. Some of them had a great memory and it would not take them long to tell a good story. The people nowadays are not at all as good as the old people were for telling stories, as well as for many other things, such as, jumping, dancing, running and many other things. About fifty years ago there lived in the townland of Drishanebeg, Skibbereen, Co. Cork, a man named Jeremiah Geaney, who was famous for his storytelling. His most famous stories were fairy-tales. Besides being a famous storyteller, he was great for reading, speaking, and explaining the Irish language, and he had a great desire for Irish dances and songs.[206]

Collected by Cáit ní Donnachadha, Lahernathee
From Donnacha Ó Donabháin, Dromadoon

Jeremiah Geaney lived in Drishane, Skibbereen. He was a great storyteller. Long ago, Barlogue Point was said to be a very wide bay, and on account of the wickedness that went on in the land, he said that the western point moved east, and the eastern point moved west, and that is the reason why Barlogue point is so narrow now. There was also another man named Patrick Burke who lived in Baile na Crapach. He was a weaver, and a great storyteller and singer. A king lived in Ireland long ago, and he had a daughter. Three men wanted to marry her. The king told them that the eldest of them would get her. One said he was very old; when he was young he said he got a shipload of razors and he never lost one or broke one, but he had them all worn except one. That must be very old, said the king. The second man said he got a cargo of needles, never lost one or broke one, but had the last worn to the eye. The third said he got a cargo of combs and never broke or lost one but had the last one worn. The first then said that if a pillow of feathers were put out on a windy hillside he would catch them all. The second said that himself would shoe the fastest steed while running, and the third said he could catch a hare. The third man got the Princess, because he was the laziest and it proved he was the eldest of them, and he married the Princess.[207]

Collected by Mícheál de Búrca, Ballyoughtera
From Seán de Búrca, Ballyoughtera

# Strong Men

There was a priest in this place one time whose name was Fr Denis O'Driscoll. At the same time a man named Colonel Beecher lived at Ballygiblin. There was a party at Ballygiblin. After the party, they went stone-throwing and a certain man, whose name we don't know, threw the stone a long distance. Beecher was asked was there a man in Carbery able to do that, and he said there was and that he would get a man to throw it father. He came to Creagh for Fr Driscoll, but he did not go at the first invitation because they were the penal days. He went at the second invitation. The Colonel pledged his word and honour that nothing would happen him, and he went to Ballygiblin and they tossed for the first throw, the stake being £100. The first throw fell on the man down the country who had to throw the stone against a very high wall. He threw and put it up about three-quarter ways. Then came the priest's turn. He fastened his overcoat and threw the stone clear over the wall. Colonel Beecher said he would give him anything he wanted, so the priest asked for a site to build a church on, and there the Skibbereen ProCathedral is built. There was another man named Bill O'Brien who lived in Droumadoon who was able to lift a five-hundred weight above his knees with a heavy stone on top of it. There was one other man whose name was John O'Regan, and he lived in Licknavar, who was only able to lift it a couple of inches from the ground.[208]

Collected by Pádraig de Búrca, Ballyoughtera
From Seán de Búrca, Ballyoughtera

# Jim Nolan

Nearly a hundred years ago there lived in Ballylinch a man named Jim Nolan. He had no land or means of livelihood. He had a cabin with a thatched roof. Necessity caused him to become a thief. He lived principally on sheep stealing. The matter was reported to the police and they tried by every means to catch him. But being a great runner, they could never catch him; they even went to the extent of bringing a couple of good runners to try to arrest him. One night when he was in his cabin, the police surrounded it. They were sure they had him captured. He had a secret hole in the thatch by which he escaped. The police followed him, but as they were gradually gaining on him, they eventually had to give up. They never succeeded in arresting him. As the storyteller said, the king never reared a soldier that would catch him.[209]

Collected by Maisie Taylor, Spain, Baltimore
From Patrick Fitzgerald, Spain, Baltimore

## A Great Seanachie

We hear of several famous people who are noted for many things such as lifting heavy bags and throwing the sledge and numerous others. There is an old man named Pat Regan and he lives in the townland of Gurteenloman, Skibbereen, Co. Cork. He is noted for his storytelling. He tells many fairy tales and stories of olden times since his youth. He is called 'a great seanachie'. He can read very well and can explain every word he reads. He can speak the Irish language fairly well also. Long ago there were a great many seanachies compared to those nowadays.[210]

Collected by Siobhán ní Donnachadha, Lahernathee
From John O'Donovan, Ballyally

# Old Schools

About seventy years ago, there were three schools in this district. Two were in Church Strand near Baltimore, and one near Lough Ine a little below where the current school is built. One of these were covered with slate, and the other two had thatch roofs. The teacher of one of the Church Strand schools was Mr Tim Shine, formerly of Kerry, he was afterwards assisted by his two sons. It is stated that his family received a salary of sixty pounds a year, one or two pence per week from each pupil according to each standard. The father died and the sons continued teaching until the present National School was build when they went to Canada. The school which was attached to the building was held by three brothers Fitzgerald. It is not known whether they received any pay except from the pupils. Those three died in the district. The subjects taught were in the English language, but Irish was freely spoken both in and outside the schools. In these schools there were stools for sitting on, and a sort of bench for writing.[211]

Collected by Maisie Taylor, Spain, Baltimore
From Patrick Fitzgerald, Spain, Baltimore

# An Old School

About a hundred and fifty years ago there was a school near the village of Baltimore. That school was built at the cross leading into the Tullagh graveyard. It was a thatched school and had one window. The teacher's name was Michael Shine. He was from the village of Baltimore. After being teaching in the school some time. He was succeeded by his brother Cornelius Shine. Those teachers got no pay only school fees. The first class gave a shilling a quarter, and the second class two shillings, and so on, a shilling higher every class. Very few went higher that fourth class in those days. They used write on slates with slate pencils. They taught all subjects except Irish. The people had great regard for those teachers. The teacher used sit on a chair and there were stools and desks for the children.[212]

Collected by Máire de Búrca, Ballyoughtera, Skibbereen
From Randál de Búrca, Ballyoughtera, Skibbereen

## LOUGHINE
# Farming, Trade and Crafts

# Animals on the Farm

The animals that we keep on the farm at home are cows, a horse, calves, pigs, and a sow. We keep six cows, and their names are Strawberry, Rosy, Lady, Madam, Summer, and Daisy. People say while driving cows, "How how", and when they want them to stop, they say, "youish anors". When a cow has calved, she is milked about an hour afterwards, and some people give the first of the milk to the cow to drink and it is called 'Beestings', and it is given to the calf for about a month. If a cow is cross while being milked, her hind legs are tied with a rope, and it's called in Irish, 'buarcu'. If a cow is apt to go over a fence, she is tied by her foremost legs, and it is called a recúal. It used to be the custom long ago after a cow had calved to light a blessed candle and burn the long hairs that are on the cow's udder. People say "suck suck" when calling calves.

The horse is the most useful animal on the farm. It is shod five or six times in the year. Its food consists of oats, chopped furze, hay, mangolds, and a drink of water twice a day. Very few around here keep sheep and goats. The domestic fowl kept on the farmyard are ducks, hens, turkeys, and geese. When people call ducks, they say "Fíonach fíonach', and hens, "tuic, tuic", and geese "beadaide, beadaide".

When eggs are put hatching, they are left about three weeks under the hens before the young chickens come out, and eggs got at a poultry station are marked.[213]

Collected by Máire de Búrca, Ballyoughtera
From Randál de Búrca, Ballyoughtera

# Potatoes

Every farmer around this place sets potatoes and they prepare the land themselves. They manure it beforehand with farmyard manure and artificial manure also, such as ammonia, guano, and superphosphate. It is in the drills the people usually set the potatoes. The drills are made with ploughs. All the people help each other in the cutting of the seeds and in setting them. The potatoes are sprayed in June with blue stone and washing soda against the blight, which would burn them down but for the spraying. Some people gather a crowd of neighbours together to dig the potatoes and they dig them in a day. The people call this a potato 'meithal'. When they have the potatoes dug, they store them in small pits in the field for about a week. Then they draw them home and put them in big pits in the haggard. Here are some names of potatoes; aran banner, aran victors, aran pilots, aran chiefs, champions, British queens, kerrs pink, epicures, and colleens. The champions are the best eating potatoes. The people used make starch from potatoes long ago. They grate the potatoes first and mix a little water. Strain the water off then and the starch remains.[214]

Collected by Siobhán ní Donnachadha, Lahernathee
From Mrs Mary O'Donoghue, Lahernathee

# Clothes

In the parish of Rath about thirty-five or forty years ago there lived an old tailor who was named James Gibson. He used go around from house to house making suits. The people used spin the wool themselves, then they used carry it to some weaver, and the weaver used spin it into cloth called frieze. This man stopped in each house until he used had the suit made. The people used spin wool also and carry it to the weaver to make flannel so that they could use it for underwear. The old people spun black and white wool and mixed it together to knit stockings out of it. They used call these pepper and salt stockings. There are no tailors like these nowadays and there are no spinning-wheels there either like there was long ago.

Collected by Siobhán ní Donnachadha, Lahernathee
From Mr Patrick Collins, Creagh

# LOUGHINE
# Local Customs

# Marriage Customs

The old people say it is unlucky to get married in May, and it is also unlucky to get married on a Monday. Some people get property and others get money. It was an old custom long ago for a big reception, a day and a night, and it was all horses and common cars that were in the wedding. It was an old custom to hang old shoes or horse's shoes to the back of the car in which the newly-married pair were as a sign of good luck.

The old people say it is lucky to get married in white or blue. People get married mostly in Shrove or between Easter and Advent. There is another saying that the man and woman to get married went to the church in different cars, and it was considered lucky that the man should go into the church first, and if the woman arrived at the church first, she should wait until the man would come. When they were coming out of the church after the marriage, their friends would push them out, so that they would come out together, as they thought whichever of them would come out first would die first.[215]

Collected by Cáit ní Donnachadha, Lahernathee
From Seán Ó Donabháin, Ballyally

The customs of marriage long ago were very different than today. The brides used stay up all night before they got married. Everyone around the place was asked to the wedding and each one was to bring a saddled horse. They used to go to the chapel. The man used hide on the last horse and the bride on the first one. They used to be charged from fifteen to twenty shillings by the priest. After the marriage, the man and his wife came home on the first horse. It is a good thing there is such a great change now-a-days because many of them used go racing coming home, and when they reached home, they had their wives lost. There was a man named Dan McCarthy from Ballyally, Skibbereen, who got married long ago. The people used to call him Domnall Bán. The night he got married, the few around he did not ask to the wedding filled cars of stones and stayed throwing them at the door all night and spoiled the wedding. The dress worn in those days was a white cap with borders of lace and a hooded cloak.[216]

Collected by Mícheál de Búrca, Ballyoughtera
From Seán de Búrca, Ballyoughtera

## LOUGHINE
# Local Cures

# Old Cures

In the old road leading from Lough Ine bridge to Creagh Post Office there are old wells called 'The Holy Wells'. People having any disease visit them on May Eve. Picking up seven small stones out of the lower well, they go around them then and say one Our Father, one Hail Mary, and Glory be to the father, and cast in one stone each time until seven rounds are given. They should go three years in succession before they are cured. They then go on their knees and say the rosary and leave some relic on the tree above the well and bring some water home with them and that water will never get bad.

To cure wildfire, write your name before it with ink. For diabetes, drink a glass of lemon juice every morning. For kidney trouble and chest infections use Irish moss. For coughs, internal ulcers, and skin diseases use ground ivy. Dandelion root is a popular remedy for kidney and liver complaints. Oak bark is used as a gargle for a bad throat.[217]

Collected by Máire de Búrca, Ballyoughtera
From Randál de Búrca, Ballyoughtera

A cure for rheumatics is to wash your feet in salt water and in weeds. People used go to a tomb in Ross, scrape the earth off the tomb and rub it to their teeth to cure toothache. To cure headaches, rub vinegar to brown paper and put it up to your forehead. Rub honey to the roof of your mouth with a cloth to cure thrush. A cure for deafness is to go to a holy well in the townland of Highfield and gather little stones, go around the well ten times, and throw one stone into the well each time until the ten times is up, then wash your ears with a rag and hang it on a bush over the well.

The people did practise these cures some years ago and used practise them very often, but they are giving them up now.[218]

Collected by P.J. Wholly, Baileuchrach, Skibbereen
From Mrs Mary Wholly, Baileuchrach, Skibbereen

# More Old Cures

There are great many diseases and numerous cures for them also. Here are some of them. It is a cure for cuts to put cobwebs into them, and a cure for hurts is wild sage; rub the juice out of it, strain it and drink it. A cure for cough is dandelion, boiled and drunk. There is a cure for boils which is to boil besom and rub the water to the boils, and besom is also used for rheumatism. A cure for headache is to rub vinegar to the forehead. There is a cure for sore eyes which is to rub cold tea to the eyes. Blackcurrant is a cure for hoarseness, sore throats, and coughs. There is a plant called Maidenhair Fern which is very good for influenza.[219]

Collected by Siobhán ní Donnachadha, Lahernathee
From Mrs Mary O'Donovan, Lahernathee

# The Natural World and Weather Lore

# Signs of the Weather

A star near the moon is a sign of rain. A red moon is a sign of wind. When seagulls fly inland it is a sign of storms. It is a sign of rain when crickets sing sharply, and it is also a sign of rain when those complaining of rheumatism have the pains very bad. When the wind follows the sun, it is a sign of good weather, and when the wind goes against the sun it is a sign of bad weather. When ducks are quacking loudly it is a sign of rain. When starlings are seen in the fields it is a sign of cold weather. When smoke rises straight into the air, it is a sign of good weather, and when the smoke falls to the ground it is a sign of bad weather. If bubbles appear in the pools while it is raining, it is a sign that the rain will continue. When flies are busy pitching on the cattle it is a sign of rain. It is a sign of rain when pigs are restless. When sounds can be heard far away, or when distant objects seem near, it is a sign of rain.[220]

Collected by Cáit ní Donnachadha, Lahernathee
From Díarmuid Ó Géanaigh, Curravally

# The Signs of Good and Bad Weather

If there is a motion in the sea without any obvious reason, it is a sign of a storm. Before rain or a change of weather, the sea usually changes its colour from blue to a grey. Short stumps of rainbows close to the horizon usually indicate strong wind. Thick black clouds passing quickly indicate stormy weather. If the sun rises with the sky red around it, it is a sign of rain. When the stars are dull and no clouds visible, it is also a sign of rain. If there is a halo around the moon, it indicates rain. When the wind is drawing south against the sun, it also is a sign of rain, and when it draws in it has the opposite effect. The seagulls come on the land and are very busy before a storm. When you hear the curlew, or when you see them in the fields, you can be prepared for bad weather. When the wind is from a westerly direction, you will have showers with bright periods, and when it blows from a northern direction you will have fine weather.[221]

Collected by Maisie Taylor, Spain, Baltimore
From Patrick Fitzgerald, Spain, Baltimore

# LOUGHINE
# History and Archaeology

# Hardships

In the summer of the year 1935 a big fire took place in Skibbereen. It happened that a draper's shop, occupied by Denis Collins and his family of Main Street, Skibbereen, caught fire and nobody knew how it happened. It was the barking of a little dog on the street that aroused the inmates from their sleep, and they immediately set to work to quench the blaze. But, in spite of all they could do to save the house and goods, everything was burned to ashes. The occupants of the house had to try and escape without being burned, and some of them had to get out through the windows. The remains of the property were smouldering for more than a week after the burning. Many of the neighbouring shops were also damaged.

There was a sad drowning accident which occurred in Lough Ine lake in August 1929. It happened that a young Skibbereen man named Harry Mahony had taken some townspeople to Lough Ine in a motor for a drive. He went swimming, and after being a little while in the water he got into difficulties and drowned. As soon as he was noticed, help was called, and a man named Jack Sheehy from Barlogue jumped into the water dressed as he was, and immediately brought out the drowned man, but when he was taken out of the water, he was dead.[222]

Collected by Cáit ní Donnachadha, Lahernathee
From Díarmuid Ó Géanaigh, Curravally

# God Bless All Here

In a little thatched cabin near the town of Baltimore there lived a man named John O'Driscoll and his wife Nora O'Driscoll. It happened at that time that Nora O'Driscoll, whilst in delicate health, gave birth to a child. After her child being born, she happened to get worse. Her husband got very much alarmed and thought she should have the doctor. The doctor arrived, examined Mrs O'Driscoll and ordered to send for the priest immediately. So, he sent a messenger to the priest house in Rath, but the priest was suffering from rheumatics at the time and unable to attend the patient but said he would go in the morning if possible. In the meantime, there was a raging storm. John O'Driscoll thought it too long to wait for the priest until morning. Mrs O'Driscoll was asked did she know any person that would go, and she said she had a nephew that would do anything she asked him. He was sent for and asked would he venture to Sherkin for the priest - he said he would. So, he went out in a small boat, and so terribly frightened of being lost on the way that he said he would not venture back again. He told the priest of the case and asked him did he know any person on the island that would row him into the pier. He got some fellows and when they came near the shore, they were afraid to venture. So, the priest went himself in the middle of the storm and before he was gone far from the shore he was drowned.

Mrs O'Driscoll who was still suffering in Baltimore thought it too long until the priest arrived. Mrs O'Brien the housekeeper was getting worried when the priest was not coming, and she was praying in the kitchen when the priest arrived. He opened the door and said, "God bless all here" and put his overcoat across the back of a chair, went to the woman's bedroom and anointed her. When he was finished, he went out into the storm again. Then Mrs O'Driscoll turned her face to the wall and died. Next morning the priest in Rath came to anoint Mrs O'Driscoll, and they told him she was anointed last night by the priest from Sherkin at half past eleven. "I am sorry to say," said he "that he was drowned at that time coming into the pier". The time is not known when that happened, but it is a long time ago.[223]

Collected by Máire de Búrca, Ballyoughtera
From Randál de Búrca, Ballyoughtera

# A Tragic Drowning

Last summer, a cargo of coal arrived to Mr Edward Shipsey, Old Court, and a young boy named Welsh came with the rest of the men on the ship. It was his first voyage. After two days, the cargo was emptied, and they all came up to the public house for a little while. The only gangboard they had was a ladder, and that was hitched to the boat with a rope at one end, and at the other to the pier. Three of the men left early in the night. This boy remained a little while with his friend. He left the public house intending to return again, but going to the ladder, he missed his foot and it swung sideways, and he fell into the water and was drowned. The Skibbereen guards were sent for. They were on the scene immediately and the body was found about half an hour after. He was taken home the next day.[224]

Collected by P. J. Wholly, Baileuchrach
From Michael Wholly, Baileuchrach

# Ringarogy

Co. Chorcaighe
Bar: Cairbre Thiar
Par: Creagh (an Ráth)
Scoil: Rinn Garóige, An Sciobairín
Oide: Máire Bean Uí Chonaill

RINGAROGY and INNISHBEG islands – the former about three miles long and one mile broad, the latter about a mile in diameter – are in the harbour, and connected with the mainland by a bridge and causeway. Like the adjacent lands, their surface is broken and rocky; and apart from the view which they afford of this singular bay, there is little to attract the notice of the traveller.

James Fraser, *Handbook for Travellers in* Ireland (Dublin: McGlashan, 1854), p.365.

# RINGAROGY
# Local Folklore and Stories

## The Priest and the Flying Horse

One day during the penal times, soldiers were hunting a priest in Berehaven. They had hunted him a long way, and they were sure of capturing him when they reached the bog, thinking he could not cross it. But they were mistaken. The priest was riding a horse and when he reached the bay, the horse rose up in the air and did not come down again till he reached the other side. The horse landed on the rock and was killed. The marks of his hoofs and knees are still to be seen. The priest fell out over the horse's head and the prints of his hands are on the ground yet. He was then on the Bantry side and the soldiers on the Berehaven side as he escaped from them.[225]

## The Sailors and the Holy Woman

About five miles from Skibbereen is a lake called Lough Ine. An old story is told about a holy woman who lived there. It is said that she used be always praying alone. Boats used pass and the sailors used to shout at the holy woman and disturb her. One day as they passed, they shouted as usual. A big disaster happened. A great storm arose, and they were all drowned. Then a big cliff fell in and the opening in the channel going into Lough Ine was closed.[226]

## The Rich Woman of Ringarogy Island

Long ago, an old woman who was very rich lived in a little hut in Reengaroga near the spot where my house is now situated. She lived alone and before she died, she buried the purse of gold which she always kept, and it is said that the sun will shine with some beautiful colours one day on the spot where she buried it.[227]

## The Hidden Treasure of Sherkin Abbey

There are not many known hidden treasures around this place, but long ago, a chalice was supposed to be hidden in Sherkin Abbey. One morning, a lot of men went to work digging in search of it, and they found it, bright and shining at the foot of a cliff.[228]

Collected by Domhnall Ó Leanáin, Donegall West

## Anson's Horse

West of Reengaroga there is a small island called Green's Island which is not inhabited now. Long ago, an old gentleman by the name of Anson lived there. He was a landlord on a small scale. In those days there were no roads in Reengaroga, only just a bridle path. When Anson used be travelling, he would go on horseback but never mounted his horse till he came to a large stone which is about 100 yards west of the school. Up to the present day this stone is called Cloc Anson. There is a story told that for a long time after his death, he used be seen riding his horse along this road which passes by the school. One man watched one night and struck him with a stick, and to his horror, the stick was burned up in his hand.[229]

## Burnt Houses

In the Western side of Reengaroga there is a place called Inane, and the old people say that there was a group of houses there long ago. They were burned by an accident and are since called the 'burned houses'. When this happened, the people of the island gathered together and built small houses west beyond the wood for those who were left homeless. To the west of the burned houses lived a man who was driven out by O'Driscoll. Another house was built for him by the people. It was built near the wood at the bog. There were five houses there owned by Simon Daly, Denis Driscoll, Patrick Cadogan, James Cadogan, and Jer. Connor. Each one of them had a piece of garden. When they died, the houses went into ruins and later the stones were used to build the school in 1913. Another version of the story of the burned houses is given by Diarmuid Mac Cariag who got it from his father. In Inane, Reenagaroga, there is a place called 'The burned houses.' Long ago, in the bad times, a lot of poor people lived there. The houses were thatched, and all were in one street together. One night, one of them took fire and they were all burned. Near this place was a protestant school and also a shop. There are only two protestants in the island now.[230]

# RINGAROGY
# People, Places and Property

# Sir Henry Beecher

Long ago, there was a landlord in Creagh called Sir Henry Beecher, and he was very hard on the poorer people. If all his tenants had not their rent paid before Christmas, they would be evicted. There were thirteen families in Gort le Sgar [sic], Rinn Garóige. They all had their rent paid and their crops set, and still they were evicted. The landlord wanted to give all the land to a family called O'Driscoll, from Turkhead. This family had it for some time. Later they put it up for auction. No one would buy it after so many being evicted, so, in the end, it was bought by Minihane from Creagh who was married to O'Driscoll's aunt. The farm is still owned by Minihanes who keep cattle there sometimes, but several stories tell of the house being haunted.

O'Driscolls in Gort na Sgar had a family by the name of Simoy lodging with them. They were 'seekers'. There was the father and mother and a daughter who was married to a man by the name of Gray. She had a son whom they used weigh in a bucket every day. They used light fires in the middle of a field and kneel down around them. Sometimes they used to give parties and invite the people of the island. To each one they would give a small drop of tea in a cup, and a quarter of an apple.[231]

# Old Houses in Jack Salter's Field

In Jack Salter's field in Ringarogy, down by the strand, there are the remains of four old houses, about two hundred years old. A man named Owen lived there and the strand is called Trág Eoghain. Long ago there was a group of homes on this island. It is now desolate.[232]

Collected by Padraig Ó Coileáin, aged 11, from Micheál Ó Coileáin

# A Well

In the island of Ringarogy there is a field called Tobar loc Cáin. The origin of the name is uncertain, but some people say, and it seems likely enough, that it was named after a man called Cahalane. This man made a well which is still used. It never goes dry, and he considered it so good that he named it after himself.[233]

# Soldier's Hill

In the Penal Days when the priests were hunted, one of them was saying mass on Cnoc Camfar at Lough Ine, about five miles from Skibbereen. When the priest saw the soldiers coming, he ran away and one of them followed him. Both horse and soldier fell down over a big cliff and were killed. It is known as Soldier's Hill.[234]

Collected by Domhnall Ó Leanáin, Donegall West,

# Farming Oysters

In the North side of Ringarogy is a strand where they used keep oysters for the landlord long ago. There is a narrow opening between this and another island called Inis Beag. There is a small house at each side of the scornach and a woman in each house paid by the landlord to look after the oysters. Peig Ní Mhuirchú was on the Reengaroga side and Máire Ní Laoghaire in the Inis Beag side. Every day at low tide they used gather the oysters & send them to the landlord.[235]

Collected by Padraig Ó Coileáin, aged 11, from Mícheál Ó Coileáin

## RINGAROGY
# Farming, Trade and Crafts

# The Local Forge

Near my house an old smith lived long ago. It is uncertain about the time but there is a little field called Comar na Gabhainn.[xxxii] It is said by some that he lived there about one hundred years ago, and that his was the only forge in the parish at the time. The remains of the walls were to be seen about fifty years ago.[236]

# Processing Wool

Long ago, the people of this island used weave the thread and make their own clothes. At first the sheep were washed to clean the wool. Then they would shear them and take the wool to the mill. The miller would pile it and it would be separated out. Then it was made into long rolls and brought home. After that, it was carded and spun, and big balls were made of it. They put it on some wall into which sticks were driven and it was made up like chains. It was then taken to the weaver and then to the tucker. It was brought home then and dried well, and the tailor would come to the house to make clothes.[237]

# Grinding Wheat

My house is situated in the middle of Reengaroga. We have two stones at home, one big and one small, in which wheat used be ground long ago. We often use it still. We put the big stone on the table and the small one on the top of it with a handle on it. The wheat is put into a hole in the small stone, and then we work it around with the handle.[238]

# Baking Cakes

About forty years ago there was a special kind of griddle used for baking cakes. It was a great flat piece of iron with two holes in the sides of it to put the hangers into. There was one in Reengaroga until lately.[239]

---

[xxxii] This probably means valley or ravine of the blacksmith.

# RINGAROGY
# Local Cures

# Local Cures

A Plant called saiste cnuic was used here in bygone times to cure a pain in the back. They used boil it and drink the juice. Another plant called macr dá h-abha was a cure for boils. They used to boil it and put the juice on boils.

Anyone by the name of Walsh was supposed to have a cure in his blood, and any person born on Good Friday and baptised on Easter Sunday had a certain cure.[240]

Collected by Máire Ní Choileáin, aged 13, Ringarogy Island

# Wild Sage

A bout fifty years ago, the people here used pick a plant called wild sage. They used put it into water, and if any person having a pain in his side drank it, he would be cured.

# RINGAROGY
# History and Archaeology

## Suppression of the Irish Language

When the English were doing their best to destroy the Irish language and to teach the English language to the people, a man was sent to Cape Clear Island to teach English. He was not succeeding very well and used beat the children. The people of the island resented his attitude. They are noted for being a big race, and one day, some of the biggest men among them took this English teacher out in a boat and threatened to drown him if he would not leave the island. He left immediately, and the effort to anglicise the island failed.[241]

## The Death House

About two miles from Reengaroga is a place called Creagh where a landlord by the name of Beecher lived long ago. His house is situated down by the bank of the River Ilen. About one hundred yards from it is a little house, dark and dreary inside. In the penal days Catholics used to be shut into this little house and left there to starve. Some were suffocated to death there. The house is still to be seen.[242]

## The Old Spinning Wheel

In my house there is an old spinning wheel which was in use about forty years ago. My father and mother remember quite well seeing the flax growing here in Reengaroga.[243]

## Barratts' Castle

In the north-east side of Reengaroga Island, Baltimore, was an old castle which belonged to the Barratts. Fearing they would build another similar castle, the masons who built it were put to death and buried in a little island which is since called Oileán na Saore. Many valuable ornaments were supposed to be hidden in the castle. The English tried hard to capture it, and the guns used during the fighting were buried in the mud and never found. Some cannon balls were found and are still to be seen, and about sixteen years ago, a big round stone with a man's head carved on it was got in the ruins. All the stones were used later in building a dwelling house.[244]

# Unrest in Rathmore

Long, long ago, there was a fight in Rathmore, Baltimore, Co. Cork, and the cause of it was a Baltimore minister. It was then the fashion that the minister should get every tenth sheaf out of the stack of corn every year when the people were threshing it. He and his men used to come around to every house that the threshing machine would be at, and he would take every tenth sheaf. After a while, the people did not want to give away the corn, so they made up a plan to keep it from the minister.

It was about September and the threshing machine was coming. When the minister heard of this, he went around for the corn, but instead, all the people gathered around and began to fight against him. The minister got an army of Englishmen and began fighting. The people of the parish won, and one man was shot. That time was called 't-am an beicrú'.[245]

# SHERKIN

Co. Chorcaighe
Bar: Cairbre Thiar
Par: Tulach (Ráth)
Scoil: Inis Arcáin
Oide: Risteárd MacCarrthaigh

The island of Sherkin forms the western boundary of Baltimore harbour, protecting it most effectively, by its interposition, from the fury of the southwestern gales and the wild waves of the Atlantic. It is separated at the north end, by a very narrow channel, from the mainland, which, as the extreme end of Aghadown parish, projects in the form of a promontory (Turk Head) between Baltimore on the east side and Roaring Water (Lough Trasnagh) on the west. The correct name of the island is Inis Arcain.

Daniel Donovan, *Sketches in Carbery* (Dublin: McGlashan, 1876), p.33

# SHERKIN
# Local Folklore and Stories

# Hidden Gold

It is said that gold was buried near Sliabh Mór in a place called Poll a 'Choiligh. There was a woman there. No one knows exactly where she lived, but the old people say that the Vikings watched over her to take the gold. Poll a 'Choiligh was the place where she put the gold, and she left a man in charge. Sometime, long ago, that man was seated near the hole. Anyone who went there to take the gold had to light two candles. If he didn't have candles, the trip wouldn't be successful. It is said that most of the gold is still in that place, and no one can take it.[246]

# Hidden Treasure

It is said that a jar of gold is hidden somewhere in Sliabh Mór. It was put there for fear of being stolen by robbers. It is told that there were two men taking care of the gold. Attempts were often made to steal the treasure, but every time anyone went near where it was, the two men ran after them.[247]

# The Ghost of Urchar

Once upon a time there was a ghost living in Urchar, that's a place near the school on this island. One night, a tailor was walking along the road, and he saw a ghostly woman. She ran after him. The tailor had scissors and took them out of his pocket. It is said that no sprite has the power to take anyone who has any steel tools in his hand. He came to the old monastery and jumped into the graveyard. The woman could not follow and had to return to the hole in which she was living. The poor tailor spent the night in the graveyard. A few days later a priest was walking over the place, and he saw the woman and drove her away to a beach outside of Ireland where he punished her by making her count the grains of sand there.[248]

# The Beach Hound

It is said that there was a dog long ago named the beach hound. My grandmother's house is very close to the beach named after the above. It is said that the dog came every night and put his paws up at the window. One night, a man was planning to go home after fishing. He saw the dog and hit it with the fish he was holding, and it is said that the dog grew as big as a horse.[249]

# The Tricked Man

A man was going to a fair once. He had no alarm clock and went to bed early because he had to get up early in the morning. While he was asleep, two boys came and put bags outside the window. The man woke up in the morning, sat up in his bed and looked at the window. He thought it was still dark so lay down in his bed again and went back to sleep. When he awoke again, the darkness was still there, and he became very suspicious. He climbed out of bed and when he opened the door, he saw that the sun was shining beautifully. It was too late to go to the fair and he had to stay home for another month.[250]

# The Lepracáin's Shoes

Long ago, a man on this island was walking through a field. He found a small shoe which he said belonged to a lepracáin. He carried it home, and that night one of his own shoes was carried away. He did not know what to do, and the next night the other shoe was taken. Next day he took the lepracáin's shoe out to clean, but he forgot it outside that night. The next morning when he went for it, it was gone. He noticed that there was nothing taken out of the house any night afterwards, and the man's own shoes were brought back that night.[251]

# The Mermaid

Long ago in the northern side of Sherkin on a stormy night, a man by the name of Gláinín went out looking for wrecks.[xxxiii] Going around the points he saw on the rocks a woman combing her hair. He went towards her and put his hand on her shoulder. She threw back her hair and looking up at him said, "As you put your hand on me now, you'll have to marry me". He said he was satisfied, but before they were married, he had to make three promises; never to kill a black sheep; never to invite a landlord to dinner; and never to kill a seal. He promised to keep all three. They lived very happily together and had three children. One morning, he said he would go wrecking (a local name for collecting the timber that is washed ashore after a storm). He met a seal which was resting on the sand and did not notice the tide going from it. The seal was quite alive when he met him. The man slipped around to a boat in the vicinity and, having procured an oar, he returned and killed the seal and brought it home on his back. When he arrived, his wife was as usual sitting on a stool combing her hair. He went in and threw the seal on the floor. On noticing the dead carcass, the wife hurried in its direction, and kneeling down took hold of one of the seal's paws, muttering at the same time, "Lapa, lapa a driothóir a croidhe thíos a Muire na cróí." The wife then asked her husband three times for a kiss, but he refused. "'Tis well for you", she said, licking around her mouth as far as her tongue would go, "For I would bite that much out of you before I'd go". She kissed her five children in succession and went back to the place where her husband first met her. Then taking a little bundle from her pocket, shook it, and immediately a black horse came to the rock. She jumped on his back and was never seen again.[252]

---

[xxxiii] This is a version, of which there are many told in the area, of The Glavin Mermaid, a story about a man who married one. In a number of the stories, the seal is said to be her brother,

## The Serpent of Sherkin

Some few hundred years ago, there lived in Sherkin a serpent who tormented the people. One morning a priest went shooting (as it was usual for him to do). The serpent at once tried to torment him. The priest loaded his gun and turning to where it lay wriggling on the bank, shot it. The hollow stone form of this serpent is still to be seen. A giant who lived on Mount Gabriel used to throw stones at the serpent. One of these stones bears the print of his fingers, this stone is near the bog which is called Fordrea.

## How Foxes Arrived on Sherkin

One day, two men from Inis Arcáin went to Drinagh Island to cut gorse. When they had cut it, they went back on the boat again. There was a dead fox on the port, and they put him into the boat. When they landed in Inis Arcáin, they threw the fox out onto the beach. No sooner had the fox hit the ground, didn't it run off like the wind. The men thought he was dead, but he was too clever for them. It was the first fox to come to Inis Arcáin, and there are still foxes today.[253]

# SHERKIN
# People, Places and Property

# Travellers

A long time ago, a poor man named John Relehan used to collect alms on Sherkin. Some of the people gave him potatoes and some of the people gave money. He put the potatoes in a bag on his back and sold them elsewhere. Sometimes he had two bags. Once upon a time, he took one bag from them and walked with it for a while. Then he would go back and walk with the second one until he had the two bags together again. He died a few years ago.

A man named John Hegarty was coming here. He always came to my father's house and used to tell stories all night. He used to sell buckets, baskets and other things.

Mickeen Crowley was nicknamed 'Beads and Scapulars', as he used to sell the two. He would drink a cup of tea in every house he went to. He gave the money he collected to the nuns. One night he came home from Skibbereen. He had no light and was looking around to see if he could find a candle, and what fell from the sky to him was just a candle.[254]

# The Graveyard

The graveyard is located on the east side of the island. There was a monastery long ago, but in Henry's time it was burnt down and then they made a graveyard out of it. The dead are buried in the south side of the graveyard and a few monks are said to have been buried on the north side.

The Monastery was built by Fineen O'Driscoll in 1460. It was built in the form of a cross. On the western window, a head is carved on stone with spots of blood on it, and on the top of the window the head of a sheep. There was another head there long ago but that is not there now. Glen-Roy Abbey is its right name. It is said that it was not the Waterford men who destroyed it but the English soldiers under the leadership of Carew. There is a tower in the centre of it with a winding staircase leading up to the top. There is a wishing-chair on top of the tower, and whoever wishes to have their wish granted must not tell anyone what it was.[255]

# My Own Area

The place where I live is called The Garrison. It's called The Garrison because there is still an old castle that belongs to Finghin the Rover. It is on the west side of the island opposite Baltimore. Nolan is the most common surname. There are only two old people who speak Irish. They can tell stories in Irish and English. Many people went to America from there. The ground is very rough. There are no rivers or lakes in the area.[256] Cill Móna is the name of my district. It got its name from St Móna who is buried there. There used to be seven thatched houses but now there are no people living in them. There are now twelve houses in the district. These houses, three of which are unoccupied, have slate roofs. There are no old people living in the area but one old woman. She cannot tell stories in Irish or English. There are only two old fortifications, and one of them is perched on a hilltop. Many people from my area went to America long ago in search of work.[257]

Collected by Máire Ní Nualláin, Cill Móna, Baltimore

# Place Names

There is a rock on the south side of this island called Poll a Chuppair [Copper Hole]. A boat once went up on it full of copper, which is why it was given that name. There is a place next to that called Losacáin. It was given that name because there were a lot of fish breaking there. It also has a cavity called Cuas Cam. It is a small cove and is very crooked. There is a low hill going down to the cove.[258]

## Old Schools, Old Trades and Marriages

The old school was next to the present one in Dún na Séad. In the past, people on this island used to make baskets with sticks growing around the place. Ships are said to have been made here and sailed to America. One of those boats was called The Margaret Hughs. She was made in the place called the Dock. Long ago, there was a tailor who would go around to the houses and work there.

Many people used to be married on this island, but now they go out to Charleville (the parish church). In the time of the penal laws, mass was held on a hillside there. There is a big rock on this island called Carraig an Afrinn. It sits in a place called An Chéim (the stage).[259]

# SHERKIN
# Farming, Trade and Crafts

## Potatoes

Potatoes are planted on the farms here every year. The ground is first dug and then manure is spread on it. Sometimes, seaweed is dug into the ground. The potatoes are planted in ridges. Holes are made in the ridges to accommodate the seed potatoes. The holes are closed again with the pucadóir (puck a taon). All the neighbors help each other plant the potatoes. Long ago, during the Great Famine, the people there plucked the eyes of the potatoes for seed and ate the rest of the potato. The potatoes are harvested in September and a hole is made in the ground. The potatoes are then placed there and covered again with straw and then clay. They are left there for a few months until a house is ready for them. They are turned a few times and the shoots are removed. A potato with no eyes at the top is called a male potato. No stem grows through this hole. A potato on which other small potatoes grow is called a bastard potato. A man from America came once and took some potatoes with him. He planted them and they brought a beautiful crop of potatoes. These are used on the island and are called Yankies.[260]

## The harvest long ago

Long ago, when a farmer was going threshing his corn, a meitheal of men came helping him. Big stones were brought into the house and every man took a sheaf of wheat and beat the ears on a stone to knock the wheat out of them. When one sheaf was finished, another was taken, and the same thing done with it. This was carried on until it was all finished. Then the corn was gathered and put into bags. When night came, they had a dance in the farmer's house.[261]

# Old Trades

Basket-making was the main occupation of the people of this island in the past. They grew a lot of sticks and cut them with a sickle. Then, while they were stiff, they made the baskets with them. They would put the long sticks down in the ground and then turn the other sticks around them until the basket was high enough. The baskets were well-made and very expensive, and the people got a lot of money that way. They were used to haul manure to the fields, and to keep potatoes and greens fresh. The people do not make any baskets now because the people here now do not know how.[262]

In Sherkin about forty years ago, the farmers kept sheep. The sheep were sheared twice a year and the wool was spun. It was then made into thread called yarn, and some of it was converted into frieze and flannel. Any of the wool, frieze or flannel that was not used was sold. This trade was carried on until the creameries were built. The people then did away with the sheep as they wanted the grass for cattle. Then again there was net-making. The nets made were trammel or puzzle-nets. It was a fine net suited to catch big or small fish as there were big and small meshes in it.[263]

In about 1867, a blacksmith lived in Kilmona. He made oars, ploughs, and all sorts of things that a farmer would use. His name was Donal Ó Drisceoil. The place where he used to work was surrounded by a large garden, now known as the Blacksmith's Garden.[264]

Figure 18. Industrial School, Baltimore (top). The Illustrated London News, 27 August 1887, p.247. Netmaking, Baltimore School (bottom), ref. L_ROY_02595, photo by Robert French, used with the kind permission of The National Library of Ireland.

# Farm Animals

The cows here are named Beauty, Sukie, Rosie, Daisy, Darkie, Polly, Starri, Cannie, Molly, and Nancy. The people who drive them say 'habha, habha'. The cows sleep in a building called the cowhouse. These are covered with sand and gorse. When the cows are put in for the night they are tied with a rope. Cows are tied in fetters while they are milking for fear of spilling milk. The hind legs are tied to attach them. Horseshoes are hung inside the cowshed to make the cows thrive.

When a cow calves, the hair of her udder is burned with a blessed candle, and the sign of the cross is made over her back three times so as to bring luck to the cow. If a person made a present of any kind of milk to another, the person who receives it puts salt in the bottom of the gallon before returning it. It is said that if this were not done the luck would pass from one to the other.

## Horses

If a horseshoe is found, it should never be left but carried home as it is a sign of luck. A horse will never drink water without first straining it through his teeth.

One Sunday, while the people were at Mass years ago, a horse that was grazing on Sliabh Mór took a turn and ran three times north and south through the hill. It was said that the fairies were hunting him. On going south the last time, he fell into a hole between two rocks. The owner was three days looking for him before he found him. The wonder was the hole was only big enough for a man to go down, so that it looked impossible for to get him up. The horse was fed for a week in the hole. One Sunday, after Mass when a crowd was gathered, they set out to liberate the animal. Sticks were placed across the mouth of the cave and ropes were tied around the horse. When they had him nearly to the top, one of the sticks cracked and the horse fell to the bottom again. After many attempts to set free the animal had failed, there was nothing left but to destroy it, so the horse was shot. The hole has since been covered over.

## Chickens

It is said that if a hen is put sitting on eggs at the time of low water, the chickens will be pullets. A light in the hen house at night is supposed to be good for making hens lay. It is said that the shape of a boat was first fashioned from a hen's back-bone. If a person wants a dozen eggs to hatch, thirteen are given, the odd one being for luck. If hatching eggs are sprinkled with hot water every day, all the birds will live.[265]

To call hens, people say 'tuic tuic.' To call geese they say, 'badaí badaí,' or 'cróiste cróiste,' and for turkeys, 'peep, peep.' To call ducks, people say 'feenie feenie,' and for chickens, 'cluch cluch' or 'cluchie cluchie.'

## Cockerels

Long ago, the cock was kept over the back door for luck. One night long ago a man was coming home late. When he reached his home, the cock began to crow and fly wildly about the man. The bird continued thus for about an hour, and at the end of that time suddenly dropped dead. It was thought that the devil was hunting the man and that the cock saved him.

## Sheep

At one time sheep were plentiful on the island, but the predatory habits of foxes and dogs caused the people to give up keeping them. The rule here was to wash the sheep every week so that the maggots would not live on the wool.

# SHERKIN
# Leisure

# Games

Counting: All the children catch hands and form a circle. Then one of them goes into the centre. That person will count to eight and the person he stops at is hunted around the circle by the person who was counting.

London Bridge: A line of children stand together. Then two of them stand out in front. The two in front choose two things. Then they say, "London Bridge is broken down", and they form an arch with their hands, and all the others pass under it. The last person is asked which would he prefer, and he will go behind the person who has the thing he prefers. When all the players have been asked their choice, both sides pull a tug-of-war.

Sally Walker: The children stand in a ring, and one child will sit in the centre. The others will say:

> Sally, Sally Walker, sprinkle on the pan,
> Rise, Sally rise, choose [a] young man,
> Choose to the east and choose to the west,
> And choose to the very one you love best.

Then she chooses someone outside. The last person chosen is to go in next.

Statues: A line of children stand away from a wall while one stands near the wall with his back to the others. The one near the wall counts aloud up to ten while the others attempt to reach the wall during the interval of counting. Should anyone be caught moving after ten has been counted, that person must return to the starting point again. The counting continues until someone reaches the wall. That person then counts while all return to the starting point again.[266]

# SHERKIN
# Local Customs

# Old Customs

Whenever it happens that anyone from the island is to be buried on the mainland, certain customs are observed. The largest boat always carries the coffin and priest. All the other boats follow in single formation, each being towed by its succeeding neighbour. Flags are sometimes flown at half-mast, and thus the procession proceeds to the mainland. When a funeral comes from the mainland to the island, the boat carrying the coffin comes to a place called the Carraig Liath, but not to Tráigh na mBráthar, the usual landing stage on all other occasions. The corpse rests east to west, facing east. Graves are not reddened [dug] on Mondays or Fridays and should not be allowed open during the night. Earth is never shovelled in any other direction but south. Two men of the one name do not dig a grave, but four of the one name carry the coffin into the church and into the graveyard. A mother who loses her first born never enters a graveyard. It is not right to bring any tobacco or cigarettes with one from a wake-house.

On St Brigit's day people fast. They don't work but have a holiday. A horse or man that does not observe this custom is not supposed to be fit for ploughing in the twelve months that follows. There is one instance, in 1891, of this custom being broken. The horse fell over a cliff and the man was drowned.

Castration is never done on Good Friday. No milk is lent on May morning for fear it would take away the luck of the cows for the year. One should never strike the ploughshare with a white stone. White stones are not used for ballast or for building.

A boat going fishing is not allowed to carry clergymen or quadrupeds on board. At the start of the season, boats strive to be in the first two leaving the harbour because the third boat out will be unlucky. Often, when the first and second boats leave the harbour, the others beat about for hours avoiding the third place. In the Isle of Man, to overcome this piseóg, three boats are placed abreast, and another boat tows the three out. Whistling is not permitted on board. It denotes a storm. Singing is allowed. It is not lucky to give a match or exchange any kind of fire with members of another boat. It is supposed to be parting with luck. Members of the same boat may exchange fire. Nets are never hauled in or out over the port side.[267]

# St Móna

There is an old church on the shoreline which is said to have been the church of St Móna. The four walls of the church are still visible and the steps leading up to the altar are also visible. Some people say that St Móna is buried in south Cill Móna in a place called Tobar na Scoile which is situated on the side of Coinne Beag. No one knows what her feast day is. There is no name of Móna on the island now. There was one there a years ago, but it is no longer there.

St Móna is the patron saint of Sherkin. She was born in North Cill Móna which was named after her. South Cill Móna is also named after her. There was a church in North Cill Móna which she established. A well is also named after her, though it is a long way away from her townland. There is an old burial ground in North Cill Móna.[268]

# Special Days

On St Brigit's day, no one should plow. There was a man plowing there a long time ago and a crustacean was thrown at him. Some other man planted an acre of wheat but harvested only half a bag. On May Day, the people bring green plants into their homes to bring in summer. The people there go to Tobar an Ghabha (the blessed well) which is on the island. On Halloween, the custom is for the young people to have a nut and an apple. They put an apple in a tub of water, and everyone tries to catch them with their mouths. On New Year's Eve the young men go around to the houses, especially the farmers' houses, and steal straw. When they have a large bundle of straw, they light it to burn out the old year and burn in the new. On St John's Night, many bonfires are lit. In a potato field, fires are lit on the side of the field from which the wind blows so that the wind will blow the smoke over the potato ridges. It is said that the smoke blesses the crops. On Ash Wednesday, if a baby wants some milk he must cry nine times before he gets it.[269]

# Butter

The butter churn was used here forty years ago. All of them were made of wood. The people themselves made them. It had a wooden cover on top and a big hole in the cover, and inside a large piece of wood called a beater. Nine or ten gallons of cream was added at a time. It was very troublesome to operate. When the people were making the butter, they had to turn the handle or work with their hands. If someone came in while they were making the butter, they had to help as it was believed if they didn't, the butter would be stolen.

When butter making, a certain colouring substance was used to take away the pale colour and give it a yellow appearance. During the summer months it was necessary to wait up until the early hours of the morning to make the butter. The wells used go dry and the days were too warm to keep the butter solid. At about three o'clock in the morning the wells used begin to fill again and this promised the only chance for washing the butter. To keep it from melting during the day it was rolled in cabbage leaves.[270]

# The clothes of the people in the olden times

Long ago, the people of this island used to keep sheep on their farms for wool to make clothes. First, they used cut the wool off with shears. Next, they used wash it and leave it dry. After that they wove it into frieze for making clothes and stockings. The women in those times used to do all their own spinning and weaving themselves. The people nowadays measure the cloth by the yard but in the time of the frieze people used measure it by the bundle.

Some of the people used to go out fishing for seals. The use of their skins was for making caps and they used the inside of the seals for making oil. This oil was used for burns and any kind of sores. There was a tailor on the island at one time. He used go around to the houses to work. This tailor lived in North Kilmona with his brother and sister.[271]

# SHERKIN
# Local Cures

# Cures

For measles, cuckle-buckles boiled in milk and the milk given to the patient. For warts, the froth which forms on the water when boiling potatoes. Also, the milky sap which comes from the stem of the spurge when broken. For heartburn, cold milk sipped slowly. For drawing thorns etc., a fox's tongue applied to the thorn or sore. For chilblains, goose-fat rendered and rubbed on. For toothache, a mouthful of cold water, letting it get into the aching tooth. For closing wounds, such as ones made by broken glass or a knife, a cobweb put into the wound and bandaged tightly. For corns, ivy leaf. Wormwood is a cure for a bad stomach. For rheumatism, boiling the roots of dandelion in water and then drink the water. For internal injuries, use wild sage juice.[272]

# SHERKIN
# Sea and Shipwrecks

# The Loss of the Alondra

In the year 1917, a ship named the Alondra was going from Spain to England, and she had a large cargo. She was crossing Oileán Dubhlainn (Kedge Rocks) when she hit a rock there and stayed there for six weeks. The Alondra crew put out a small boat and eight of them went into it. As they were heading for Oileán Dubhlainn the boat capsized. The crew drowned. The other men who stayed in the Alondra and were rescued the next day.[273]

---

### STEAMER WRECKED OFF CORK COAST

### PLIGHT OF CAPTAIN & CREW
### EFFORTS AT RESCUE
### Skibbereen, Friday

Early this morning the large steamer Alondra, during a fog and storm, struck on the Kedges Rock, two miles outside Baltimore Harbour. The vessel was bound from Lisbon to Liverpool, and was laden with wines, corks, oil, powder, and sardines. She carried a crew of 40, the master being Captain Taylor, of Liverpool. Fifteen of the crew left in the ship's boat, and, up to the time of wiring, have not turned up. One of the sailors was drowned. The captain and engineers are still aboard the vessel, which is likely to break up. Six of the sailors, partly dressed, arrived here.

### Skibbereen, Later

The steamship Alondra of Liverpool, 1,700 tones, laden with wine, resin, minerals, hides, powder, etc., now lies in a precarious position between the outer Kedge Rock and the second rock off Baltimore Harbour, and is rapidly breaking up.

During the day several unsuccessful attempts have been made by motor and other boats from Baltimore to rescue the captain and crew remaining on the vessel. A very heavy sea is running outside, and the boats have not yet been able to approach the dangerous rock. The rocket apparatus from Baltimore is also in the vicinity, but up to the present is unable to render any assistance.

The ship left Lisbon on the 26th, but off the South Irish coast encountered storm and fog, and struck the Kedge Rocks at 1:30am yesterday morning. The crew were first under the impression that the vessel had struck a mine.

---

The captain ordered the boats to be lowered and fifteen of the crew got into one boat, which has not since been heard of. Six got into another, and after a terrible struggle with the tempestuous sea, arrived at Ballyally Coastguard Station at 8:30am, where they were hospitably treated by Mr Connell, the chief officer, his wife and family. Mr W. G. Wood, auctioneer, Skibbereen, agent of the Shipwrecked Mariners' Association, then attended to the wants of the men with the greatest care and consideration.

The names of the six men landed at Ballyally are Dave Rowson, A.B., 14 Palmerston Street, Liverpool; Thomas Upton, fireman, 27 Tavistock Street, Liverpool; Laurento Caldron, fireman, Spanish Boarding House, Park Lane, Liverpool, Charles Decker, mess steward, 33 Park Road, Liverpool; Charles Victor Olsen, chief cook, 18 Wesley Avenue, Apelcourt, Cheshire; and James Williams, A.B., Dollins Street, Liverpool.

Up to the time of wiring, there is no information as to who left in the ship's boat which is missing, but is stated that the captain, officers, and engineers are still on the vessel.

*Freeman's Journal*, 30 December 1916, p.5.

# The Wrecking of the Ailsawald

The steamship Ailsawald left Liverpool on 20th December, 1900. She was bound for Hampton Roads, South America. On passing the Fastnet two days after she left Liverpool, a terrific north westerly gale arose, causing her to break her propeller shaft. She was driven helplessly before the wind down the bay north of Cape Clear, and about ten o' clock that night she struck the rocks north of Sherkin. The people of the Island saw her distress signals and hurried to where she was. With the aid of ropes and a boat they succeeded in taking the crew off safely. The crew were taken to the houses on the Island. The Ailswald was not refloated until March the 18th, 1901, and during that time there were divers working underwater repairing holes in her bottom. She was then towed off by tugboats and taken to Rushbrook Docks to be refitted for sea again. Sometime afterwards it appeared in the papers that she was lost in the English Channel with all hands in the Winter of 1902.[274]

---

**OFF BELFAST**

The storm in Belfast and neighbourhood was the most severe experienced for years. Considerable damage was done to property, and eight persons were injured by falling slates. One schooner has gone ashore in Belfast Lough, but owing to the heavy seas it has been impossible to render her assistance. The steamer, Magic, from Liverpool, sustained deck damage.

A large steamer in ballast, name unknown, is on the rocks of Sherkin Island, near Baltimore, County Cork, and will probably become a total wreck. The crew reached shore in safety.

A later telegram says that the steamer proves to be the Ailswald of Newcastle-on-Tyne, from Cardiff for Bermuda. She carried a crew of 24, all of whom landed on the island.

Nottingham Evening Post, 21 December 1900. p.3.

---

## The wreck of the Little Florence

On the 23rd of April 1893, the Little Florence of Newry foundered with all hands, between the Kedge and Whale rocks, as she was coming from the fishing ground in a southerly gale. All the other boats went to different harbours, only one, the Eleanor of Sherkin that came to Baltimore, saw her crew in the water, but as there was a terrible storm they could not rescue the drowning men.[275]

## The Wrecking of the Mullion

Long ago there was a ship coming from Spain with a cargo of cork. The night was very foggy, and the crew did not know where they were going. The ship drifted towards the north of Cape Clear and the first idea the crew got of the danger they were in was to hear the draw breaking on Drollán Rock. The captain immediately tried to turn the ship around, but it was too late as the boat was already on top of the rock. Four of the crew swam ashore and the rest were drowned. Since then, the rock has been known as the Mullion, called after the name of the ship that was lost. This ship was lost on 9th December 1878.[276]

# The Loss of the Thomas Joseph

Once a man had a new boat. He went to Crookhaven, and when they were coming home the night was very dark. No one was paying attention to the direction they were going, and the boat went on top of a rock. The captain and two engineers were drowned. Five or six of the tourists on board were drowned too. A girl jumped out of the boat onto the rock. A man was going to Baltimore in a boat in the middle of the night and he saved her. Everyone was sad when they heard the news. The lost boat was called the Thomas Joseph, and the place where it foundered is called Rí na Bó [King of the Cows]. It has been said since then that the lost boat is occasionally seen at nighttime when the wind is south-westerly.[277]

## SHERKIN
# The Natural World and Weather Lore

# Weather Lore

When dark clouds run across the horizon it is a sign that we will have rain. When the stars are sparkling that is a sign that we will have frost. When places that are far away from us are thought to be closer to us, we will have rain. When there is a large ring around the moon, and when it is getting bigger, that is a sign that we will have a bad weather. There is a rock at the mouth of Baltimore harbor called Black Point and when it is heard screeching, we will have a storm. There is a rock on the north side of this Island called the Mill. If the waves are breaking against that rock, it is a sign of a storm. There is a rock between Inis Cléire and Inis Arcáin called Carrickmore. If you see the rock shining, we will have bad weather. When waves break on the rocks of Drinagh Island it signals a north westerly wind. When waves break on Eoin Mór beach, then we have a westerly wind. When the sky is red in the morning, we will have rain and wind, but when it is red in the evening, we will have beautiful weather. If you saw the rays of light from the lighthouse on Carraig Aonair [the Lonely Rock, also known as the Fastnet] above Cléire island up in the sky, we would have rain.[278]

# SHERKIN
# Local Songs

# The Flower of Sherkin Isle

The Summer sun shone brightly on the parish of Lisheen,
O'er hill and dale and valley lay a mantle of pure green.
The Sabbath bells being chiming, we went and prayed a while,
Then said I to a welcomed friend, we'll stray to Sherkin Isle.

The boat we anchored at the dock and hurried on to meet,
The loving hearts that always flocked the strangers for to greet.
Then to the inn to get a drink we marched in double file,
But there I had not hoped to find the flower of Sherkin Isle.

Bright Sol withdrew his golden rays a mist o'er set the moon,
We dined and hurried on our way to search the shore full soon.
Three jolly youths conveyed us where young lovely females smile.
where first I saw fair Venus or the Flower of Sherkin Isle.[279]

# History and Archaeology

## The Evil World

In the bad old days, when the farmers had harvested the potatoes, the people would go rooting again, looking for any potatoes that were still in the ground. At that time the Protestants said that the Catholics were hungry as they were too immersed in their faith. There were up to a thousand people on the island at that time, but none of them took the abyss [converted to Protestantism]. There were up to six Protestant families in the area, but now there is only one family. The present family go over to Baltimore praying. The site of the soup house can still be seen near where O'Connor's family now resides.[280]

## The Holy Well

The holy well is situated on the hillside overlooking Horseshoe Bay. It is a small well surrounded by small fuchsia bushes. There is an old legend connected with it that people get cured there. On that account, it is visited at certain times such as May Eve and St John's Night. If a little bird is heard chirping when a person suffering from and disease is praying there, it is considered a very good sign of being cured. It is the custom of the people to take something with them when they visit it, such as a part of a rosary beads, a medal, a bunch of flowers, or a bit of rag. People usually cross the hills when they visit the holy well. It is said the well takes its Irish name, Tobar na nGabha, from an old smith in the old times. The water in the well is always quite fresh and it never goes dry. When a person wants to get his wish, he must walk around the well and say four hail Marys each time he walks around. Once, in the month of January, there were primroses seen there while there was not a primrose to be seen anywhere else.[281]

Figure 19. The Cork Society Soup House. *Illustrated London News*, 16 January 1847.

# The Landlords

Long ago, the people used have a very bad opinion of the landlords and their agents. Beecher was the name of the old landlord of this place. There were several families evicted from their homes here. Some of them went to England, and others were given smaller houses by the landlords but with very little land. Some people were turned out, although they'd paid their rents, because someone else wanted their houses and farms. One family by the name of Mahony was evicted from this island and went over to England. About three years ago one of them died and left thirty-two thousand pounds and a lot of property as well.

The landlord furnished the slate and lime for the construction of the houses. The tenant had to supply the stones and pay and feed the men. The agent collected the rents once a year, and occasionally the landlord came to the island by yacht to inspect the holdings. On such an occasion, the tenants were always on the lookout to see that everything was in proper order as they always lived in fear of eviction. Such small things as broken fences, thistles on the land, dirty yards etc. were factors to ultimately cause an eviction.

At one time, this island was stocked with hares by one of the landlords, and these were reserved for their own use to furnish material for a hunt whenever he chose to pay a visit for that purpose. Grave penalties were inflicted on the locals should they be caught injuring or killing one of the hares. The local tenants were forbidden to keep dogs, and any that were in existence prior to that had to be destroyed. A priest was the first to introduce dogs in defiance of the landlord, and from this onwards the dogs began to increase in numbers and the hares to dwindle until finally they became extinct here. Foxes swam in from the mainland and helped to lessen the number of hares. Since then, foxes have become permanent settlers here and it was eventually necessary to poison them. The island, at one time, was cleared of foxes but in the past few years they have returned again.

In the days of the landlord, the best farmer was always on the lookout to see how he could gain more land. Such were known by the name of 'grabbers'. There was one instance here of how one of these grabbers kept a bull and used him for the purpose of evicting poor people. This bull was led to a house where a poor woman and her family lived. The grabber played on the superstition of the woman and allowed the bull in on the floor while himself remained outside hidden. When this happened several times, the woman became alarmed and thought to leave the place altogether as she concluded the house was haunted. Every year since it is thought among the islanders that the bull can be heard roaming on the anniversary of the eviction.[282]

# Food of the people long ago

Long ago, the people used have three meals a day. They would always have a day's work done before breakfast. Their breakfast consisted of milk and cake. Only on churning days did they have butter. For their dinner they had potatoes, home cured fish and skimmed milk. For a change sometimes, they had triapán instead of fish. Their Sunday treat was pig's cheek and cabbage. The supper and tea were all one in those days. At this meal they used have yellow meal stirabout with plenty milk. The cakes were made with oneway and sometimes with meal. The oneway cake was called baróid.[xxxiv] There was another cake which was called a bucaidín. On St. Patrick's Day and Easter Sunday, a pot of eggs was boiled. On Good Friday it was the custom to have limpids for dinner.

At one time potatoes were a luxury here. When times began to improve and white flour was introduced into the island, the people were ignorant as to the making and mixing of the cake. They heard that a certain amount of bread-soda was used as an ingredient, and it is said that one housekeeper used an over amount in the mixing. When the cake started to bake, it raised the cover off the pot, and the man of the house noticing such, concluded that some evil spirit was at work and immediately ran for a stone and placed it on the cover of the pot, as he thought the cake was going to leave the pot and go out the doorway.

Long ago the people used to make their own flour from wheat. First of all, the wheat was heated in a pot for to harden it for if the grains were not heated, they would not crack so well when put in the quern. The quern consisted of two stones, one of which was shaped much like the cover of a cocoa-can. Another stone had a handle which fitted into the other stone.

---

xxxiv Oneway cake is another name for soda bread.

Next the wheat was put into the lower stone, the stone with the handle was twisted, and the wheat came out through a hole in the underneath stone.

Potatoes and fish were the main food of the people in the past. They had three meals a day, and had potatoes, fish and sour milk at each meal. Sometimes they cooked cakes and porridge made of yellow flour, and ate the porridge before going to sleep. The people went fishing every night. When they had enough fish, they cleaned them and spread some salt on them. Then they hung them up in the chimney until they were yellow. When the people were eating their meals, they would put a long bench at the table as they did not have enough chairs at that time.[283]

## Houses of the Old People

Long ago, the poor people's houses were built with clay, mortar, and stones, and were thatched. They had mostly one storey, but other houses had two and were roofed with slate from the quarry, a place on the south side of this island which is still called by that name. They had a large hearth with bellows to blow the fire. They used not sleep in the kitchen but in bedrooms on big wooden bedsteads. For a fire they used turf, furze, and coal.

There was once a house in Slievmore which was roofed with sods. People by the name of Scannel owned the house. It was situated on the side of a hill, and the south side of it was level with the ground. One day, as the people were eating their dinner, a cow happened to be grazing on the hillside, and on seeing the long grass, went up on it to feed. The weight was too much, and she crashed on the dinner table underneath.

There were only two rooms in each house, some of them had a bed in the kitchen. There was a certain little box erected over the door for the cock to sleep in. The cock was supposed to be blessed, and he was supposed to keep away harm. If a beggar came to a door for a night's lodging, a bed was made on the settle for him. They had an open hearth called the hob. If the fishermen caught any fish, the old women would put it on a string and hang it above the hob to dry.[284]

# The Harvest

Long ago, when threshing machines were unknown, the corn was threshed by smashing the sheaves against a big stone. The threshing machine is used now. The farmers would always help each other in turns. When one farmer would go to help another one, the farmer he helped would give him a day's help in return. The corn used to be cut with a sickle or reaping hook. This was a narrow, curved knife with teeth in the cutting edge, and a wooden handle. The reaper caught a fistful of straw with his left hand and holding the sickle with his right hand he cut the straw off close to the ground. He then laid the straw close together on the ground, and the binder came along later and bound it into sheaves with a fistful of straw twisted around them. They were then stood in stacks. After a few days, it was taken home and made into a stack. It was then put in a field and threshed with flails.[285]

# The Old Castle

There is an old castle in the garrison on this island. Finghín Ó Drisceoil once lived there. Ships from Waterford once came into the harbor for shelter, and Finghín went on board. There was wine in it and he took it. They went back to Waterford and came again to break up the castle.

To the east of the island sits Dún na Long castle. It was the castle of Finghín Ó Drisceoil. A piece of cannon used by Finghín Ó Drisceoil was on a beach to the north of the castle, until about thirty years ago, but they took it to Baltimore and it is still there. To the west of the castle was the great door, and there was a stair going up from the door to the top of the castle. The tower is square and has two small rooms in the walls. There is a high wall to the east and at the top of that wall is a small tig called the dog's kennel. The guard dogs are kept there. It is said that there was an underground tunnel going from the castle down to the sea, but it is now closed.[286]

Figure 20. Sherkin Castle, Baltimore (top), ref. L_IMP_2124.
Sherkin Abbey (bottom), ref. L_CAB_05209.
Photos by R. French, used with the kind permission of
The National Library of Ireland.

# Skibbereen

Co. Chorcaighe
Bar: Cairbre Thiar
Par: Abbeystrowry
Scoil: An Sciobairín
Oide: Micheal Ó Cuileanáin

# Skibbereen
# Local Folklore and Stories

## Stories of the Famine around Skibbereen

The famine began in the year 1845. Hundreds of people died on account of this terrible plague. I heard a very interesting story about the famine from an old lady. She told me that one night during the famine at about twelve 'o clock, she saw men with five victims on their shoulders. They buried them in gárdín na much. Hundreds of other people died also and were buried in the dead of night. The famine was caused by the terrible blight of potatoes in Ireland. It is said that the servants in the workhouse in Skibbereen used to give meal to the starved people twice a day. It is said that when the meal was to be given, the poor people were so eager to get the food that they used to trample over the poor weak people and kill them. May the lord have mercy on their soul's.[287]

Collected by Kevin O'Hara

## Tom Gearun's Survival

Very little is to be read in the modern History books, about the Famine around Skibbereen. I will now write a short account about it which I got from my grandmother. I suppose the most interesting story of the Famine is that of Tom Gearun. Tom Gearun was a poor man, who had no home and had to go into the workhouse where all the poor and dispossessed were detained. At that time people died in hundreds from starvation. Anyhow, it came to pass that when Tom Gearun died, he was taken to the Abbey graveyard. At that time the dead people used not be coffined. When Tom was buried, one man struck the sods that covered the grave, at that moment, he heard some-body say, "Let me out, let me out, let me out". They opened the grave, and Tom jumped out, afterwards it was found that Tom was only in a trance.[288]

Collected by Cornelius Daly

Figure 21. Old Chapel Lane, Skibbereen (top); Skibbereen from Clover Hill (bottom). The Illustrated London News, 13 February 1847, pp.100-101. Illustrations by James Mahony.

## Mass Burial at Derrygrenaugh

Our ancestors suffered very much during the Great Famine. Never had the Irish people suffered as much until the potato crops failed and then they died in thousands.

In my grandfather's land in Derrygrenaugh to the east of Bantry, there is a big hole surrounded by a wall 30 yards in circumference, one yard high, and it is supposed to have been 100 feet deep the first day. After several hundred people were buried there, including three priests, it got filled up. It is certain that people were buried there because my grandfather heard his father talking about it. In a rock behind Cnocáin na n-Éan in my grand-father's next-door neighbour's land, there was a place for giving out food.

During that time, there was a very fat man in Bantry, and there was a cousin of Lord Bantry visiting him. A Bantry man met him one day and they began talking about appetites. "I'll bet you", said the Bantry man, "that I'll get you a man to eat fifteen loaves of bread, two chickens, and ten pints of milk on condition that you'll pay all costs." "I'll give ten to one on it," said the other man. The eater was got, but he was after a good meal before that. When he had eight loaves eaten, he said in Irish, "I can't eat no more Jim." The gallant had no Irish, so he asked what he said and was answered, "He said that he could eat thrice as much." With that he walked away, and the other got his hundred pounds to the ten pounds he had down.[289]

Collected by Philip O'Neil

# Famine in Skibbereen

'After leaving this abode of death, we proceeded to High-street, or Old Chapel-lane, and there found one house, without door or window, filled with destitute people lying on the bare floor; and one, fine, tall, stout country lad, who had entered some hours previously to find shelter from the piercing cold, lay here dead amongst other likely soon to follow him.'

The Illustrated London News, 13 February 1847, p.100

Uncoffin'd, unshrouded, his bleak corpse they bore,
From the spot where he died on the Cabin's wet floor,
To a hole which they dug in the garden close by;
Thus, a brother hath died – thus a Christian must lie!

'Twas a horrible end and a harrowing tale,
To chill the strong heart – to strike revelry pale.
No disease o'er this victim could mastery claim,
'Twas famine alone mark'd his skeleton frame!

The bones of his grandsire and father too, rest
In the old Abbey-yard, by the holy rites blest;
Their last hours were sooth'd by affections fond cares,
Their last sighs were breath'd midst their friends' tearful prayers!

Unshriven, untended, this man pass'd asway,
Ere time streak'd one hair of his dark locks with grey,
His requiem the wild wind, and Ilen's hoarse roar,
As its swollen waves dashed on the rock-girded shore.

C.C.T

Figure 22. Harrington's Hut, Church Cross, The Illustrated London News,
13 February 1847, p.100. Illustration by James Mahony.

# Skibbereen Abbey

It is said that long ago when the Abbey was first built, it was built on the other side of the river. Every morning when the masons came, they found that the building was transferred to the side where the Abbey is now. At last, they discovered that it was to be built at the place where it is now, and they built it there.

The right name of the Abbey is Mainistir na Sruthrach, but on account of this story it is sometimes called Mainistir an Fhormaid. The field where they were building it at first belongs to Mr James Barnett and is called to this day Páircín an Fhormaid.[290]

# Buried Gold on Cuileanach Hill

It is said that there was gold buried in Cuileanach Hill. It was said to be very far under the ground in an old fort on top of a table, and that there was a cat minding it. If anyone went near the gold, the cat would tear him. The only way to get it was to take a big bit of meat with you and throw it to the cat, and while the cat would be eating the meat you could take the gold. It was said that some foolish man went looking for it, and after spending some time there, went home downhearted.[291]

Collected by Seán Mac Cártha

# Leathceannta na Riabhaiche

There was once an old grey cow and she was afraid she would die in the month of March, and when March was gone, she was delighted and said, "March is gone now and I will live another year." When march heard this, he borrowed three days from April, and they were so cold and wet that the old cow died.[292]

Collected by Pádraig Ó Tuama

## The Murder at Doire Liath

It is said that a rate collector was passing Derryleigh Bridge one night with the rates she had collected, when she was attacked by a robber who struck her with an iron bowl. He threw her body into the lake, and it was afterwards found there. The robber was found out and when he was going to be hanged, he said to the audience that the gold was hidden in Cuileanach.[293]

Collected by Seóirse Ó Donnabháin

As I was out for a walk one day, it started to rain. I went into a forge nearby for shelter. The smith was idle at the time, so he started to tell me some stories which he had heard in his younger days. One of the stories he told me was about a robber who lived in a cave in Cuileanach Hill. One evening, as a woman who had been collecting rates around Leap was returning home, the robber knew her and when he saw her coming, he struck her with a bowl on the head and killed her. He then took the money from her and threw her body into the lake and when her people at home found she was not returning home they went out looking for her. They saw the blood on the road, so they got a blessed candle and tied a stem of wheat around it, and it floated over the place where the body was. Suspicion was put on the robber, and he was arrested and found guilty. Before he was hanged, he was asked was there anything he wished to say. So, he asked was anyone from Skibbereen there, and if there was, he said that the was gold hidden in the cave where he used to live.[294]

Collected by Seán Mac Cártha

Folk stories, such as those above, often contain elements of truth. The theft of money from a woman, her murder, and the disposal of her body in a lake were reported in newspapers across Ireland and the U.K. in April 1826. If this was the source of this story, the facts are somewhat different.

**Globe, 24 April 1826**

# DREADFUL MURDERS

Skibbereen – April 19. – The following are the particulars of the above unprecedentedly cruel and cold-blooded deeds, and by giving insertion to them in your valuable paper, much good may accrue to the deluded people of this truly unfortunate country.

About two months since a wedding took place in the neighbourhood of Bantry, to which the principal part of the relations of the bride and bridegroom were invited; unfortunately the fumes of the whiskey soon began to be felt very sensibly by the guests, and a quarrel was of course the consequence; but whether it originated in any former dispute or not, I have not been able to learn; suffice it was that a blow was inflicted upon an infatuated man, of which he soon afterwards died. The person suspected immediately absconded, and, notwithstanding the vigilance and activity of the police (although it is an ascertained fact that he had been lurking and sheltering very near to this place), he has not been as yet apprehended.

In such a state of anxiety and suspense, the wife of course, with the consent of her friends, determined upon disposing of her cattle and other effects preparatory to accompanying him to America, when opportunity offered, and for which it appears by the evidence of her brother, she put together the sum of £35. All arrangements being finally settled about the 1st inst. she set off to join her husband, who was then understood to be in or near Castletownshend, and being a stranger to that part of the country, she called at the house of a person named Collins Cambaws, who knew all the movements of the husband, in order that some persons of his family might accompany her part of the way, and direct her to the place.

Accordingly, the eldest son left the house in company with her, for this purpose, about four o'clock on Saturday fortnight last, and after escorting her about one mile (according to his own statement) returned home. It will be recollected that the Cambaws were in the secrets of the husband, and that, of course, they knew of the woman's having the money.

The following day she was missed by the brother, who, it seems, had also appointed to meet her at the rendezvous, and after the necessary inquiries were made of the parties whom she had last been with, suspicion fixed upon them, and naturally enough, as no other person near the place could know of her having the money. A vigilant search has been kept ever since without success till this day, when, horrible to relate, she was discovered sunk in a lake by two immense stones, with her skull dreadfully fractured in two places. The Cambaws, who have been apprehended, underwent a partial examination, but as yet nothing has appeared by which this horrible transaction could be fixed upon them.

# Labarach Ó Loíngseach

The most interesting story that I have heard is about Labhar O Loíngseach, a chieftain who lived in Loughine in the olden times. It is said he had ears like a donkey. Whenever he used to get a clip, he used always kill the barber for fear of the secret. At last, when no other barber was to be got, he asked a poor widow's son to come. She asked Labhar to spare her son, he said he would try to do so. When the boy had finished, he told him not to tell the secret to anyone. The boy's health got bad with the weight of the secret in his mind. One day he whispered it to a tree, and the tree was cut down and made into a harp. When the harp used to be played, the only tune it would play was 'Tá dá chluais asail ag Labarach Ó Loíngseach' [Labarach Ó Loíngseach has two donkey ears]. The chieftain got ashamed of this and was last seen in his chariot at a place called Barlogue.[295]

Collected by Séan Ó Donobháin

# Cáit Ní Ceállaig

There is a hill called Cáit Ní Ceállaig half ways from Trawle bane, a townland about four miles to the east of Bantry and Dromore Chapel. It is said that Cáit had her castle on the summit of the hill and she was very rich. The British soldiers robbed all the gold and they buried it in the hill. One day they were getting the gold from where they buried it. At the mortal spot, Cáit appeared and turned into stone. That stone is there to the present day and is still called Cáit Ní Ceállaig.[296]

Collected by Pilib Ó Néill

# SKIBBEREEN
# People, Places and Property

## Carraig Phóilín

About a mile from Skibbereen there is a rock known as Carraig Phóilín, about two hundred feet over the river. It is said that a giant used this as a seat to bathe his feet in the River Ilen. This giant used to go to the top of Letter Scanlan, and if he saw a ship coming inside the islands, he would throw rocks at it to drive it away. That is why there are so many rocks in the sea near the mouth of Baltimore Harbour.

## Gleann na mBan Áluinn

In Mr Burke's land near Upper Bridge Street, Skibbereen, is a big glen called Gleann na mBan Áluinn. An old man living in this place said that he could hear the fairies singing and that they could be heard at Ballydehob.[297]

Collected by Conchubhar Ó Confhaolaidh

## Crosses

The cross boreen is situated in High Street by Mr McCarthy's house. It is a short cut to Chapel Lane. In the winter days it is very wet, and you could not walk on it.[298]

Collected by Donnchadh Ó Drisceóil

## Roads, passages and Wells

The Blind Boreen is in the townland of Gortncloghy near Mr Daly's house. Bóithrín Daoimhín is near the Bank of Ireland in North Street. The Croppies' Well is situated in the Windmill. Harrington's Well and Guggy's Well are situated in Upper Bridge Street.

# Local Place Names

There are many place names in this town and district whose names are not to be found in the map. We have names for wells, pools, boíthríní, etc. I shall give a few of these here.

The stony field is in Mr Hosfords land. The cabhachán is on the top of Upper Bridge Street. Sruatháinín na mBan runs through Mr Burkes land and then across the road. Long ago the women used come bare footed as far as the srutháin, they'd wash their feet in the water and put on their shoes going into town, and coming back they used take them off again. Cnuc Cán Fhínn is a big hill between Mar Dyke and Upper Bridge Street.

The Soldier's Hole is near the town park, at the back of Mr Kearney's shop, in the River Ilen. The Rock Hole is also in the River Ilen, up by the Weirs in Mr Jack Coughlan's land. Poll na Rab is a great fishing hole in the River Ilen, in Mr McCarthy's land. The Farthing hole is situated in Russagh. The crossroads also have names such as, the Lake Cross, Callaghan's Cross, the Four Crosses, the Three Crosses, Asolus Cross, and many others. The Round Pool is near the pound up in High Street.[299]

Collected by Séan Mac Cártha

# The Fenians

About sixty years ago there was a secret society in Ireland called the Fenians. It originated in Skibbereen and O'Donovan Rosa was their leader. Their object was to free Ireland from England. They rose in rebellion in which they failed, and after that the Fenian army fled to America. Others of them were captured and cast into prison. It is said that O Donovan Rossa and his followers held meetings in the place where Mr Wolfe has his garage now. And they used to drill in a field of Mr Kington at Bourabille.[300]

Figure 23. View of Skibbereen (top), ref. EB_1096. View of Skibbereen from the river Ilen (bottom), ref. EB_0136. Photos by William Lawrence, used with the kind permission of The National Library of Ireland.

Figure 24. Main Street, Skibbereen (top), ref. L_CAB_07985. Main Street, Skibbereen (bottom), ref. L_ROY_10243. Photos by Robert French, used with the kind permission of The National Library of Ireland.

Figure 25. Bridge Street, Skibbereen (top), ref. L_ROY_10241. View of the West Cork Hotel (bottom), ref. EB_0143. Photos by William Lawrence, used with the kind permission of The National Library of Ireland.

## SKIBBEREEN

# Farming, Trade and Crafts

## Trades that have died out

Most of the old trades have now gone. It would not pay the people to buy these things made by the tradesmen when they can get them cheaper in the shops. All hand-made work is much better than factory work. Some of the trades now dead that flourished here are as follows: nail making, weaving, boot making, and many others. The last of our weavers is Mike Keefe who is still alive. Basket making has also died down. The only basket maker in this town now is Mr Maloney. There are also other basket makers living in the country such as Jeremiah Collins and T. Kearney who make fine baskets also.[301]

Collected by Padraig Ó Donnchadha

## Old Trades

Long ago people did all their weaving and other things at home. During the past few years, these trades have died down altogether in Skibbereen.

Basket making was a popular trade long ago, but now it has nearly died down. It is said that where Mr Roycroft's Mill is now, was situated a distillery. It is also said that a brewery was in North Street where Barry and Sons are now. The old people did almost everything at home. They kept spinning wheels to spin their wool. Spinning wheels are kept yet in Connemara and in Donegal. Nail making was one of the best trades in Skibbereen long ago. Some of the old people say they remember five weavers in Skibbereen.[302]

Collected by Caoimhín Ó Róich

# Old Trades

| | |
|---|---|
| Weaving. | There were four weavers in Skibbereen and the last one who is left is Mr O Keefe who gave it up about ten years ago. |
| Nail-making: | All the nails were made by the nailers, but the factories destroyed the trade. |
| Coopering: | Coopering was a great trade in Skibbereen long ago, but the factories killed it with their ready-made barrels. Tom Young was the last cooper we had here, he died a few years ago. |
| Shoemaking: | The shoemakers made shoes locally in their own houses in this district forty or fifty years ago, but the ready-made shoes destroyed them. Some of these old shoemakers are still alive. |
| Brewing: | A brewery flourished in North Street where Mr Barry has his store now; some people alive now remember it. Mr Maloney over in Bridge Street made his own Lemonade while he was alive, but he is dead now. |
| Tanning: | There was a Tannery long ago where the Munster and Leinster Bank is now, and it produced as good a leather as was made then.[303] |

Collected by Níall Ó Briain

# Skibbereen
# Local Customs

# Blessed Wells

A round Skibbereen there are several blessed wells, but I know only a couple of them. Sceabar well is situated near Lough Ine. On the 30th of April every year crowds of people are to be seen praying and making the rounds. Every time a person goes around the well, they drop a white stone into it, and alongside there is a white thorn bush. On this bush people tie old rags, but the last couple of years very few people are to be seen praying around it. There is another well called St Brigid's well and there is an old church a couple of yards away.[304]

Collected by Diarmuid Ó Drisceóil

T here is a blessed well in Mr Carey's land; it is known as St Peter's and Paul's well. It is about a mile and a half from Skibbereen. Hundreds of people go to this well on the 29th of June every year. The people take a piece of bread or cloth with them usually. There are two blessed eels in this well. It is said that long ago a blind woman and a lame man were cured there and that you must see one of the eels before you can be cured. I heard that six unbaptised children were buried in a mound of earth near the well. May the lord have mercy on their souls. The water that flows into this well drops from a rock that is over the well. If a person looked up, he could see the drops falling down. Why people take a piece of bread with them is because they say that the eels will live on that much food for the year.[305]

Collected by Caoimhín O'hEadhra

# Local Customs

L ong ago, the old people used to carry out many customs which are not carried out at all now. I heard an old woman telling a story about two farmers who were enemies. At that time cows used to get a disease called blue quarter, and it was said that if a person threw a piece of a cow which had died of blue quarter into another person's land on a May morning with the intention of injuring him, that ill-luck would fall on him.[306]

Collected by Seóirse Ó Donnabháin

# May Customs

M any customs are practised on May morning. The young children go around to the nearest wood and bring home branches of every kind of tree. These are put hanging on the doors and windows. These things are done to welcome the Summer.

In another custom, children gather a bunch of nettles and then follow some other youngsters and nettle them in the feet and hands. Some children get up very early on May morning and go out and wash their faces with the dew. That will keep them very fresh during the day. Some people say that if you could hear the cuckoo with your right ear, you would have good luck for the rest of the year.

Another custom is getting a snail and putting it on top of a plate of flour, and when the snail would creep, he would make a sign, and these were the letters of the name of the man who the girl would marry. This snail is called a dhúchtín. The first person that gets a bucket of water out of a well on May Day will be very fortunate for the day. The old people say that it is very unlucky for youngsters to be out after nine o'clock on May evening.[307]

# Nósa na Samhna

T he last night of October is called Oidhche Shamhna or Hallow Eve. There are piseógs in connection with Hallow Eve. They say that if you looked into a mirror, you should see the person you are going to marry. My mother usually makes a barmbrack with a ring, a stick, and many other articles. It is believed that the person who gets the ring will be married first.

Some people believe that fairies, púcaí and spirits, are out on Oidhche Shamhna. On Oidhche Shamhna, apples are suspended from the ceiling by means of a bit of string and each person tries to bite the apple, and if they succeed in getting the apple, they will get the apple for themselves. In another game, a tub of water is placed in the centre of a floor, some apples are put floating in the water and each person tries to catch an apple.[308]

Collected by Conchubhar Ó Dálaigh

## Customs at Wakes and Funerals

Many customs are practised during the night of a wake. The men usually stay in the kitchen and the women sit around the corpse. After the person dies, the clock is immediately stopped to show the hour. It is better to have the corpse removed to the Church on that night to give the household time to sleep, and to get prepared for the funeral. The Rosary is usually said at twelve o'clock in the house, and in the Church when the corpse is brought in. The coffin is usually shouldered by people of the same name as the deceased to the graveyard. The screws of the coffin are then loosened for fear the person would be in a trance. Every man present at a wake gets a pinch of snuff and also a clay pipe to smoke. People say that if you did not say some prayer after taking the pinch of snuff that the fairies would have power over you.

Sometimes when a person dies, his eyes stay open, and a penny is placed on the eye lids to close them. A stitch is usually put on the toes of the stockings the dead person is wearing so as to keep his legs together. The room he is laid out in usually has white sheets all around the walls on which a cross made out of black crape is put. It is said that the mother should not go into the graveyard in the funeral of her first child.[309]

Collected by Seóirse Ó Donnabháin

# Attending a Wake

The first thing a person does when he goes into a wake-house is to say to the nearest relation of the dead person, "I am sorry for your troubles", then he kneels alongside the bed of the dead person and says a few prayers. Then he is given a pinch of snuff and then he says, "may the Lord have mercy on his soul and may the souls of all the faithful departed through the mercy of God rest in peace amen." The body is not usually coffined till the priest prays over it. The nearest relatives, as a rule, don't touch it. When the coffin is taken out, it is placed on two chairs which are turned upside down. When the body is removed, the coffin is always taken feet forward. The old roads are always followed to the graveyard. Sometimes these roads are very rough and bad, and put miles of a round on the funeral, but they are followed just the same. If there is a cabhlach in the graveyard, the funeral generally goes round it before coming to the proper grave. This is not done in Skibbereen, but it is at Creagh, Tullagh, and Castlehaven.[310]

Collected by Caormín O' Roic

# Tending the Dead

Long ago, women used wash the corpse, but it is now done by nurses except in the country. After being washed, a man is dressed in a clean shirt trousers and waistcoat but no coat. A habit is got, and he is put into it. The habit is generally a Franciscan one and can be got at the nearest convent where the nuns make them. The hands are then joined, and a bead placed between the fingers. If the mouth of a dead person is open, a couple of prayer books are placed under the chin to close it. Long ago, a bandage called a marbfáisch was tied round the head for the same purpose, but that is not done now. When a corpse is fully laid out, a small table is placed at the foot of the bed. On this table five candles are placed in brass candlesticks. If the people of the house have not got brass candlesticks, they borrow them from some neighbours who have them. In the same way some of the neighbours lend sheets for the laying out.

A saucer of snuff is also placed on this table and a saucer of tobacco, which is generally cut by the oldest male relation of the dead person. Several times during the night a person goes round with the snuff and another person takes round the tobacco and clay pipes.[311] The smokers fill their own pipes with tobacco or take a new clay pipe from the plate and pray for the repose of the soul of the deceased.

There are certain days on which it is not lucky to dig a grave - Monday and Friday in this district. In that case, a sod is dug off the grave on Sunday or Thursday. This is called reddening the grave. All the work of opening and closing the grave is done by relatives or friends of the deceased. When a person is to be buried, all the old coffins in the grave are taken up and the new coffins put at the bottom, and the old boards and bones thrown in beside it. This is an ugly practice and should be stopped.

Collected by Tadhg Ó Conchubhair

# Names of certain parts of the year

There are certain names for parts of the year, and these are mostly all Irish. The following are some. Sgairibhín na g-Cuac usually falls on the beginning of May. It is the time when the cuckoo sings. The weather is generally very hard and blowing at the time.

## Shrovetide or Inid

The period from Christmas to Ash Wednesday is known as Shrove or Inid. During this time all marriages used take place long ago. The last day of Shrove is called Shrove Tuesday or Máirt Inide, and nearly everybody has pancakes for supper on that night.[312] It is said that all the unmarried men and women have to go to Sceilg Micil on that night as a penance for not having got married during the Shrove. The 1st of April is called Lá na n-Amadán or All Fool's Day. People delight in making fools of others on that day.

The 24th of June is St John's Day or Lá Sain Seáin. On the Night before, called Oíche Sain Seáin, large bonfires are lighted in honour of St John. Each street has a bonfire of its own and for weeks before the boys have been collecting turf and timber and bog deal for the fire. A bush is burned on every field where crops are grown, and prayers are said for the crops. Long ago people used stay dancing around the bonfire till morning.[313]

Collected by Liam Ó Nualláin

## Snares for birds and beasts

There are many ways used for catching birds such as bird baskets and birdlime, but now birdlime is illegal.

Splintering: on the night appointed, a number of men gather together and set off to where birds are to be got together. They shine a light into the birds' eyes which dazzles them, and then they are struck on the head with a stick. This is a very cruel manner of killing birds.

Snares, traps and ferrets are used in catching rabbits. When a rabbit is known to be in a burrow, nets are put up to the mouths of it and then a ferret is put in to hunt out the rabbit. This is a very easy way of catching them. Snares are mostly always put in rabbits' tracks, and when the rabbit is out in the night-time, he cannot see where he is going, and into the snare he is sure to go.

Bird-baskets are four-sided, coming to a point on top. They are about square at the ground. They are raised off the ground by a twig. The bird to be caught perches on this twig and its weight brings down the basket. Of course, the basket must be baited first.[314]

Collected by Seán Ó Donnabháin

Birdlime is put on a twig about a foot and a half long, and the twig is put on top of a bush standing up straight. Then a songbird in a cage is put on a fence nearby. Another bird comes to see the bird in the cage. He perches on one of the bird-limed sticks or twigs and is thus caught.[315]

Collected by Donchadh Ó Drisceoil

Rabbit Snares: Rabbits have become so numerous lately that some farmers cannot plant wheat on account of them. To catch them, snares are made. Making a snare is very simple. In order to make a good snare, four strands of copper wire are necessary. These must be rolled between the hands till they adhere together. A loop is then made at one end. The other end is then put through this loop and the snare is made.[316]

Collected by Pádraig Ó Donchadha

# SKIBBEREEN
# Local Cures

# Traditional Cures

Warts: If a person has warts, it is said that if he puts a stone into a purse and puts it on the road, the first person that gets the purse will get the warts. Another old cure is to tie a piece of string around the warts for a few mornings. Potato water, that is the water left when the potatoes are boiled, is said to be a cure for warts. It is said that forge water is a cure for warts. If a dog licked a person's warts it is said that they would disappear.

Sore Eyes: A cure for sore eyes is to rub your fasting spit every morning for about three or four mornings. Another cure is to rub cold tea to it for a few days.[317]

Nettle Stings: The juice of the dock leaves rubbed to a nettle sting is said to be a very good cure.

Rheumatism: To roll yourself in a bunch of nettles is said to be a cure for rheumatism.

Bee stings: The cure for a sting of a bee is to rub a blue-bag to the sting. Another cure for it is to rub a raw onion to the sting.[318]

Burns: If a person gets burned, a raw potato is put on to the burn and this is a cure. It is said that a dock root is a cure for a burn from a nettle.

Bleeding: If a person's hand or leg was bleeding, a cobweb put around the wound would stop the bleeding.[319]

Headache: If a person had a very bad headache, the best thing to do is to tie a piece of cloth around his head tightly and then to rest in bed.

Sore Throat: If a person has a sore throat, a cure for it is to tie the left stocking around it[320]

Collected by Pádraig Ó Donnchadha, Séamus Ó hAirt,
Conchubhar Ó Dálaigh and Seán Ó Donobháin

# History and Archaeology

## Ringforts and Raths in the District

There are many Forts in this district. There is a fort in Dan O Mahonys land in Cúl Na gCorán named Páirc an Leasa, and it is said that John Hurley went looking for gold there. There is also a fort in Mr Newmans land in Doire Guail. Some people think that there was gold hidden there also. There is another fort in Mr Swanton's land in Lic a' Phóna. It is overgrown with long grass and ivy. It is about thirty yards long and about twenty yards wide. There were many forts in Ireland long ago, but they were knocked down or else ploughed up.[321]

Collected by Seóirse Ó Donnabháin

Mr Coakley's fort is situated in Coolnagrane. It is one of the best forts in the district. There are about three ditches around it. It is about two hundred yards from the road. Mr McCarthy's fort is situated in Gortnaclohy. It is at the side of the road. Only one ditch is around it now, but at one time there were three. You could see two or three other forts from this one. Mr O'Mahony's fort is situated in Coolnagrane, about a hundred yards in from the road. The field where the fort is is called Páirc a' Leasa. It is said that a man went looking for gold there. This fort is not as good as Mr Coakley's. There are holes going under it, but Mr O Mahony filled it in about a year ago because some of his cows broke their legs there.[322]

Collected by Seán Ó Donnabháin

There is a fort in Mr Duggan's field in High St and it is surrounded by two big walls. When they were digging the foundation for Mr Power's house, they came across an underground fort in which they found a stone hammer and some coins. This fort is now built upon. Mr Power's residence covers the site.[323]

# INDEX

# REFERENCES

1 Vol.297, p.223.
2 Vol.297, pp.225-226.
3 Vol.297, pp.228-229.
4 Vol.297, pp.222-223.
5 Vol.297, pp.226-227.
6 Vol.297, pp.231-232.
7 Vol.297, pp.215-216.
8 Vol.297, pp.228-229.
9 Vol.297, pp.229-230.
10 Vol.297, p.224.
11 Vol.297, pp.216-217.
12 Vol.297, p.218.
13 Vol.297, pp.219-222.
14 Vol.297, pp.232-232.
15 Vol.296, p.31.
16 Vol.296, p.32.
17 Vol.296, pp.72-73.
18 Vol.296, p.37.
19 Vol.296, pp.51-52.
20 Vol.296, pp.63-64.
21 Vol.296, p.65.
22 Vol.296, p.68.
23 Vol.296, pp.53-54.
24 Vol.296, p.45.
25 Vol.296, pp.75-77.
26 Vol.296, p.40.
27 Vol.296, p.38.
28 Vol.296, pp.81-82.
29 Vol.296, p.41.
30 Vol.296, p.80.
31 Vol.296, pp.77-78.
32 Vol.296, p.42.
33 Vol.296, p.49.
34 Vol.296, pp.70-71.
35 Vol.296, p.50.
36 Vol.296, pp.66-67.
37 Vol.296, p.48.
38 Vol.296, pp.35-36.
39 Vol.296, p.39.
40 Vol.296, p.47.
41 Vol.296, pp.43-44.
42 Vol.296, pp.57-59.
43 Vol.296, pp.60-61.
44 Vol.298, pp.221-222.
45 Vol.298, p.223.
46 Vol.298, pp.223-224.
47 Vol.298, p.224.
48 Vol.298, p.225.
49 Vol.298, pp.225-226.
50 Vol.298, pp.230-231.
51 Vol.298, p.231.
52 Vol.298, p.232.
53 Vol.298, p.233.
54 Vol.298, p.235.
55 Vol.298, pp.235-236.
56 Vol.298, pp.236-237.
57 Vol.298, pp.238-239.
58 Vol.298, pp.237-238.
59 Vol.298, p.238.
60 Vol.298, pp.239-242.
61 Vol.298, p.256.
62 Vol.298, p.247.
63 Vol.298, pp.244-246.
64 Vol.298, p.264.
65 Vol.298, p.258.
66 Vol.298, p.243.
67 Vol.298, p.258.
68 Vol.298, p.259.
69 Vol.298, pp.259-260.
70 Vol.298, p.261.
71 Vol.298, p.260.
72 Vol.298, pp.261-262.
73 Vol.298, p.260.
74 Vol.298, p.257.
75 Vol.298, pp.262-263.
76 Vol.298, p.231.
77 Vol.298, p.263.
78 Vol.298, pp.263-264.
79 Vol.298, p.36.
80 Vol.298, pp.22-23.
81 Vol.298, pp.24-25.
82 Vol.298, pp.37-38.
83 Vol.298, pp.39-40.
84 Vol.298, pp.12-13.
85 Vol.298, pp.14-15.
86 Vol.298, pp.6-7.
87 Vol.298, p.33.
88 Vol.298, pp.18-20.
89 Vol.298, pp.8-9.
90 Vol.298, p.9.

91 Vol.298, pp.20-22.
92 Vol.298, p.28.
93 Vol.298, pp.26-27
94 Vol.298, p.29.
95 Vol.298, pp.31-32
96 Vol.298, p.34.
97 Vol.294, pp.243-244.
98 Vol.294, pp.265-266.
99 Vol.294, pp.249-250.
100 Vol.294, pp.251-252.
101 Vol.294, pp.257-258.
102 Vol.294, pp.255-256.
103 Vol.294, pp.237-238.
104 Vol.294, pp.231-234.
105 Vol.294, pp.263-264.
106 Vol.294, pp.235-236.
107 Vol.294, pp.239-240.
108 Vol.294, pp.259-261.
109 Vol.294, pp.267-268.
110 Vol.294, pp.241-242.
111 Vol.294, pp.269-270
112 Vol.294, pp.245-246.
113 Vol.294, pp.253-254.
114 Vol.297, p.95.
115 Vol.297, pp.98-99.
116 Vol.297, pp.99-102.
117 Vol.297, pp.105-106.
118 Vol.297, p.93.
119 Vol.297, pp.84-85.
120 Vol.297, p.90.
121 Vol.297, pp.87-89.
122 Vol.297, pp.91-92.
123 Vol.297, pp.96-97.
124 Vol.297, p.86.
125 Vol.297, pp.103-104.
126 Vol.298, pp.149-150.
127 Vol.298, pp.131-132.
128 Vol.298, p.137.
129 Vol.298, pp.136-137.
130 Vol.298, p.160.
131 Vol.298, p.159.
132 Vol.298, pp.122-124.
133 Vol.298, p.152.
134 Vol.298, pp.151-152.
135 Vol.298, p.139.
136 Vol.298, p.153.
137 Vol.298, pp.145-146.
138 Vol.298, pp.111-112.
139 Vol.298, pp.141-142.
140 Vol.298, pp.143-144.
141 Vol.298, p.102.
142 Vol.298, pp.51-52
143 Vol.298, p.53.
144 Vol.298, p.66.
145 Vol.298, pp.56-58.
146 Vol.298, p.74.
147 Vol.298, p.75.
148 Vol.298, p.61.
149 Vol.298, pp.69-70.
150 Vol.298, p.67.
151 Vol.298, p.55.
152 Vol.298, p.71.
153 Vol.298, p.54.
154 Vol.298, p.54.
155 Vol.298, p.62.
156 Vol.298, pp.59-60
157 Vol.298, p.73.
158 Vol.298, p.63.
159 Vol.298, p.68.
160 Vol.298, p.70.
161 Vol.298, p.72.
162 Vol.298, p.73.
163 Vol.298, p.71.
164 Vol. 0296, pp.18-21
165 Vol. 0296, pp.22-24
166 Vol. 0296, pp.27-29
167 Vol. 0296, pp.11-13
168 Vol. 0296, pp.8-10
169 Vol. 0296, pp.14-15
170 Vol. 0296, pp.16-17
171 Vol. 0296, p.6
172 Vol. 0296, pp.3-5
173 Vol. 0296, p.7
174 Vol. 0296, pp.25-26
175 Vol.295, pp.247-249.
176 Vol.295, pp.251-255.
177 Vol.295, pp.260-262.
178 Vol.295, pp.273-274.
179 Vol.295, p.244
180 Vol.295, p.280.
181 Vol.295, pp.281-282.
182 Vol.295, pp.277-278.
183 Vol.295, pp.241-243.
184 Vol.295, pp.237-239.

185 Vol.295, p.259.
186 Vol.295, p.279.
187 Vol.295, pp.275-276.
188 Vol.295, pp.271-272.
189 Vol.295, pp.267-268.
190 Vol.295, p.243.
191 Vol.295, pp.263-264.
192 Vol.295, pp.256-257.
193 Vol.295, pp.239-241.
194 Vol.297, pp.113-114.
195 Vol.297, p.115.
196 Vol.297, p.116.
197 Vol.297, pp.117-119.
198 Vol.297, pp.120-123.
199 Vol.297, pp.109-110.
200 Vol.297, p.111.
201 Vol.297, pp.111-112.
202 Vol.297, p.13.
203 Vol.297, p.37.
204 Vol.297, pp.27-28.
205 Vol.297, p.3.
206 Vol.297, pp.6-7.
207 Vol.297, pp.16-18.
208 Vol.297, pp.40-42.
209 Vol.297, pp.31-32.
210 Vol.297, p.61.
211 Vol.297, pp.35-36.
212 Vol.297, pp.73-74.
213 Vol.297, pp.81-82.
214 Vol.297, pp.71-72.
215 Vol.297, pp.8-9.
216 Vol.297, pp.19-20.
217 Vol.297, pp.25-26.
218 Vol.297, pp.54-55.
219 Vol.297, pp.67-68.
220 Vol.297, pp.4-5.
221 Vol.297, pp.29-30.
222 Vol.297, pp.10-12.
223 Vol.297, pp.21-24.
224 Vol.297, pp.52-53.
225 Vol.296, p.95.
226 Vol.296, p.93.
227 Vol.296, pp.94-95.
228 Vol.296, p.101.
229 Vol.296, p.96.
230 Vol.296, pp.98-99.
231 Vol.296, pp.86-88.
232 Vol.296, pp.105-106.

233 Vol.296, p.94.
234 Vol.296, p.102.
235 Vol.296, pp.104-105.
236 Vol.296, p.97.
237 Vol.296, pp.88-89.
238 Vol.296, p.97.
239 Vol.296, p.93.
240 Vol.296, p.89.
241 Vol.296, p.93.
242 Vol.296, p.91.
243 Vol.296, pp.91-92.
244 Vol.296, pp.86-88.
245 Vol.296, pp.85-86.
246 Vol. 0295, p.169
247 Vol. 0295, pp.231-232
248 Vol. 0295, p.170
249 Vol. 0295, pp.170-171
250 Vol. 0295, p.171
251 Vol. 0295, pp.226-227
252 Vol. 0295, pp.196-197
253 Vol. 0295, p.231
254 Vol. 0295, pp.187-188
255 Vol. 0295, pp.224-225
256 Vol. 0295, p.192
257 Vol. 0295, p.193
258 Vol. 0295, p.178
259 Vol. 0295, p.176
260 Vol. 0295, pp.202-203
261 Vol. 0295, p.228
262 Vol. 0295, p.179
263 Vol. 0295, pp.179-180
264 Vol. 0295, p.180
265 Vol. 0295, pp.206-209
266 Vol. 0295, pp.182-183
267 Vol. 0295, pp.198-201
268 Vol. 0295, pp.212-213
269 Vol. 0295, pp.204-205
270 Vol. 0295, pp.210-211
271 Vol. 0295, pp.211-212
272 Vol. 0295, pp.181-182
273 Vol. 0295, pp.173-174
274 Vol. 0295, p.174
275 Vol. 0295, p.233
276 Vol. 0295, pp.174-175
277 Vol. 0295, p177
278 Vol. 0295, pp.172-173
279 Vol. 0295, pp.189-190
280 Vol. 0295, p.191

281 Vol. 0295, pp.194-195
282 Vol. 0295, pp. 13-215
283 Vol. 0295, pp.216-218
284 Vol. 0295, pp.220-222
285 Vol. 0295, pp.219-220
286 Vol. 0295, p.223
287 Vol.297, p.127.
288 Vol.297, p.129.
289 Vol.297, p.131.
290 Vol.297, pp.183-184.
291 Vol.297, pp.182-183.
292 Vol.297, pp.199-200.
293 Vol.297, p.179.
294 Vol.297, pp.180-182.
295 Vol.297, pp.184-185.
296 Vol.297, pp.186-187.
297 Vol.297, pp.187-188.
298 Vol.297, pp.197-198.
299 Vol.297, pp.196-197.
300 Vol.297, p.139.
301 Vol.297, pp.173-174.
302 Vol.297, pp.176-177.

303 Vol.297, pp.174-176.
304 Vol.297, p.141.
305 Vol.297, pp.143-145.
306 Vol.297, pp.161-162.
307 Vol.297, pp.158-160.
308 Vol.297, pp.163-164.
309 Vol.297, pp.165-167.
310 Vol.297, pp.167-169.
311 Vol.297, pp.169-171.
312 Vol.297, p.200.
313 Vol.297, pp.202-203.
314 Vol.297, pp.208-210.
315 Vol.297, pp.210-211.
316 Vol.297, pp.211-212.
317 Vol.297, pp.189-190.
318 Vol.297, p.190.
319 Vol.297, pp.191-192.
320 Vol.297, pp.192-193.
321 Vol.297, pp.204-205.
322 Vol.297, pp.205-206.
323 Vol.297, p.207.

# Also Available

## MIZEN: RESCUED FOLKLORE FROM IRELAND'S SOUTHWEST

In 1937, just fifteen years after the establishment of the Irish Free State and at the dawn of the new republic, the Irish Folklore Commission charged the students of Ireland's schools with the rescue of the country's folklore. After centuries of oppression, emigration and occupation, this fundamental element of national heritage risked extinction. The children, representatives of a new, free generation, accepted their brief with enthusiasm and vigour, talking with family members and neighbours, young and old, and writing down local stories, histories and songs in school exercise books. Now in the National Folklore Collection (UCD), these books form a wonderful snapshot of oral tradition, painting a vivid picture of an old but familiar Ireland.

This book is a transcription of stories, songs and histories from the Mizen Peninsula, collected between 1937 and 1939 by the National Schools at Crookhaven, Lissagriffin, Goleen, Toormore (Altar), Lowertown, Schull, and Ballydehob. Here you will find tales of local life, trade, farming, shipwrecks, superstition, and the supernatural. Songs, some still performed today, others lost, are presented, the various versions illustrating the power of word of mouth. For those who live in the area today or whose families are amongst the emigres from this most south-westerly of Irish headlands, some stories and names will be familiar. Visitors, and those who hope to visit (and I recommend you do) will find that though much has changed, the people (warm and friendly) and places (wild and windswept) are as instantly recognisable as those depicted in this rescued folklore.

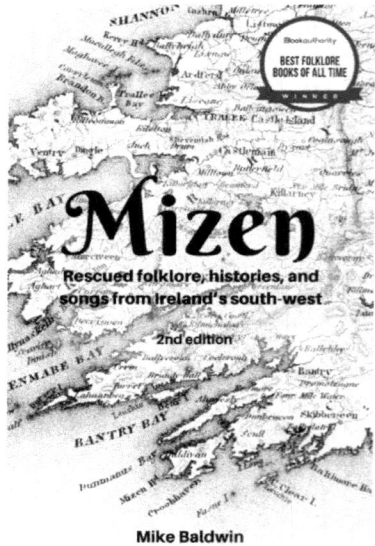

www.ingramcontent.com/pod-product-compliance
Lightning Source LLC
Chambersburg PA
CBHW060303030426
42336CB00011B/917